A Guide for Preachers on Composing and Delivering Sermons

The *Or ha-Darshanim* of Jacob Zahalon

A Seventeenth-Century Italian Preacher's Manual

Volume XI in the **Moreshet Series**, Studies in
Jewish History, Literature and Thought

A CENTURY OF ACHIEVEMENT

1886–1986
תרמ״ו־תשמ״ו

A Guide for Preachers on Composing and Delivering Sermons

The *Or ha-Darshanim* of Jacob Zahalon

A Seventeenth-Century Italian
Preacher's Manual

Henry Adler Sosland

THE JEWISH THEOLOGICAL SEMINARY OF AMERICA

New York 1987/5747

Library of Congress Cataloging in Publication Data

Zahalon, Jacob, 1630–1693.
   A guide for preachers on composing and delivering
sermons : the Or ha-darshanim of Jacob Zahalon :
a seventeenth-century Italian preachers' manual.

   (Vol. 10 in the Moreshet series)
   Title on added t.p.: Or ha-darshanim.
   "Yotse la-or mi-tokh sheloshah kitve yad 'im meḵorot
ve-he'arot"—Added t.p.
   Bibliography: p.
   Includes index.
   1. Preaching, Jewish—Handbooks, manuals, etc.—Early
works to 1800.   2. Zahalon, Jacob, 1630–1693.
3. Rabbis—Italy—Biography.   I. Sosland, Henry Adler.
II. Title.   III Title: Or ha-darshanim.   IV. Series: Moreshet series ; v. 10.
BM730.Z3413   1987.   296.4'2   85–23754
ISBN 0–87334–026–4

MANUFACTURED IN THE UNITED STATES OF AMERICA

DISTRIBUTED BY KTAV PUBLISHING HOUSE, INC.
HOBOKEN, NEW JERSEY 07030

לזכר
אבי מורי
בנימין ב״ר יצחק ע״ה

ולזכר
חמי מורי
הרב צבי ב״ר מרדכי ע״ה

ולזכר
חמתי מורתי
עטל בת ר׳ אריה לייב ע״ה

ותיבדל לחיים ארוכים
אמי מורתי
לאה בת שלמה זלמן

האבות עטרת לבנים
(משלי יז:ו)

בה חלק ראשון על ד' התורה

ספר שמו

אור הדרשנים

מורה כאלבע הסימנים · מכל דברים וענינים ·
של מאמרי חכמים · שבילקוט שבנים שונים ·
מעיל לבחורים וזקנים · להקל טורח המעינים ·
וערוך מדליק לפניהם נרות · מלאכת הדרשה
מאירות · בחבור יפה ובאמירות · לעשות
דרוש ישרות : יגעתי בכח על מעלת הדרושה
מוהרך הרב טוב לעמו · ברומא שבנסך הר'
קאטאלאני וארמוניסי י"ן כמוהר' יעקב
בכמוהר' יצחק צהלון ז"ל
לשם הבורא יתיאמן לרווחה :

הועתק על יד הבחור שלמה בלאא יצחק ד"ל
קיטטה עטיאם עזו בלונדרש בענת הרע"ן:

Title Page of JTS Ms. of *Or ha-Darshanim*

Contents

Hebrew Section

Preface

The Jews of Rome in the mid-seventeenth century were socially, economically, and religiously in a state of decline. The cumulative effects of the papal legislation that had instituted the ghetto system along with other forms of degradation in 1555—followed in subsequent years by forced attendance at conversionist sermons, severe limitations on the choice of occupations, occasional forced baptisms, and other forms of humiliation—might have been enough to explain the low spiritual state of Roman Jewry. When, however, to these external difficulties were added internal confusion and despair in the wake of the apostasy of the mystical messianic figure Sabbatai Zevi, the situation became even worse.

Jacob Zahalon, among the luminaries of post-Renaissance Italian preaching, combined within himself the practical and scholarly knowledge of a consummate physician with the wisdom and religious sensitivity of a learned rabbi. The late Cecil Roth, in a letter to this writer dated February 20, 1970, described Zahalon as an "overlooked figure." Noting that the Roman ghetto "was in a period of full decadence" in the seventeenth century, Roth referred to Zahalon as almost its only " 'spiritual' leader of real force." Actively immersed in the Jewish community of Rome and its affairs, as well as in the task of regular and thoughtful preaching, Zahalon set out to heal some of the ills of his people.

He had already written a complete index to the *Yalqut Shimoni* in order to aid himself, and other preachers as well, in the task of preparing sermons. To this index he now added a comprehensive thirteen-chapter treatise on how to compose, organize, adorn, deliver, and evaluate sermons which might inspire and meet the needs of the Jews of his day. Although various suggestions had been made by earlier writers, this was one of the first Hebrew preachers' manuals ever written, to our knowledge. In it Zahalon discusses the subject-matter, the quality, and the length of the sermon, as well as the use of voice and gestures, and even how the preacher should care for his health. The first version of this manual, entitled *Or ha-Darshanim,* "A Light for Preachers," appeared in 1660, and it was later expanded around 1672.

Zahalon reminds rabbis of the purpose of preaching, and one can sense his deep concern for his people. He decries forced preaching and carelessness. There is reason to believe that he was partly referring to attempts by local preachers in Italy and elsewhere after 1666 to justify Sabbatai Zevi through bizarre and inauthentic use of texts.

There are many similarities between Zahalon's published medical textbook and his advice to preachers. His training as a physician and his sensitivity to patients and their symptoms make him unusually alert as a preacher to the needs of his listeners and their responses to the sermon.

Although the Catholic Hebrew scholar Bartolocci gave a favorable description of Zahalon's manuscript in 1675, and a reader of Hebrew books from the Holy Office found in it nothing contrary to the Catholic faith in 1693, the *Or ha-Darshanim* was banned by the Inquisition one year later, fourteen months after Jacob Zahalon had died. What he so very much wanted to impart to his colleagues remained unpublished in the Biblioteca Casanatense in Rome, with only two other copies extant, in New York and in Oxford, apparently ignored and forgotten until the present time.

In January of 1967, after spending many months trying unsuccessfully to discover an area of Jewish learning in which to pursue doctoral studies, I was in the process of continuing my search when Dr. Menahem Schmelzer, Librarian of the Jewish Theological Seminary of America, brought the manuscript of the *Or ha-Darshanim* to my attention. This work represents an extensive revision and expansion of the dissertation, which was submitted in the spring of 1977.

A much neglected figure in the history of the Jews of Italy,

Jacob Zahalon was, nevertheless, a prolific writer on subjects ranging from theology, both Jewish and Catholic, philosophy and mysticism, commentaries on books of the Bible, *halakhah, aggadah,* confessional prayers, and *piyyutim,* to symptomatology and the latest and most effective cures in medicine. Only two of his many works were ever published, *Margaliot Tovot,* "Choice Pearls" (a study guide to the *Ḥovot ha-Levavot* of Baḥya Ibn Paquda) and *Oẓar ha-Ḥayyim,* "The Treasure of Life" (a compendium of medical advice for physicians, and for laymen in emergencies, on diseases and how to treat them).

From the moment that he first made me aware of the *Or ha-Darshanim,* Dr. Schmelzer has most generously given of his time, and whenever this study seemed to reach out into many other areas, he has always helped me to see the forest for the trees. Without his presence as Librarian and friend, I do not believe this book would have been written.

During my sabbatical year spent in Jerusalem, 1969–1970, I devoted much more time to the project than ever before, working at the Jewish National and University Library. Its staff was most cooperative. In addition, I found the library and staff at the Ben Zevi Institute extremely helpful, especially the man who was then its director, Dr. Meir Benayahu. Dr. Benayahu sustained me in the work on Zahalon's biography and in unraveling the Casanatense manuscript, and offered valuable insight and assistance in my efforts. Professor Joshua O. Leibowitz shared with me his medical researches on Jacob Zahalon and the *Oẓar ha-Ḥayyim.* Dr. Abraham David, then at the *Encyclopaedia Judaica,* where I also worked part-time, gave valuable suggestions. On my return to New York, Professor Isaac Barzilay read the biographical material on Zahalon which had been composed by that time, and offered important criticism and recommendations concerning that, as well as preliminary chapters I had written.

Others who expressed interest in the *Or ha-Darshanim* and its author, and provided occasional insight into areas of research, were Professors Gerson D. Cohen, Simon Greenberg, Shalom Spiegel, Abraham Halkin, Shraga Abramson. Ismar Schorsch,

Jose Faur, Moshe Greenberg, and Tovia Preschel. I am grateful to
Professor David Weiss Halivni for his suggestions concerning
improving the Hebrew text of the manual. Professor Ivan Marcus
was very helpful in his comments on the English text, and a source
of much encouragement on the book. Rabbi Judah Brumer provided much assistance with the Hebrew text during the process of
publication. Professor Avraham Holtz was most gracious in reading the entire work and making innumerable useful comments on
content, clarity, and style. Needless to say, none of the scholars
mentioned above can be held responsible for any errors which may
be found in my work.

The library staff of the Jewish Theological Seminary extended
themselves in so many ways over the years. The Union Theological
Seminary Library was most hospitable and helpful. I am also
indebted to the Bodleian Library at Oxford, the British Museum,
and the Comunità Israelitica in Ferrara (representing the library of
the *Talmud Torah*) for their permission to make use of manuscripts of Zahalon's works. Especially am I grateful to the Biblioteca Casanatense in Rome for providing the microfilm of the *Qol
Ya'aqov,* apparently the handwritten copy of Jacob Zahalon himself.

To my congregation, the New City Jewish Center, I am most
appreciative for their understanding and encouragement of
my regular absence one day each week over these years for the purpose of pursuing these studies.

Last but by no means least, let me record here my gratitude to
my children, Morton Daniel, Rachel Ann, and Abigail Nelson, for
their patience and interest, and, most of all, to my wife,
Judith, for her love, for her support of this project, and for her
helpfulness in countless ways: *"T W Sh L B O."**

Henry Adler Sosland

New City, New York
April 22, 1986
13 Nisan 5746

* "Finished and completed, praised be the Lord, creator of the universe!"

On Transliterations, the Use of Manuscripts, and Translations

I have followed the general guidelines concerning the transliteration of Hebrew as found in the *Encyclopaedia Judaica* (Jerusalem, 1971). The one exception has been with the name Zahalon.

References to talmudic sources are all to the Babylonian *Talmud* unless otherwise indicated.

Detailed descriptions of the three manuscripts on which the critical edition of the *Or ha-Darshanim* is based will be found in the Introduction, n. 41 (for the Casanatense MS.), pp. 34–35 (for the Oxford MS.), and n. 291 (for the JTS MS.).

In my notes to the Hebrew text of the *Or ha-Darshanim,* I have indicated the different *girsa'ot* (versions) as follows:

a. The letter *Quf* stands for the Casanatense MS., 217, dated 1672–1680.
b. The letter *Nun* stands for the JTS MS. R. 1339, placed in R 84a, or Adler 2247, dated 1717.
c. The letter *Aleph* represents the Oxford MS., 2268.1 in the Bodleian, dated 1733.

Rabbinic literature is very elliptical. I have not made a *literal* translation of the Hebrew texts but have tried to convey the full sense of Zahalon's words in English, attempting to translate idiomatic Hebrew or Aramaic into idiomatic English. Biblical verses and rabbinic sayings which are found incomplete have been quoted more fully, if not completely. In all cases, however, to indicate precisely what is contained in the Hebrew and what is not, I have enclosed with brackets any words added to the text in order to convey the full meaning. For the textual evidence, the reader should consult the Hebrew. I have made use of all three manuscripts, creating a conflate Hebrew text, with notes indicating variants. Regarding precedents for Zahalon's writings in the *Or ha-*

Darshanim, I have not made an exhaustive study of all possible material. However, where I am aware of any earlier parallel, I have tried to indicate it in the notes to the translation.

A Guide for Preachers on
Composing and Delivering Sermons

The *Or ha-Darshanim* of Jacob Zahalon

A Seventeenth-Century Italian
Preacher's Manual

Henry Adler Sosland

I. Introduction

The objective and intention of the preacher should be to refine the people and to draw them ever closer to the service of the Lord. [At the same time it is] to draw them away from transgression and to teach them the *Torah* of the Lord, all for the sake of heaven, and not for [the preacher's] own glorification or to show off his intellect. (*Or ha-Darshanim*, ll. 649–653)

Introduction

1. Roman Background

[The preacher] should seek to learn what it is that [his] congregation is most anxious to hear about, for example, whether [they are concerned] about [the prospect for] *Ge'ullah* (redemption) and the reasons for the length of the *Galut*. Or, [they might prefer hearing] an account of some events [which occurred and what can be learned from them].

(*Or ha-Darshanim*, ll. 285–290)

"Now . . . that they are sick of the [oppressions of the Roman] government, they are eager to hear words of Scripture and *haggadah!*"

(*Ibid.*, ll. 415–417, quoting a *Midrash* in the *Yalqut*, II, 986, 535a)

Abundant hardships of our [present] time have diminished our abilities and increased our forgetfulness . . .

(*Ibid.*, ll. 196–197)

History has amply recorded the works, and most of the lives, of many mid-seventeenth-century religious thinkers of renown. John Milton published his *Areopagitica,* subtitled "The Liberty of Unlicensed Printing," in London in 1644. Arguing vigorously against any form of censorship, he denounced "expurging Indexes that rake through the entrails of many an old good Author, with a violation worse than any could be offered to his tomb." The object of his scorn was the licensing ordinance of the largely Presbyterian Parliament seeking to control the press.

In 1667 the first edition of Milton's *Paradise Lost* appeared, in which he prayed for divine illumination to "assert Eternal Providence, and justify the ways of God to men." Meanwhile, in Amsterdam, Rembrandt van Rijn had been drawing, painting, and etching many biblical scenes (among his other works), not at all unusual for an artist of the baroque period. He also chose numerous contemporary Jews for his subjects, including Ephraim Hezekiah Bueno, depicting a moment around 1647 when Bueno was about to leave home to care for a patient. Rembrandt reveals

5

not only the physician's warmth and compassion in his painting, but his own sympathetic conception of the "Jewish doctor."

The focus of religious concern during these times was far from monolithic even in the same city, as evidenced by Benedict (Baruch) Spinoza, who developed early biblical criticism in his *Theologico-Political Treatise,* which he published anonymously in Amsterdam in 1670. Arguing against Maimonides, he maintained that the domain of Scripture was strictly to teach and inculcate moral virtues, leaving the area of correct beliefs and religious truths to the philosophers.

In America, somewhat earlier, Roger Williams was formulating his concept of social reform and freedom of conscience partly through his mystical interpretations of the Bible. He wrote a letter in 1663 in the town of Providence, Rhode Island, drawing an analogy, like a good preacher, between a colony and a ship with passengers of many faiths, commanded by a captain who had to practice toleration to them all. And he described the period in which he lived as "wonderful, disputing, and dissenting times." These words would hardly have been appropriate to describe the Rome of his contemporary, Jacob Zahalon.

One cannot properly understand the Rome of Zahalon's day without some awareness of the papal legislation which had instituted the ghetto system in that city. Through his infamous bull, *Cum nimis absurdum,* Pope Paul IV had on July 14, 1555, less than two months after his ascending to the papacy, attempted to segregate Roman Jewry completely from the rest of the populace. Within two weeks after the issuance of the decree, the ghetto had been established.[1] Jews now had to live within a sharply secluded

---

[1] Using this date as a starting-point for examining seventeenth-century Jewish life in Rome is, admittedly, somewhat arbitrary. One could as well begin with an earlier papal bull, *Cum sicut nuper,* issued by Julius III in May 1554, reaffirming the order given in September 1553—on *Rosh Ha-Shanah* according to the *Encyclopaedia Judaica* (hereafter cited as E.J.), XIV, 248—which led to the public burning of thousands of volumes of the Palestinian and Babylonian

quarter, shortly afterward surrounded by a wall, which included a few narrow streets on the left bank of the Tiber River and from the Quattro Capi Bridge to the modern Piazza of Tears. The entire Jewish population, consisting then of 3,000 souls, was now concentrated into an area which had been inhabited by Jews since ancient times. It was a malodorous and highly unsalubrious section, often

Talmud, along with many post-talmudic Hebrew books and manuscripts, on the Campo de' Fiori in Rome. The destruction of the *Talmud,* carried out by the Grand Inquisitor Gian Pietro Carafa (later Pope Paul IV), who personified the spirit of the Counter-Reformation, had as its goal the removal of what was regarded as a principal means of defense by Jews against conversion. *Cum sicut nuper* enunciated this policy clearly in one line: "Jews are tolerated . . . so that . . . led by our kindness . . . they may convert." Although ten years later Pius IV removed this ban on the *Talmud*—provided that only expurgated copies without title pages be permitted—his intention was in no way different from that of his predecessors. Censored versions of the *Talmud* were to be tolerated in order to facilitate conversion through the use of quotations by Catholic preachers from the Jewish texts in the houses of catechumens, or prospective converts (see below, pp. 12-14). While the *Talmud* had been condemned for centuries because of alleged "blasphemies," the Inquisition's present concern was not that there was any harm to the Church, but that it wanted to deprive the Jews of any means whereby "their impiety is encouraged or increased and their conversion is delayed." Ultimately, however, despite policy variations back and forth concerning the *Talmud,* what eventually prevailed was the view exemplified by Andreas Masius, a Flemish scholar of Hebrew and Greek, who argued in 1553 that "no book is more appropriate to convince the Jews than the *Talmud.*" This summary of the Church's attitude toward the *Talmud* during the Catholic Reformation and the quotations are taken from the analysis of Kenneth R. Stow in his "The Burning of the *Talmud* in 1553 in the Light of the Sixteenth Century Catholic Attitudes toward the *Talmud,*" in *Bibliothèque d'Humanisme et Renaissance* 34 (1972): 435–459. Another view similar to that of Masius was that of Giles of Viterbo (d. 1532), a cardinal who had been elected prior-general of the Augustinian order in 1507 and was very close to several popes, who expressed a commonly held opinion that kabbalistic texts could be used as a device through which Christians could convert Jews, especially when the Hebrew text of Scripture was interpreted by means of the secrets of *Kabbalah* (J. W. O'Malley, *Giles of Viterbo on Church and Reform* [Leiden, 1968], p. 109).

flooded when the Tiber overflowed, and the occupants of the Roman ghetto had to endure the worst conditions found in all of Europe at that time.[2]

Obviously, therefore, this Jewish quarter was dangerously inadequate in spite of the fact that it was enlarged from time to time. In 1526–27, out of a total population in Rome of 55,035,

---

[2] Cecil Roth, *History of the Jews of Italy* (Philadelphia, 1946), p. 329. On the precise sequence of events in the full implementation of *Cum nimis,* see Attilio Milano, *Il Ghetto di Roma* (Rome, 1964), pp. 74 ff.

Cum nimis was interpreted, expanded, and implemented through the legal tract *De Iudaeis et Aliis Infidelibus* (Venice, 1558; reprinted 1568 and 1589, Venice, and 1601 and 1613, Frankfurt), written by Marquardus de Susannis of Udine, Italy, a jurisconsult, or lawyer specializing in the writing of *consilia,* the Catholic equivalent of *teshuvot* (responsa) in Jewish law. A popular manual, *De Iudaeis* started with the assumption that "modern Jews are religious enemies of Christianity (as opposed to civil enemies). Nevertheless, the Church and Christianity receive them and sustain them out of piety and charity" (I, 2, as quoted in Kenneth R. Stow, *Catholic Thought and Papal Jewry Policy 1555–1593*, hereafter cited as CTPJP [New York, 1971], p. 81). De Susannis's work includes a fervid sermon in which he preaches that "the end of the world is near," and just as the Spaniards have already converted many in the New World, so must a major effort be made to convert all infidels, especially Jews (pp. 131, 145–147). Stow argues that de Susannis's tract complemented *Cum nimis* by adapting the spirit of Paul IV's bull to Jewry law (Church laws applying to the Jewish people, as opposed to Jewish laws, originated by Jews themselves). He maintains that Jewry law became an instrument designed to bring about the conversion of the Jewish people through all manner of exclusions and prohibitions which served to dramatize their subservient status more than ever before, thereby driving them to the "logical" conclusion of conversion as the means to overcome their intolerable legal status (pp. 166–170). For the eschatological yearnings of Cardinal Carafa (later Paul IV) and his despair over the events of the times and his belief that the world was ready for the fulfillment of the messianic prophecies of the Gospels and for the conversion of all non-Christians, along with an analysis of his personality, see Stow's excellent psychological and religious portrait (pp. 109, 266–277). The comparison of Paul IV, Giles of Viterbo, and de Susannis, their belief that their "world was coming apart" and their consequent emphasis on inner discipline as a way to hasten the millennium, is especially valuable for our purposes because of the similar turning inward and anticipation of the coming of the Messiah that was occurring among Jewish mystics in the second half of the sixteenth century (see

there were 1,750 Jews. By 1592, the overall population had grown to 97,000, and the number of Jewish souls to 3,500. To appreciate the size of the city's Jewish populace, one must remember that in 1552, Venice, the center of Jewish publishing efforts and a significant center in its own right, had only 902 Jews in a general population of 158,067.[3] Understandably, Roman Jewry was one of the largest Jewish communities in Christian Europe. During the seventeenth century, the population grew 400 percent, converting the ghetto into a veritable slum. Zahalon refers to a population of 4,127 Jews in 1656, just prior to the outbreak of the plague.[4]

Fire and the danger of a wall or building collapsing held ghetto residents in constant fear. In 1647 and 1660, the Tiber River overflowed, inundating the Jewish quarter and doing much damage besides causing considerable impoverishment. Many homes within the ghetto had only one bed, which was used around the clock alternately by different members of the family. Jews needed passes to go outside the ghetto, and were not even allowed to look out of the windows of their homes during certain Christian holidays, as from Holy Thursday to the Saturday following.

There were over thirty religious and communal organizations in the Roman ghetto, a testimony to the advanced degree of social welfare in the Jewish quarter. The functions of the various societies included fasting, praying for the Messiah to come speedily, studying, helping the indigent, aiding women about to give birth,

below, n. 85). Zahalon's entire *Margaliot Tovot* [Venice, 1665] was surely an outgrowth of the prevailing religious outlook (also see Ibn Yaḥya, *Sefer Shalshelet ha-Kabbalah* [Jerusalem, 1962], p. 108, for his conviction that the Messiah would appear in 1598).

3. D. Gnoli in *Descriptio Urbis,* Archivo of the R. Societa Romana di storia patria, XVII, 384, as quoted in Salo W. Baron, *A Social and Religious History of the Jews,* XIV (New York, 1969), pp. 67, 144, and notes on pp. 332 and 358.

4. *Oẓar ha-Ḥayyim* (Venice, 1683), p. 21b. A Jewish population of 3,000 in 1555 and 4,500 in 1655 continued to grow in spite of the loss of 800 in the plague, and many more due to conversions.

succoring prisoners, visiting the sick and providing them with medicine and food, burying the dead (a *Ḥevrah Qaddisha*), and aiding widows and orphans.[5]

In spite of the extensive social concern which these organizations manifested, the Jews of Rome sought to prevent too many poor and untrained people from moving into the ghetto, so as to prevent increased competition, taxation, and overcrowding in the limited space. Here, obviously, Jews had a definite degree of autonomy in passing on each new applicant's desirability as a resident of the ghetto.

We can surmise that there was frequent social intercourse between the ghetto Jews and their non-Jewish neighbors, judging from an Inquisitorial decree of 1598, renewed in 1628, that "Christians attending Jewish circumcisions, accepting breakfasts or unleavened bread, serving in the homes of Jews, conversing with them in a familiar vein, or discussing matters of faith with them shall be punished, together with those very Jews, by the Holy Office."[6] Such ambivalence, Baron comments, was quite common in Judeo-Christian relations, and the entire matter depended on local enforcement agencies, which were very susceptible to the influence of judiciously administered bribes.

The legislation which first appeared in 1555 reenacted all of the humiliating laws instituted by the predecessors of Paul IV and only enforced from time to time. These included the wearing of yellow caps and head shawls and of the Jewish badge,[7] prohibitions on owning real estate and on dealing in corn and other necessities, and the relegation of Jews to dealing in old clothes and second-

---

5. Baron, p. 364.

6. *Ibid.*, pp. 121–122.

7. *Cum nimis* specified that these items of clothing should be worn, "in full view a hat or some obvious marking," as signs of disgrace, classing Jews with prostitutes and slaves as opposed to people of virtue and Christians (as explained in *De Iudaeis,* see Stow, CTPJP, pp. 94 and 295).

hand merchandise.[8] Jewish physicians were not allowed to treat Christian patients and were forbidden to respond even when called. The prohibition concerning treating Christians was renewed in 1608 and in 1631.[9] Yet we find that in Zahalon's early years, specifically from 1640 to 1655, a certain bishop had the right to grant Jewish doctors the permission to treat Christians "in view of the scarcity of Christian physicians."[10] We know, too, as Friedenwald points out, that despite all the opposition and bitter Church attacks on Jewish physicians, they were still preferred by many popes, papal officials, monks, and nuns.[11] Guedemann

8. In his "Prayer for [Sufficient] Sustenance," Zahalon alluded to these hardships: "let the cruelty of mankind or of our enemies not prevent me from earning a livelihood . . ." (*Margaliot Tovot* 10a, see below, p. 37).

9. Harry Friedenwald, *The Jews and Medicine* (Baltimore, 1944), II, 589.

10. *Ibid.*

11. *Ibid.*, p. 590. Heinrich Graetz notes that although the ecumenical council of Basel (1431–1437) ordered that Christians were not to consult Jewish physicians, the popes and cardinals ignored the ruling. For example, Alexander VI had a Jewish physician from Provence, Bonet de Lates, who later also served Leo X (*Divrei Yemei Yisro'el*, trans.by S. P. Harkavy [Warsaw, 1893],VI, 210). During the Renaissance nearly every pope had a Jewish physician. Samuel Sarfati ministered to Sixtus IV, who confirmed certain privileges which had been granted to him earlier under Alexander VI. Isaac Sarfati was physician to Clement VII, Jacob Mantino to Paul III, who appointed him professor of medicine at the University of Rome in 1539, one of the few instances of a Jew's holding such a position at this time (see H. Vogelstein, *Rome,* trans. by M. Hadas [Philadelphia, 1941], pp. 245–246). Baron comments concerning the rejection of Guglielmo Portaleone's right to have his medical license renewed in 1636 that "the decision . . . could not have been made without Urban VIII's approval. . . . Fewer Jewish physicians functioned after that date." Yet this same Guglielmo of Mantua, or Benjamin b. David Mi-Sh'ar Aryeh, as he was known in Hebrew, was granted a renewal three years later by the same pope, as was another Portaleone in 1655, under either Innocent X or Alexander VII. Even with the renewed license to practice medicine, Jewish physicians might have had to endure other indignities, such as rejection by the local medical society, the use of Catholic religious references to the Virgin Mary and local patron saints in the procedure of licensing doctors, and possible religious observances required of all physicians in a particular community (pp. 64 and 109, p. 330, n. 61).

explains this preference for Jewish medical men as due to their scientific thoroughness, loyal devotion, and unselfishness.[12] Further, Graetz suggests that with all the intrigue rampant in Rome at that time, each man looked at his companion as a potential enemy, and Christians simply were not worried, when asking medical help from a Jewish physician for a pope or cardinal, about the possibility that the sick person might be given a "poisoned cup instead of a salutary remedy."[13] Graetz further maintains that there were very few competent Christian physicians at the time.[14]

Another sign of the times in which Zahalon lived was the number of forced conversions that occurred. In 1635, it was ruled that if the head of a household was baptized, his entire family could also be converted if he so desired.[15] Many Jewish men were forcibly carried off to the Casa dei Catecumeni, and prospective women converts to the Monastero delle Convertite.[16] The snatching up of children and forced baptisms were surely some of the most frightening aspects of Jewish daily life in Rome. Roth describes them as the principal cause for emigration outside the area of papal rule.[17] The poignancy of the situation is particularly evident in the prayer that Zahalon composed for a *Mohel* to say when circumcising his own son or the sons of others:

> and may those who are circumcised by me, as well as all the children of Israel, Your people, never convert from their religion or their faith either willingly or under duress. Rather, may they be strong in their faith in the *Torah* of Moses even to the day of their

[12] Moritz Guedemann, *Sefer ha-Torah ve-ha-Ḥayyim be-Arẓot ha-Ma'arav bimei ha-Beinayim* (Warsaw, 1896), trans. by A. Friedberg, from *Geschichte des Erziehungswesens und der Cultur der abendlaendischen Juden* (Vienna, 1880–88), II, 157.

[13] Zvi (Heinrich) Graetz, *Divrei Yemei Yisro'el,* VII, 38.

[14] *Ibid.,* VI, 267.

[15] Roth, p. 378.

[16] See nn. 20 and 21 below.

[17] Roth, p. 381.

death. May You make them strong in the face of those who disparage their faith. Cause their resistance to be as firm as metal against their detractors that they may never have reason to be ashamed in this world, nor to be humiliated in the world to come.[18]

In 1639, an earlier bull of Julius III was enforced once more, whereby the baptism of Jewish children without their parents' consent was outlawed with the threat of having to pay a fine of 1,000 ducats and suffer suspension from public office.[19] The bull had made it a crime to convert by force and not through persuasion. Baron explains that the term "persuasion" was now given a broader meaning, however, thus diminishing the degree of protection afforded to the Jewish community. So, for example, in 1639, a woman responsible for converting a three-year-old Jewish girl without her parents' knowledge was merely warned not to repeat such actions.

The entire Roman Jewish community had to listen to conversionist sermons on the Sabbath, and any adult or child over twelve who was not present could be severely punished. The Dominicans who preached on such occasions often cited the same scriptural texts that had been read that day in the synagogue service in order to refute them.[20] Jews were taxed for the support of the conver-

---

[18] *Margaliot Tovot* 9b. Especially remarkable is a phrase below this: "And grant me the privilege of bringing new converts under the wings of the *Shekhinah* (Divine Presence), as Abraham our father did" (see Sanh. 96b).

[19] Baron, p. 60. De Susannis in his *De Iudaeis* rules that no one should ever be baptized against his will, i.e., with *coactio praecisa* (absolute force) when the baptized person is *pati quam agere* (totally passive). If such were to occur, the baptism would not "effect its indelible imprint." However, when the baptizer makes use of force, and no objection is raised over a long period, then the baptism is considered valid (III, 2, 4, and 11, referred to in Stow, CTPJP, p. 172).

[20] Although conversionist sermons existed since the thirteenth century, the papal bull *Sancta mater ecclesia,* issued September 1, 1584, by Gregory XIII, began with the observation that "each day we consider whence more opportune provisions can be made for the conversion and salvation [of the Jews]." It provided that "qualified persons, wherever possible expert in Hebrew," should

sionist preachers, their assistants, and the houses of catechumens, all of which was deeply resented.[21] Within these institutions, devoted to the training of converts, were often found many renegade Jews who delighted in inflaming the feelings of the authorities or populace against their former fellow Jews through deliberately misinterpreting Jewish teachings.

The frequency of conversions among Roman Jews lessened somewhat after 1634. From then until 1700, 1,195 Jews were baptized, or about 18 per year. Between 1700 and 1790, about 1,237 were converted, averaging 14 per year.[22] According to Baron, there was no doubt a higher percentage between 1555 and 1634, due to the effects of the Catholic Reformation and much more anti-Jewish persecution.

Economically, the Jews of Rome were surely on the decline during Zahalon's lifetime, a factor which must have played a part in his eventual move to Ferrara between 1678 and 1680.[23] In 1647, the Roman Jewish community, in desperate need of funds to meet the exorbitant demands of the papal treasury, had been forced to borrow large amounts from the Monti di Pieta, paying an additional bribe to the authorities for allowing it to borrow the money. In 1668, the Jews of Rome had a floating debt of 250,000 scudi.[24]

---

explain the weekly scriptural portions in the synagogues each Sabbath. Earlier, in 1577, Gregory XIII had ruled that one hundred Jewish men and fifty Jewish women should be sent by the community every Saturday afternoon to listen to conversionist sermons given in a church near the ghetto. In addition to these conversionist sermons, houses of catechumens had been established already in 1543 by Paul III in his bull *Illius cui.* These were houses meant for newly converted Jews, where they could live and be further indoctrinated (Vogelstein, *Rome,* p. 291; see pp. 291–295 for descriptions of the houses of catechumens and how they were conducted).

[21] Baron, p. 61.

[22] E. Natali, *Il Ghetto di Roma,* p. 245, cited in Baron, p. 328, n. 59.

[23] See below, pp. 51 and 54.

[24] Baron, p. 331, n. 63. On the background of the church-run loan banks, see Gilbert S. Rosenthal, *Banking and Finance among Jews in Renaissance Italy* (New York, 1962), pp. 14–22. The scudo (pl. scudi) was a silver coin first issued in the sixteenth century and used in Italy until the nineteenth century, worth approximately one dollar. Cf. below, n. 60.

There is evidence of frequent insults and beating of Jews in the streets of Rome from the law, renewed in 1630, 1632, 1634, and a few times thereafter, threatening anyone who attacked a Jew with three lashes and a fine of 200 scudi.[25] Baron points out that the necessity of reinstituting this law so frequently demonstrated its inefficacy in putting an end to the gross popular amusements and "scandalous vexations" to which the Jews had become victims.

In addition, the Jews of Rome had to endure further indignities. Each year a number of nearly naked older Jews were made to run a race which was calculated to subject them and the whole Jewish community to the most terrible humiliations. This yearly event was abolished in 1668 out of practical rather than ethical considerations, but another ceremony was put in its place: now certain Jewish leaders had to appear before the local *conservatori* dressed in a particular prescribed degrading manner.

A further way in which Roman Jewry were reminded of their subservient position was through the ritual they had to observe after each papal election. Near the Arch of Titus, symbol of Jewish defeat, Jewish officials had to present the new pope with a *Sefer Torah,* which he very often would return to them in a most offensive manner. Such indignities were, nevertheless, a far cry from the physical dangers faced by the Jews of Poland in the Chmielnicki massacres of 1648 and subsequent pogroms which lasted until 1655. Yet, doubtlessly, this may have been little comfort to Roman Jewry because of the multitude of subtle and not-so-subtle pressures they had to contend with.

[25] *Ibid.,* p. 58. The law had originally been passed in 1595 through the insistence of a Roman governor. Regarding physical danger to Jews, autos-da-fè had been seen often in Rome. Marranos consciously avoided living in the papal states, which accounts for the dearth of Marranos killed. Yet on June 23, 1566, during the reign of Pius V, one Marrano is listed as having been put to death in such an "act of faith." In 1565 four Marranos, and in 1578 seven, were executed in autos-da-fè under Gregory XIII. Other public burnings of individual Jews took place in 1628 and 1641. Of course, Jews were not the only ones who perished in this way. Such a prominent liberal Catholic as Giordano Bruno was also a victim of the Counter-Reformation, accused of heresy and burned at the stake on the Campo dei Fiori in Rome in 1592.

One sign of Jew-baiting carried on in Rome can still be seen to this day. There is a church very near the old ghetto, a short distance from the Great Synagogue and just opposite the bridge of Quattro Capi. On the front of the building, in addition to a painting of the crucifixion, one can see printed clearly in Hebrew as well as in Latin translation the verse from Isaiah 65:2, "I have spread out My hands all the day unto a rebellious people, that walk in a way that is not good after their own thoughts." According to Gregorovius, this biblical verse was put there by a converted Jew to flatter his newly adopted religion.[26] The sight of such a verse from the Hebrew Scriptures could only have aroused sadness and deep humiliation in the local Jewish populace.[27] It was into this Jewish community that Jacob Zahalon was born in the year 1630.[28]

[26] F. Gregorovius, *The Ghetto and the Jews of Rome*, trans. by Moses Hadas from the 1874 ed. (New York, 1966), p. 80.

[27] Zahalon's "Prayer for the Acceptance of Prayers" (see p. 37 below) alludes to another form of attack on the Jewish religion, *viz.*, on Hebrew as the language of prayer: "And why do the wicked say, 'Your holy language is without value in making your prayers ascend before the King of kings, the Holy One, praised be He. Who asked you for such [prayers]? It is a worthless commandment. "Your strength is spent in vain" (Lev. 26:20)'? Now, my God [in the face of all these attacks], hear the prayer of Your servant . . ." (*Margaliot Tovot* 12b). Arguing similarly against the efficacy of Jewish prayers, de Susannis had written over a century earlier in his *De Iudaeis* that Jews should be able to see that their "perfidious synagogue" has been rejected in favor of the Church, for while they no longer engage in idol-worship or human sacrifice, "they dwell in perpetual calamity, and they have lived destitute of all divine aid 1,555 years" (Stow, CTPJP, p. 138).

[28] In the light of so many forms of oppression and degradation to the life and spirit of Roman Jewry, one source comments: "It is not remarkable that in the age of the Ghetto there were few scholars or communal leaders of any distinction, the case of the courageous and erudite Tranquillo Vita Corcos (1660–1730) being exceptional" (E.J., XIV, 250). Jacob Zahalon would seem to be a second such exception.

Stow ascribes the weakened cultural life which had even earlier produced this lackluster quality of Roman Jewry to two principal causes: the loss of the Talmud and other rabbinic works in plentiful supply to the masses after the book-burning

2. The Early Life and Education of Jacob Zahalon

"Now, Lord my God, You have placed me in a position of authority, and You have appointed Your servant in place of my father,
and I am only a small lad, with no experience in leadership" (I
Kings 3:5). You have given to Your servant "a skilled tongue, to
know how to sustain with a word him that is weary" (Isa. 50:4).
("Prayer for One Who Preaches Publicly," *Margaliot Tovot,* p. 3b)

While Zahalon's writings abundantly reveal his attitudes and
concerns, personal references about his life and family are extremely sparse. Zahalon himself provides no direct light on his family
background or communal role except in two instances.[29] In his
detailed account of the epidemic in Rome in 1656 and 1657,
although he tells little about his own role, he mentions that he
delivered two *derashot* under extraordinary conditions and that he
was involved in a controversy with a Catholic doctor over the
diagnosis of a patient.[30] Further, in a note on the title page of the

---

of 1553—though a limited number of copies obviously existed—from which
trauma the people had never truly recovered (see above, n. 1), and the
prohibition against making use of so many religious and educational buildings
which had been allowed prior to 1555 (see below, n. 40). He, too, following
Milano, bemoans the lack of more than a very few competent rabbinic authorities
in the entire three hundred years during which the Roman ghetto existed, which
simply worsened an already poor state of Jewish learning (CTPJP, p. 186).
Milano documents the widespread scarcity of all forms of learning, secular as well
as religious. Secular studies, he notes, were viewed as distinctly harmful to Jewish
well-being (*Il Ghetto di Roma,* pp. 385–396).

[29] We have not included the many seemingly personal references found in the
Vidduyim, or confessionals, in *Shuvu Elai,* an unpublished work mentioned below,
p. 70; we have referred to prayers concerning Zahalon's wife in n. 221. Further, in
his prayer for forgiveness, under the Hebrew letter *Tav,* Zahalon prays that God
will remember the merit of his father Isaac "who prayed for me . . ." See below, n.
224. How much of this material can be considered autobiographical, and how
much is for the sake of completing the *Vidduyim* and the prayers for forgiveness,
we cannot know for sure.

[30] *Ozar ha-Ḥayyim,* p. 21b; see below, p. 25.

Casanatense manuscript of the *Or ha-Darshanim,* which Zahalon appears to have personally edited, he indicates the number of years he spent as a rabbi in Rome.[31] Building a composite portrait of the physician-rabbi's life has to be done, therefore, on the basis of biographical clues from his writings together with historical and bibliographical works dealing with his times.

The Zahalon family were Sefardic Jews who apparently migrated to Italy and Near Eastern countries after the Spanish Expulsion.[32] The shadow of the Inquisition hung over Jacob's life to the very end, and that ecclesiastical authority was ultimately responsible for the fact that the work with which we are chiefly concerned, the *Or ha-Darshanim,* was never published. A little more than one year after his death, the manuscript was relegated to the Holy Office archives, "never to be printed in any form nor . . . returned to anyone claiming ownership of it."[33]

Concerning the early history of the family, an ancestor, Moses b. Abraham Zahalon, copied one of the manuscripts of Mordecai Comtino in 1495.[34] Another forebear, according to Bartolocci, was Abraham b. Isaac Zahalon of Safed, who completed his commen-

---

[31] L. 19. See below, n. 41.

[32] Giulio Bartolocci, *Bibliotheca Magna Rabbinica de Scriptoribus et Scriptis Hebraicis,* I (Rome, 1675), 32, 33. Bartolocci describes Abraham b. Isaac Zahalon as a "Sefardic Jew, born in Safed, which is in Upper Galilee." In this same entry on the man who was known as the Raviẓ, Bartolocci adds: "The Zahalon family's origins in Rome were with those exiles, among whom it held a significant place (*Familia Tzahalonica etiam Rome inter exulantium coetum reperitur . . .*). The family almost always had learned men (if such there be among the Jews), and today in that family there is now Jacob Zahalon, a doctor of medicine and a *Morenu* in the synagogue . . . about whom we shall deal in his place" (p. 33). The words in the parentheses read *si qui sint inter Iudeos.* Later, however, in Bartolocci's entry on Jacob Zahalon (III [Rome, 1683], 852–854), there is no mention of the origins of the family. See below, p. 51.

[33] Casanatense MS. of *Or ha-Darshanim,* recto of the first page; see below, p. 93.

[34] H. Vogelstein and P. Rieger, *Geschichte der Juden in Rom,* II (Berlin, 1896), 268, n. 1.

tary on the Book of Esther, *Yesha Elohim* (Venice, 1595), while in Baghdad.[35] He was also the author of a work comparing the Jewish, Christian, and Islamic calendars, *Yad Ḥaruzim* (Venice, 1595), and an ethical treatise based on the work of the founder of the modern *Kabbalah,* Rabbi Isaac Luria, *Marpe la-Nefesh* (Venice, 1594).[36] He complained that he had to travel too much. According to one source, this Zahalon, known as the Raviẓ after the initials of his name, lived in Italy, and "enlightened the rabbis of his generation through the works which he composed."[37]

The father of Jacob Zahalon, Isaac Zahalon, is mentioned on the title page of the *Or ha-Darshanim*[38] with the designation *K M H R R,* "Our honored master and teacher," which is also used to describe his son, except that Jacob is referred to as "The Honored Outstanding Physician" in addition. This may merely be a pious filial gesture, and if so is insufficient reason for inferring that our author's father was, indeed, an ordained rabbi. According to

---

[35] In the introduction to this work, its author refers to his father, Isaac Zahalon, as "from those who dwell in Upper Galilee, Safed, may it be speedily rebuilt in our days." That Yom Tov Zahalon of Safed (1559–after 1638) may in some way have been related to Jacob Zahalon of Rome is not impossible, and interesting to consider.

[36] On the title page of this work, the title of which means "A Healing for the Soul," the author writes, "In this work will be found balm and healing for false opinions." It is an interesting coincidence, and nothing more than that, that this possible ancestor of Jacob Zahalon used such medical terminology. If there is a relation between the Raviẓ and our author, it becomes a curious historical fact that what an earlier Zahalon wrote about in a figurative sense (*Marpe la-Nefesh*), a later Zahalon was to write on in a very literal sense (i.e., Jacob's medical treatise, *Oẓar ha-Ḥayyim*). Scholem describes the *Marpe la-Nefesh* as one of "the penitential classics of the Lurianic school" (*Sabbatai Ṣevi: The Mystical Messiah,* p. 294 and n. 263). Jacob Zahalon was later to exhibit an obvious spiritual kinship with that mystical school through his inclusion of the *Yedid Nefesh* and other works of Azikri in his *Margaliot Tovot* (see below, n. 85).

[37] Bartolocci, III, 852.

[38] Hereafter cited as the *Or.*

Bartolocci, the term *Morenu* was used for the most distinguished rabbis, obviously equivalent to what we would call ordination.[39]

The Zahalon family was affiliated with the synagogue of Cataloni and Aragonesa in Rome, which apparently represented a merger of two separate synagogues.[40] It was to this congregation that Jacob was called to preach around 1651.[41] That he was accepted into the University of Rome and able to earn the title of *Doctoris Philosophiae ac Medicinae,* or *Artium ac Medicinae,* would seem to be no small accomplishment. The number of Jews who completed their studies in the faculty of medicine in Rome in Zahalon's time was extremely small in comparison with the number that we know of at the University of Padua.[42] The period

[39] III, 852. Bartolocci writes "inter precipuous Rabbinos, quos Morenos appellitant, connumerari meruerit." This reference to Jacob Zahalon by his prominent Catholic contemporary as "deserving of being counted among the great rabbis called *Morenu*" would seem to be significant testimony to the high regard in which Zahalon was held in the Roman Jewish (and non-Jewish) community.

[40] One of the provisions of *Cum nimis* in 1555 had been that the Jews "should have one synagogue alone in its customary location, and they may construct no new synagogue. . . . Accordingly, they must demolish and destroy all their [other] synagogues except for this one alone" (quoted in Stow, CTPJP, p. 295). Before 1555 there had been nine separate congregations, each in its own building. Although all congregations remained after that date, they were forced to share one building. By the end of the sixteenth century, there were only five: Cataloni, Aragonesa, del Tempio, Nuova, and the Sicilian congregation (see Gregorovius, *The Ghetto and the Jews of Rome,* p. 97).

[41] See the Casanatense MS. (hereafter cited as Cas. MS.) of the *Or* for what seems to be Zahalon's own note on the title page of this autographic MS., ll. 16–19. According to Gustavo Sacerdote, *Catalogo dei Codici Ebraici della Biblioteca Casanatense* in *Cataloghi dei Codici Orientali di Alcune Biblioteche d'Italia,* VI (Florence, 1897), 648–649, the Cas. MS. is no. 217, in one volume, measuring 20 by 12.5 cm. with 268 folio pages. This MS. is no. 3074 in the Jewish Theological Seminary microfilm collection. Cf. below, pp. 93–94.

[42] J. O. Leibowitz, "R. Ya'aqov Zahalon Ish Roma u-Fizmono le-Shabbat Hanukkah mi-Shnat 1687," in *Sefer Zikaron le-Hayyim Enzo Serini, Ketavim al Yahdut Roma,* edited by A. Milano, Sh. Nakhon, and D. Karpi (Jerusalem, 1971), p. 166. Elsewhere Leibowitz comments on the policy of the medical schools in

during which Zahalon completed his medical studies has been described by Cassuto as one of decline for the cultural life of Italian Jewry and for Jewish participation in science and medicine.[43] Friedenwald notes that there are very few references to Jews practicing medicine in Italy in the first half of the seventeenth century.[44] We have already referred to several strictures against

Perugia (in central Italy) and in Padua as being more liberal in their acceptance of Jewish students than the University of Rome. See "Jacob Zahalon: A Hebrew Medical Author of the XVIIth Century (1630–1693)," in *Actes du Septième Congrès International d'Histoire des Sciences* (Jerusalem, 1953), p. 431. Leibowitz states there: "The eminent historian, Professor Umberto Cassuto, doubted that Zahalon studied at Rome," though Leibowitz does not give his source for this reference. Bartolocci's statement that "Doctorisque titulum in Philosophia, & Medicina in Romana Uniuersitate recepit" ("He was granted the degree of Doctor of Philosophy and Medicine by the University of Rome"), III, 852, would appear to be rather solid evidence of Zahalon's acceptance there inasmuch as Bartolocci knew Zahalon personally and was professionally interested in gathering objective facts about Jewish authors for his work on rabbinic writings.

Clearly, the Church had been most ambivalent concerning the right of Jews to study and practice medicine (see Friedenwald, *The Jews and Medicine*, II, 589 on this, especially the appointment of Jacob Mantino as professor of medicine at the University of Rome in 1539). In 1558 in his *De Iudaeis* de Susannis noted that it was commonly accepted that Jews were not permitted to receive a doctorate in law, medicine, or theology, because that would confer an honorary status upon them. He added, however, that they were allowed to become physicians but not to minister to the pope or emperor(!). *Cum nimis* had spelled this out in its tenth provision, that Jewish physicians "even if they are summoned and requested may not come forth and attend to the care of Christians." *De Iudaeis* specified that the general rule applying to Jewish physicians might be set aside (a) during a plague when all doctors would be in great demand, and (b) if the Jew is the only one who knows how to cure a particular illness (Stow, CTPJP, pp. 113–114). In 1618, Paul V had ruled that the University of Rome should not admit Jews for studies leading to the doctorate in medicine, maintaining that the previous practice of admitting Jewish candidates had been illegal and should not have been allowed (Baron, pp. 108–109).

[43] M. D. (Umberto) Cassuto in *Encyclopaedia Hebraica,* II (Jerusalem, 1950), 797–798, s.v. "Italia."

[44] II, 589; see above, n. 9.

Jewish doctors healing Christians or preparing medicines for them, and various indignities endured by Jews in medicine.[45] Quite clearly, the Church hardly created an atmosphere that would have encouraged Jewish men to enter the medical profession.

Bartolocci adds that, outside of the study of Judaism, "in his youth [Zahalon] pursued the learning of Latin, the humanities, philosophy, and medicine . . ."[46] Simultaneous with his pursuits in secular fields of knowledge, Zahalon maintained his religious studies. He never ceased studying the *halakhah* through the talmudic literature. From his index to the *Yalqut Shimoni* we have clear evidence of his considerable mastery of the *aggadah,* and from other sources we assume that he continued to train himself to become an authority in *halakhah.*[47] Zahalon appears to have achieved excellence in preaching at an early age. It would seem that by the age of twenty-six he had entered both professions, for he was both a *darshan* and a physician in the year of the plague, 1656–1657. In fact, according to his own note on the title page of his manuscript of the *Or,* he had already begun his preaching career when he was between the ages of twenty-one and twenty-three.[48]

---

[45] Above, pp. 11–12.

[46] III, 352.

[47] See below, pp. 64–66. An earlier Italian preacher known for having started his career at a young age was Rabbi Leone da Modena (1571–1648), who began preaching in the great synagogue of Venice at twenty-two. Da Modena himself wrote that "in the days of his youth" he began "to show the peoples and princes what God had graciously done [for him in blessing him with special talent] in the work [of composing] *derashot* in Venice" in many synagogues and houses of learning there and in other communities (*Sefer Beit Leḥem Yehudah* [Venice, 1625], 2b). See below, n. 58. In 1564, in a written proposal to create a Jewish college in Mantua, David Provenzalo, himself a great preacher, included among his many suggestions for the curriculum the idea that young Jewish college students, religious in spirit, "will gradually be taught to speak in public and to preach before congregations," quoted in Jacob R. Marcus, *The Jew in the Medieval World* (Cincinnati, 1938), p. 382.

[48] Using the statement in the *Or,* ll. 16–19, that he had been twenty-seven years in Rome, and working backwards according to Vogelstein and Rieger, II,

3. Zahalon's Role in the Plague of 1656–1657

> *Question:*—What was the nature and circumstance of the plague which occurred in the city of Rome in the year 5416, 1656 according to their calendar, specifically, what occurred in the ghetto at the end of 5416 in *Tammuz* and the beginning of 5417?
>
> *Answer:*—In the year of the creation 5416, 1656 according to their calendar, in the month of July before the plague, there was an outbreak of a disease called *morbilli* (measles) in children . . .
>
> (*Ozar ha-Ḥayyim,* p. 21a)

That Zahalon's efforts to improve his preaching ability bore fruit is evident from his position in the Roman Jewish community by the year 1656, when the epidemic which he described as *morbilli* struck the city, including the ghetto, later developing into the plague.[49] From his account in the *Ozar ha-Ḥayyim,* we may reasonably assume that he was recognized both as a responsible medical man and as a *darshan* to be taken seriously.[50] Writing in this work, which was published in 1683, Zahalon describes the events that occurred twenty-seven years earlier, when he was only twenty-six years old, not only as a matter of important medical history, but also as a means of teaching some practical lessons in treating and controlling an epidemic.

From the *Ozar ha-Ḥayyim*[51] we learn that some three months before the end of *Tammuz* 5416, or June 1656, the plague broke out in the non-Jewish areas of Rome. By the middle of the summer,

269 (who maintained that Zahalon remained in Rome until 1680), or according to Bartolocci, III, 854 (who says that "four or five years ago" our author and his family left Rome for Ferrara, meaning that Zahalon went to Ferrara in 1678 or 1679, as the third volume of Bartolocci's *Bibliotheca* appeared in 1683), we would arrive at the conclusion that Zahalon was officially titled *Morenu* between 1651 and 1653, when he would have been between twenty-one and twenty-three. See p. 51.

[49] Alfonso Corradi in his *Annali Delle Epidemie Occorse in Italia,* II, 208–225, and V, 547, indicates that this was an outbreak of *plague.* Why Zahalon refers to it as *morbilli,* or measles, we cannot determine.

[50] Pp. 21a, 21b. We cannot tell whether he was a graduate physician.

[51] Hereafter cited as the *Ozar.*

the disease reached the ghetto, at first affecting only children, all of whom perished. Afterwards, adults contracted the disease, and death normally occurred three days after the symptoms were first noted. For nine months the pestilence ravaged the Jewish population, taking 800 lives out of a population of 4,127.[52]

We learn from the parallel but slightly varied account of Cardinal Gastaldi, published one year after the *Oẓar,* that the experience gained in fighting the plague among the general population of Rome was utilized to advantage when the disease reached the ghetto. The Church authorities had feared that, due to the overcrowded situation and poor sanitary conditions, the epidemic would take an unusually high toll in the Jewish quarter. As a result, special regulations were passed to empty the ghetto homes of all excessive belongings and store such possessions, carefully recorded and marked, in the boarded-up synagogues and schools.[53] A committee of fifteen was appointed to act on behalf of the Jewish population on the outside of the ghetto, purchasing provisions and acting as intermediaries within the city of Rome at large. In the Jewish quarter proper, seventeen districts were set up with overseeing doctors and with regulations for handling those suspected of having been smitten by the disease as well as those already diagnosed positively. For this purpose, special *lazzarettos,* or "fever-hospitals," were established. Burial procedures were

---

[52] *Oẓar,* p. 21b. J. O. Leibowitz in "Magefat ha-Dever be-Ghetto Roma (1656) lefi Zahalon ve-ha-Cardinal Gastaldi," in *Qorot,* IV, secs. 3–4 (Jerusalem, Sivan 1967), 166, refers to an account of the plague by Cardinal Hieronymus Gastaldi entitled *Tractatus de avertenda et profliganda peste politico-legalis* (Bologna, 1684). There are slight variations in this work from Zahalon's account. Leibowitz calls attention to Gastaldi's claim that over 1,400 Jewish lives were lost, but he concludes that Gastaldi may have included other deaths besides those specifically from the plague. Zahalon's role made him much closer to the scene, and his account in the *Oẓar* appears, therefore, more accurate. Cf. Roth, p. 330.

[53] This detail is found only in Gastaldi's account, according to Leibowitz, "Magefet ha-Dever be-Ghetto Roma," pp. 163–164. Leibowitz notes that this method of setting aside belongings of potential and actual plague victims is related to the biblical method of treating plague, p. 167.

worked out in such a way as to prevent contamination of the still-healthy population by those who had perished from the pestilence.

All Jews were prohibited from leaving the ghetto and were only allowed on the ghetto streets during certain hours. Three Jewish doctors are mentioned by Zahalon as having charge over the patients. One of them was a first cousin of our author, a certain Isaac Zahalon, a "skilled surgeon" who died toward the end of the epidemic.

As to the exact medical role Jacob filled, we have no direct knowledge. He does relate an incident, however, in which his diagnosis of one of the patients differed from that of a non-Jewish physician. A certain Sabbatie Cohen's condition revealed symptoms common to both *morbilli* and another disease. Zahalon insisted that Cohen was *not* suffering from the plague, asserting thereby that he would not have to be isolated from his neighborhood. The Catholic doctor maintained, on the contrary, that Cohen was suffering from the pestilence. A post-mortem examination confirmed Zahalon's diagnosis, to which he comments, "I was saved. Blessed is He who redeems and saves."[54]

Our author also refers to himself as if he might have been at that time a physician or at least a medical assistant, for he says: "I was greatly aided through the help of God that I made a *cauterio* (seton) on my left arm from which blood and pus flowed."[55] This detail follows his statement that the attending physicians brought with them a large torch of burning tar and placed theriac in their mouths as a prophylactic measure against the plague.[56] Obviously, Zahalon was closely involved in working with the medical teams that had been organized, even if he was not a graduate physician by that time.

[54] *Oẓar*, p. 21b.

[55] *Ibid.*

[56] Harry A. Savitz, in "Jacob Zahalon, and His Book 'The Treasure of Life'," in *New England Journal of Medicine*, Vol. 213, No. 4 (Boston, July 25, 1935), 26, suggests that the vapor of the burning tar impregnating his clothes may have made the physician an undesirable host for fleas, thus giving him some immunity.

He is hardly more specific about his precise role when he discusses the two sermons he delivered in 1657, although he describes the circumstances very carefully, perhaps because of the dramatic and extraordinary nature of the settings in which he delivered these sermons.

> Inasmuch as none of the people were permitted to attend the synagogue, on the Sabbath of *Parshat Toldot*, the second day of *Kislev*, 5717, I, Jacob Zahalon, preached a sermon on the Via Catalena from the window of the corner house of David Gatigno, and the congregation, may their Rock protect and guard them, stood in the street to hear the *derashah*. On another occasion, I preached on the Via Toscana, standing at the window of Judah Gatigno's home, while the people stood below on the street to hear the sermon. Similarly, on the other streets scholars delivered lessons on *Torah* from the windows of their homes, as no one but doctors was permitted to be on the streets all day except at certain fixed times.[57]

Zahalon does not describe the content of his sermons or the response they received. We may wonder whether the idea of delivering sermons from such places was his own special innovation. He was obviously only one among many *darshanim*. Yet the fact that he specifies so clearly the places and occasions of his sermons is perhaps an indication that his participation in this form of preaching was somewhat unique. He is, in general, noteworthy for the paucity of references about himself, particularly in regard to details that might appear complimentary. This is true not only of the *Oẓar* but also of the introduction to the *Or*.[58]

Zahalon's description of the plague in the ghetto of Rome is an

---

[57] *Oẓar,* p. 21b. Vogelstein and Rieger, II, 268, say the dated sermon was on November 18, 1656.

[58] Contrast this with da Modena's comments in his *Ḥayyei Yehudah* (Kiev, 1911), pp. 18, 25, 31, on the reception of his sermons. Consider, too, Zahalon's self-deprecating description of his writing of the *mareh maqom* to the *Yalqut, Or,* ll. 190–196.

important document. It provides us with much insight into the functioning of this Jewish community in a time of grave crisis. It furnishes details about the prevailing institutions of social welfare.[59] For example, our author records that there were 2,624 Jews on the rolls of the poverty-stricken out of a total Jewish population of 4,127 souls.

He also spells out the allotments that were distributed to these underprivileged people. To the already overburdened Roman Jewish population was now added the necessity of providing 1,036 scudi, 9 giuli, and 9 baiocchi weekly for those in need.[60] In the light of these economic hardships, how very understandable are the references to being saved from becoming a charity case in the prayers Zahalon wrote for the *Margaliot Tovot*.[61]

An earlier outbreak of plague occurred in the community of Padua in 1631. There had been 665 Jews there out of a general population of 35,463 in 1615, and 721 in 1631, immediately before the outbreak of the epidemic, but their number was reduced to 300 as a result of the disease! Obviously, in comparison with the plague in Padua, where the Jewish community had sustained the loss of 41 percent of its populace, the Roman Jewish community in

[59] Salo W. Baron, *The Jewish Community* (Philadelphia, 1948), II, 329–330. *Oẓar,* p. 21b.

[60] *Oẓar,* p. 21b. He also specifies the amounts needed daily for each man, woman, and child. See Roth, p. 408, where we are told that by 1668 the Roman Jewish community was in debt over 250,000 scudi, 166,000 funded from a debt to the Monte di Pieta, and thousands more to individual non-Jews as creditors. See above, n. 24, for the value of the scudo, pl. scudi. According to the *Standard Catalog of World Coins* (Iola, 1982), pp. 192 and 1940, the monetary system in the papal states had these equivalents: 10 giuli equaled 1 scudo, and 10 baiocchi equaled 1 giuli. Therefore, 100 baiocchi made up 1 scudo. If the scudo could be equated to a dollar, the giuli would have been worth a dime, and the baiocchi a penny.

[61] "May I be able to feed my children . . . in dignity, and not with humiliation and disgrace," p. 9a, in "Prayer for Parents Concerning their Children." The idea of being self-sufficient is also reflected in the "Prayer for Physicians," in that they should not *have* to accept a fee from the indigent but rather be able to heal them without charge, p. 7a.

Zahalon's time was extremely fortunate, with only a 19 percent mortality rate.

Aside from the information concerning the functioning of the Jewish community, Zahalon also provides an important chapter in the history of epidemiology. Many early medical details are furnished to those interested in the background of public health.[62]

A further interesting detail of the account of the events of 1656–1657 in Rome in the *Ozar* is the annual prayer of thanksgiving instituted by the committee of fifteen who supervised purchases and other affairs outside the ghetto. This prayer was meant to be said every year by those who were saved from perishing in the pestilence. Zahalon also relates that the leadership of the ghetto formed a charitable society called *Ḥevrat Ḥayyim ve-Ḥesed,* which met every Wednesday at the home of one of the members to study *Torah.* In addition, recalling the miracle of their survival, every year on *Shabbat Ḥanukkah,* those who had been spared would gather at "the synagogue of *Arba Rashim,*"[63] where the local rabbi would deliver a *derashah* recalling how this community of Jews had been miraculously saved from being utterly destroyed by the plague. Fifty pillows were distributed every year to the poor, and various other needs were also provided.[64]

---

[62] Leibowitz, "Magefet ha-Dever be-Ghetto Roma," pp. 161–162.

[63] Zahalon is probably referring to the Great Synagogue, located just opposite the bridge of Quattro Capi (*Arba Rashim*).

[64] P. 21b. The custom of recalling days of deliverance or particular community miracles each year was also carried out in Ferrara every *Shabbat Ḥanukkah* after a seemingly uncontrollable conflagration was providentially extinguished by a torrential rain. The fire, which began in a bakery, and the rescue of the people, occurred in 1687, and Zahalon himself wrote a moving poem to commemorate the event. See below, pp. 64–65, and notes 192 and 193. In the *Talmud,* Ber. 54a, the injunction to say a blessing in thanksgiving for a miracle done to a large body of Jews led to the practice on the part of Jewish communities, or families, of recalling the anniversaries of their having been saved with special prayers and observances. Over a hundred of these special Purims, as they were called, are listed in the E. J., XIII, 1395–1400.

Most significant for our purposes in all the information gleaned from the *Oẓar,* in conclusion, were the famous "window sermons." Leopold Zunz in his history of Jewish preaching singles out Zahalon for special mention for these *derashot* given during the quarantine period.[65] It might be said that these now-famous occasions of preaching during the days of the plague in Rome are illustrations of the talmudic dictum that "some are marked for immortality in one moment."[66] They were unusual and truly poignant examples of how the message of the *Torah* may be brought directly to the people. The very fact that the Church authorities permitted such public *derashot* to be given outdoors, conceivably even in earshot of non-Jews who might have been impressed and influenced by them, is in itself remarkable, and explainable due to the fact that the local synagogues had been closed because of the special dangers of the pestilence in such closed spaces. It suffices to say that these sermons, together with what we are able to surmise from his writings, mark Jacob Zahalon as a dynamic, sophisticated, sensitive, and community-minded *darshan.*[67]

---

[65] *Ha-Derashot be-Yisro'el* (Jerusalem, 1954), p. 200, and n. 59, p. 526. (This is the Hebrew translation of *Die gottesdienstlichen Vortrage der Juden historisch entwickelt* [2d ed.; Berlin, 1892] by Ḥ. Albeck.)

[66] A.Z. 10b.

[67] See especially *Or,* ll. 431–450 (Chap. 3:1), where the author speaks of fitting the sermon to the place, the time, the weather conditions, and the abilities of the *darshan* himself. In ll. 303–306 (Chap. 1:5), he cautions against exhibitionistic preaching and urges preachers to aim at producing good deeds on the part of their listeners. In ll. 650–653 (Chap. 10:1), he defines the purpose of preaching as "refining the people and drawing them closer" to their Creator, and away from transgression. In ll. 654–657, he urges avoidance of self-righteousness, and cautions against shaming others with reproofs, recommending that the *darshan* include himself in his reproofs. Above all, the concern of the preacher must be for the moral betterment of his listeners, and not with his own homiletic expertise, though he must utilize all of the rules of good preaching to produce effective results.

His contemporaries were apparently not unaware of his strong communal role at a time of extreme stress and urgency. We find that his yearly salary as a preacher and community secretary, or recorder of decisions and ordinances, was increased in 1656 from 40 to 46 scudi. It was Zahalon who began a new record book for "Dekrete und Capitoli," or ordinances and *taqqanot,* and he held this communal position until 1680. He received an additional 8 scudi for keeping this book. Among the records were found different accounts concerning expenditures during the plague.[68]

4. Zahalon's Other Communal Responsibilities

> I pray that I may be among those righteous to whom it is said, "Preach, Rabbi, preach, because for you it is appropriate to preach" (Sanh. 100a), for "you preach well and *practice well*" (Ḥag. 14b, italics added).
>
> ("Prayer for One Who Preaches Publicly," *Margaliot Tovot,* p. 4a)

On the twentieth of *Kislev,* 5422 (December 12, 1661), following Zahalon's completion of the prototype of the manual,[69] Joshua Menagen, senior rabbi of the Jewish community of Rome since *Elul,* or around September 1660, suggested before the committee of sixty leaders that certain teachers be appointed to supervise the dissemination of knowledge of the Holy *Torah* among the people. For this purpose, three well-known men were selected: Moses b. Shalom Passapaire, Elisha b. Joseph Menagen, and Jacob b. Isaac Zahalon.[70]

Was this perhaps to guard against some of the numerous attempts to persuade unsuspecting members of the Jewish fold to

---

[68] A. Berliner, *Geschichte der Juden in Rom,* II (Frankfurt a. M., 1893), 192. Our translation of "Capitoli," a term used by Berliner, as *taqqanot,* is based on the explanation of Daniel Karpi, *Pinqas Va'ad Q"Q Padua, 1577–1603* (Jerusalem, 1973), p. 554. I am indebted to Dr. Ivan Marcus for this note.

[69] See below, Chap. 13.

[70] Berliner, II, 55.

convert to Catholicism? We have referred above to the many efforts that were being made at this time to win over Jewish souls.[71] Or were the three teachers appointed to protect their fellow Jews against purely internal factors that were weakening the community's religious life? While we cannot answer these questions, we can at least know from this appointment that Zahalon must have been keenly aware of the religious and communal problems that were occurring in Rome.

It is of note that Zahalon found time to assume this supervisory role in addition to his duties as recording secretary of the Jewish community, fulfilling the responsibilities of a physician, continuing his scholarly endeavors, not to mention his role as an active *darshan,* which, by his own testimony, was in itself a considerable cause of exertion. Could it have been that the task of overseeing instruction in Scripture, to which he was appointed in 1661, eventually led to Zahalon's including in his *Yeshu'ot Ya'aqov* a list of biblical verses which might be used in instruction improperly, even blasphemously?[72] Whether this appointment was to guard against incipient heterodoxy within the community we may never know. Yet we do know from other sources, as well as from oblique references in Zahalon's manual and introduction, that the middle of the seventeenth century was a time of religious ferment. Matters were to become still more complex five years later, specifically, in August 1666, with the arrival in Rome of Sabbatai Raphael, the personal emissary of Sabbatai Ẓevi. The same Joshua Menagen was among those who were extremely apprehensive about the cataclysmic events beginning to take shape at that time.[73]

---

[71] See above, especially pp. 12–14.

[72] See our description of *Yeshu'ot Ya'aqov,* p. 33.

[73] Gershom Scholem, *Sabbatai Ṣevi: The Mystical Messiah, 1626–1676* (Princeton, 1973), hereafter cited as *Sabbatai Ṣevi,* p. 509, referring to the correspondence between Samuel Aboab of Venice and Joshua Menagen, and M. Benayahu, "Yedi'ot me-Italia u-me-Holland al Reshita shel ha-Shabbeta'ut," in *Ereẓ Yisro'el,* IV (1956), 194–205.

ספר

מרגליות טובות

דהלא רהוא קצור כפר
חובת הלבבות ובראשיתו
תפלות לדרשנים ולרופאים
ולאבות על הבנים ולמוהלים
ועל המזונות ועל קבלת
התפלות ובסוף כל שער ושער
צדיקים יבאו בו ימצאו
תפלה הגונה מעניני של
אותו שער.

חברו מעלת הרב המופלא הרופא
המובהק כמהדר יעקב בכמהר יצחק
צהלון זכל לזכות את רבים זכלית
בכס סגדיל תושיה לכסויק עניניו
הרבים בדברים מועטים וחלקו לחלקים
ימים לאכן ירוץ קורא בו אלי יום כיומו
ויסלימוסו אלי קדש כתלסו

בויניציאה

במצות השר הגדול

אנדריאה פוריסיני

בסכת בשיח נגיד לפק

Appre. Domeni. Vedela.
Con licenza de Supriori.

Title page of *Margaliot Tovot*, Venice, 1665

5. Biographical Information from Zahalon's *Margaliot Tovot*

> The fifth [work of our teacher Rabbi Jacob Zahalon] is the *Sefer Margaliot Tovot* . . . small in quantity but great in quality, filled with reverence for the Lord and saintliness. It is [Zahalon's] first work [written] in his youth.
>
> (Joab ben Baruch de' Piattelli, from the first page of his introduction to Zahalon's *Margaliot Tovot*)

During this same period, before 1665, the date of the publication of the *Margaliot Tovot* in Venice, Zahalon had been keeping busy with his rabbinic writing. In the introduction to the *Margaliot*, Joab ben Baruch de' Piattelli[74] lists five works already completed by Zahalon by that time:

a. *Morashah Qehilat Ya'aqov,* which de' Piattelli calls "a charming explanation, written for the cultured person, of *Sefer Mada, Ahavah,* and *Zemanim* by the great Eagle, the Rambam, of blessed memory."[75]

---

[74] Dr. Daniel Karpi has told this writer that the Italian version of Joab's name would have been Dattilo qui Benedicti de' Piattelli. For biographical details about him, see notes 90, 127, and 251.

[75] See below, Chap. 13, for our discussion of the prototype of the *Or* found in the introduction to this work. De' Piattelli lists only these sections of Maimonides' work, but the title page of the actual MS. lists them somewhat differently as *Sefer ha-Mada—Hilkhot Yesodei ha-Torah, Hilkhot De'ot, Hilkhot Talmud Torah, Hilkhot Akum* (laws relating to idolatry), and *Hilkhot Teshuvah* (laws of repentance). An autographic MS. of this work is found in the British Museum collection, Or. 10044, Gaster 407. It has 279 pages, and is dated Rome, 1660. At the end of the introduction, containing the prototype of the *Or,* on 6b, are two *haskamot,* one by Ḥiyya Dayyan, dated with the Hebrew word *Tagel* (equivalent to 5433, or 1673), and one by Sabbatai Baer, dated *Talad* (5434, or 1674). On pages 107a to 113a (in the midst of *Hilkhot De'ot*) are found some Latin medical aphorisms in Hebrew transliteration, which had originally been written by Maimonides. At the end of the work there is an alphabetical index of the laws included here, and the last page of the MS. is signed "*Yosef Yare* . . . Ferrara." It is no. 7129 in the MSS. collection at Hebrew University.

b. *Yeshu'ot Ya'aqov,* described by de' Piattellli as "a very edifying commentary on the entire book of *Isaiah,* as well as on those verses in the *Torah, Prophets,* and *Holy Writings* on which teachers have incorrectly (i.e., blasphemously) based some of their teachings concerning the *Torah* in contradiction to the *halakhah* (i.e., normative rabbinic interpretations of law)."[76] According to Vogelstein and Rieger, a manuscript of this work *was* in the library of Dr. Med. Ascarelli in Rome and contained 404 pages.[77] However, no copy of this manuscript appears extant in any library collection at the present time. This work might have been concerned with the intensified though frequently subtle polemics between Christians and Jews. If so, it might have evolved out of Zahalon's efforts in supervising the teaching of *Torah* after his appointment in 1661.[78]

[76] The words of de' Piattelli are *ha-moreh panim ba-Torah shelo ka-halakhah,* which are very similar to a phrase in M. Avot 5:8: *hamorim ba-Torah shelo ka-halakhah,* meaning those "that teach the *Torah* not in accordance with the *halakhah.*" The phrase used by de' Piattelli is perhaps a conflation of the reading in Avot 5:8 along with an earlier one there in 3:12, *ha-megaleh panim ba-Torah shelo ka-halakhah,* meaning one who "is contemptuous towards the *Torah,*" or, quoting the *Maḥzor Vitry,* one who "seeks to ascribe disgraceful or improper meanings to the contents of the *Torah*" (translations from Judah Goldin, *The Living Talmud* [New York, 1957]).

[77] II, 269, n. 2. See JQR, V (1893), 697. In a review of a doctoral thesis dealing with a sixteenth-century MS. on *Isaiah,* the reviewer, A. Neubauer, refers to "other interpretations which have turned up since 1877," such as Zahalon's *Yeshu'ot Ya'aqov* on "Isaiah, and controversial passages in other prophets." Neubauer mentions the MS. in the possession of Ascarelli as if it were currently available to scholars who might care to pursue the subject further. Ettore Ascarelli (d. 1919), who is described as "descended from a family of exiles from Spain . . . a successful businessman . . . a lover of history and owner of a large library" (Ruth Bondy, *The Emissary: A Life of Enzo Sereni* [Boston, 1977], pp. 28–29), may have come to possess that book collection from an earlier ancestor, possibly Attilio Ascarelli, a nineteenth-century scholar in forensic medicine (see E.J., III, 677).

[78] See above, p. 30. I am indebted to Dr. Isaac Barzilay for the suggestion of Jewish-Christian polemics.

c. *Titen Emet le-Ya'aqov,* according to de' Piattelli, "a honeycomb, words of rare sweetness, sermons fashioned around all of the weekly portions (of Scripture)." The Adler collection lists this work as 278 (numbered R90 in the Jewish Theological Seminary). However, according to Rabbi Jacob Brumer, Cataloguer of Manuscripts at the Seminary, only two folio pages of the manuscript are by Zahalon, while the work is actually a collection of sermons by another author. One of the pages by Zahalon is the title page, which reads: "*Titen Emet le-Ya'aqov* . . . attractive sermons on all the weekly portions, and in the introduction he [the physician Rabbi Jacob Zahalon] has brought all the precautions and rules necessary to know in order to compose a fitting sermon, and 'he has taught knowledge' (Eccl. 12:9) on preaching in an attractive way to find satisfaction in the eyes of God and man (cf. Prov. 3:4) with the sermons that the wise man will preach."[79]

d. *Qol Ya'aqov,* described by de' Piattelli as "pleasant to behold in that it indicates the place of every saying in the *Yalqut.*" (*Qol Ya'aqov* was an alternate name on the title page of the Casanatense manuscript, but there it has been deleted finally in favor of the name of *Or ha-Darshanim*).[80] De' Piattelli in no way refers to the preacher's manual. Perhaps its original place was not in this work, but in the *Morashah Qehilat Ya'aqov,* and it was only later expanded and included in the *Qol Ya'aqov* (later called the *Or*). Neppi-Ghirondi lists the *Qol Ya'aqov* as an index to the *Yalqut* and comments: "This book is also called *Or ha-Darshanim.*" A few lines later he adds this parenthetical note: "*Or ha-Darshanim* is

[79] *The Catalogue of Hebrew Manuscripts in the Collection of Elkan Nathan Adler* (Cambridge, 1921), p. 16, under "Homilies." There is also some possibility that the collection of sermons bearing no title or introduction in the Ferrara *Talmud Torah* collection, numbered 84, no. 2475 in the Hebrew University microfilm collection, is a MS. of *Titen Emet le-Ya'aqov.* Of the two folio pages found in the Adler collection, there are two sides of text, the title page, and a blank side. The pages of text apear to be some very early thoughts on preaching by Zahalon which may have preceded the prototype of the manual discussed below, n. 245.

[80] See below, n. 283, for some explanation of the different names used for this work and possible reasons for the changes.

found in manuscript form in the treasures of 'Haraḥ Michal,'"[81] a reference to the collection of Ḥayyim Michael in Hamburg, subsequently acquired by the Bodleian Library at Oxford.[82] This is the most recent of the three manuscripts we are using in our critical edition of the *Or*, and it is numbered 2268.1 in the Bodleian,[83] and is dated 1733. R. Sabbatai Bass, in his *Siftei Yeshenim* (Amsterdam, 1680), also lists all the works mentioned in the *Margaliot Tovot*, under no. 325.

e. *Margaliot Tovot*, described by de' Piattelli as "an abbreviated version of *Ḥovot ha-Levavot*,[84] small in quantity but great in quality, filled with reverence for the Lord and with saintliness, the author's first creative work in his youth." Brief prayers written in poetry are found at the end of many chapters.[85] Most important for our purposes, however, the work includes six very thoughtful

---

[81] H. Neppi and Sh. Ghirondi, *Toldot Gedolei Yisro'el u-Gaonei Italia* (Trieste, 1853), pp. 129, 131.

[82] Cf. M. Steinschneider, *Ozrot Chajim Katalog der Michael'schen Bibliothek* (Hamburg, 1848), p. 336, no. 30.

[83] This corresponds to Hebrew University microfilm collection no. 20549.

[84] A philosophic work originally written in Arabic by Baḥya ben Joseph Ibn Paquda (ca. 1050?–ca. 1120?) in Saragossa. It was translated into Hebrew by Judah Ibn Tibbon and Joseph Qimḥi (the latter version has been lost). Zahalon's work divides the teachings of Baḥya into thirty short chapters, meant to be studied regularly over the days of the month.

[85] I. Davidson, *Ozar ha-Shirah ve-ha-Piyyut* (New York, 1933) lists Zahalon's prayers under *Aleph* 6058, 8750; *Yod* 1326, 1328, 1372, 1436; *Resh* 288, 362, 445, 503, 520; *Shin* 907, and 1646. All are from prayers in the thirty chapters of *Margaliot Tovot*. Following the thirty chapters Zahalon has included under the title of *Tefillah*, or "Prayer," on pages 61a–61b, three *piyyutim*, or love poems to God, by Eleazar ben Moses Azikri (1533–1600) of Safed, all of which are acrostics. Two bear one of the names of the author, "Eleazar" and "Azikri." Both are found in various editions of the *Sefer Ḥaredim* of Azikri (Venice, 1601), such as that published in Brno, 1795, pp. 54b–55a, with minor variations in the text from that published by Zahalon. (I am grateful to Dr. Aryae Wineman for calling this to my attention.) Davidson lists these as *Aleph* 507 and 2037. The third *piyyut* included in this section of the *Margaliot Tovot* is *Yedid Nefesh*. Written with an acrostic of the tetragrammaton, *Yedid Nefesh* was probably composed in 1584 by Azikri. Davidson lists it as *Yod* 407. For a long time this *piyyut* had been ascribed

long prayers in its introduction. Each of these is said by the
members of a certain profession on a regular basis, or by individuals on special occasions: (1) for *darshanim* before they deliver
each *derashah*,[86] (2) for physicians, to be said daily,[87] (3) for a

to Judah Halevi or to Israel Najara (see E.J., III, 1008–1009). Zahalon must have
seen the first two *piyyutim* in the *Sefer Ḥaredim*, a very popular compendium of
ethical teachings of the aggadic and *musar* literature. Finally, at the very end of
his book, Zahalon has placed four pages of *Remazim*, or mnemonic references to
the negative and positive commandments listed in the order given by Maimonides. Each commandment is referred to with one or two words. According
to Scholem, the presence of kabbalistic poetry and prayers written by mystics
such as Azikri and Israel Najara (see below, n. 193) from Safed became widespread in Italy and elsewhere. "Preachers in Italy and Poland began to speak of
kabbalistic matters in public, and kabbalistic phraseology became public prop-
erty." Scholem also refers to the prevalence of penitential manuals based on kabbalistic customs emanating from Safed (*Kabbalah* [Jerusalem, 1974], pp. 76–77).
The *Margaliot Tovot* was clearly one example among a whole genre of such
manuals. This literature, ultimately aimed at preparing the Jewish communities
for the coming of the Messiah, made its appearance in the second half of the
sixteenth century. The inclusion in Zahalon's work of these poetic prayers was a
distinctive feature of this period, between 1550 and 1750, during which a spate of
popular moral literature along with kabbalistic teachings made their appearance.
(See below in my n. 72 on the text of the *Or*, in which kabbalistic references are
conspicuous for their absence!) As Scholem points out, the homiletic literature of
this period (within which Zahalon was later to make such an important contribution in his writing of the *Or*) was very much affected by these emphases on ethics
and mysticism (see *Kabbalah*, p. 196, and *Major Trends in Jewish Mysticism*, pp.
250–251). For Catholic eschatological anticipations, see above, n. 2.

   [86] Mentioned in the *Or*, ll. 677–689 (Chap. 10:4): "When he is ready to begin
the sermon, he should pray to the Holy One, praised be He, with all his heart and
soul that He help him in delivering the sermon . . . to reconcile the people with the
Almighty, that they should perform good deeds and that all who have sinned
should repent. The *darshan* thereby prays that he should become one who
'preaches well and acts well' (Ḥag. 14b). I have already written in my book
Margaliot Tovot a lovely prayer which would be appropriate for one who is accustomed to preach regularly." See Appendix C for translation of this prayer, and
Appendix B in the Hebrew section for text of prayer. For additional possible
influences on the *Or* of the subject of the *Margaliot Tovot, viz.,* Bahya's *Ḥovot
ha-Levavot*, see my textual notes below, 14, 34, and 110.

   [87] Cf. Friedenwald, I, 268–279, on this prayer, also H. A. Savitz, "Jacob
Zahalon, and His Book, 'The Treasure of Life,'" 167–176. See below, n. 164.

father about to perform the *brit milah* of his own son, or by a *mohel* before performing the *brit milah* of another child, (4) for parents concerning their children, (5) for sufficient sustenance, and (6) for the acceptance by God of our prayers.[88] Published in Venice by D. Vedelago, with the date indicated by the Hebrew words *Mashiaḥ Nagid* (numerically equivalent to 5425 in the Hebrew calendar, or 1665, and meaning "Messiah Ruler").[89] At the end of this volume in a colophon the date is given as "17 August 1665, the fourth day of the week, first day of *Rosh Ḥodesh Elul,* in the year 'All that are the words of God WE SHALL DO and we shall heed' (see Ex. 24:7)." Here the word NA'ASEH, meaning "we shall do," is meant to be the date, as it has a numerical value of 5425, equivalent to the year 1665.[90] This work was republished later in Amsterdam in 1681, 1695, and 1701, and in Frankfurt am Main in 1708.[91]

[88] These prayers are referred to in *Sefer Ḥemdat Yamim,* written sometime after 1662. Abraham Yaari, *Ta'alumot Sefer* (on *Sefer Ḥemdat Yamim,* its authorship, and its influence) (Jerusalem, 1954), p. 17, quotes that text as saying, "and already our predecessors have ordered proper prayers and *nusaḥ* for those who lead in prayers, and of them all none were more beautiful than the words of the author of the work *Margaliot Tovot.*" This is found in *Ḥemdat Yamim* under *Elul,* end of Chap. 4, p. 29.

[89] In his copy of the first edition of *Margaliot Tovot,* found in the Ben Ẓevi Institute in Jerusalem, Dr. Isaiah Sonne wrote this notation: "an echo of the appearance of Sabbatai Ẓevi," referring to these words used in the dating. See below, Chap. 6, for our discussion of Zahalon and his attitude to Sabbatai Ẓevi and its possible influence on the *Or.*

[90] Actually de' Piattelli misquotes the verse in *Exodus,* which reads *kol asher dibber ha-shem na'aseh ve-nishma,* meaning, "All that the Lord has said we shall do and we shall heed," instead of *kol asher dibber Elohim* NA'ASEH *ve-nishma* Here, too, the author appears to indicate a sense of expectation and readiness regarding the events of his day. Leibowitz, however, comments that this second dating, with NA'ASEH, indicates some doubt or hesitation on de' Piattelli's part, in "R. Ya'aqov Zahalon Ish Roma u-Fizmono le-Shabbat Ḥanukkah mi-Shnat 1687," in *Sefer Zikhron le-Ḥayyim Enzo Serini, Ketavim al Yahdut Roma,* ed. by A. Milano, Sh. Nakhon, and D. Karpi (Jerusalem, 1971), p. 172. Scholem (*Sabbatai Ṣevi,* pp. 482–483) notes that by the end of 1665, much asceticism was already practiced by Jews of Rome in anticipation of the appearance of Sabbatai Zevi, and in Siena newborn children were named Sabbatai already in December 1665 (p. 479). As to whether Zahalon shared this anticipation, see below, p. 48.

[91] Ch. B. Friedberg, *Bet Eqed Sefarim,* II(Tel Aviv, 1952), 676.

Plainly, Jacob Zahalon was already a man of considerable literary accomplishments by 1665, the date of his first published work. Also of special interest in the *Margaliot Tovot* is the imprimatur of the Rifformatori dello Studio di Padova, or University Commissioners of Padua. This particular document, added to a published work, could only be given when three members of the Rifformatori had carefully examined the text and found nothing in it that they considered harmful to the Catholic faith. This printed stamp of approval, given to Zahalon's first published work, is the first known to exist in any work published in Venice.[92]

We might consider for a moment the range of Jacob Zahalon's intellectual interests and communal responsibilities at the rather young age of thirty-five, to give some further insight into the life of the versatile rabbi-physician. From his work prepared at least fifteen years earlier on the *Yalqut,* we see our author as a master of the *aggadah.*[93] Yet from that time until 1665, he was also able to publish a practical guide to the philosophical-ethical treatise of Baḥya, to prepare a homiletic commentary on Maimonides' code of Jewish law (particularly the theological sections of that code), to formulate a treatise on one of the most controversial biblical books (*Isaiah*) in order to defend the Jewish faith both within and without, and to compose sensitive prayers expressing the aspirations and anxieties of physicians, *darshanim,* parents, and ordinary folk at a time of economic and social upheaval in the Roman ghetto.

Moreover, Zahalon did all of this while continuing to function both as a *darshan* (even writing a volume of sermons) and as a physician, not to mention his communal role as a recorder of decisions and ordinances and as one of the supervisors of the methods of teaching Scripture within Rome. He had expressed his own admiration for the extraordinary organizational abilities of

---

[92] M. Benayahu, *Haskamah u-Reshut bi-Defusei Veniẓia* (Jerusalem, 1971), p. 234, 343.

[93] See below, Chap. 12.

Maimonides in his introduction to the *Or*.[94] Surely Zahalon himself was able to encompass a wide range of scholarly activities with considerable skill in ordering various bodies of knowledge. If he did not come up to the level of the man whom he referred to as "The Brightly Shining Sun,"[95] he was, nevertheless, remarkable for all that he had achieved by the age of thirty-five.

6. Sabbatian Reverberations

> He should always place at the end of the sermon a verse of comfort and redemption for Israel, which gives promise of future salvation [for the Jewish people].
>
> (*Or ha-Darshanim*, ll. 697–699)

Although we have virtually no specific knowledge of Jacob Zahalon's life during the next seven years, from 1665 until 1672, a fair amount of information is available as to events in Rome during that period. We have already mentioned the appearance of Sabbatai Raphael in August 1666.[96] Less than two years later, following the apostasy of Sabbatai Ẓevi, Nathan of Gaza, the Sabbatian prophet, journeyed to Rome with the intention of carrying out a mystical ritual. Although his purpose there in early 1668 was a secret, according to Scholem, it was not to win followers for the Sabbatian movement. Rather, Nathan appears to have been performing some kind of *tiqqun*, or act of rehabilitation or redemption, of the forces of Edom parallel to what his master would do for the forces of Ishmael, or Islam.[97]

While in Rome, Nathan took a scroll on which it was written that within one year Rome would be overturned and threw it into

---

[94] Ll. 127–138.

[95] Ll. 581–582 (Chap. 7:2).

[96] See above, p. 31.

[97] Scholem, *Sabbatai Ṣevi*, pp. 771–774. Whether this *tiqqun* had the intention of destroying Rome or merely bringing it to repentance, is not clear.

the Tiber River. According to Sasportas,[98] Nathan told some of the believers that the divine punishment of the nations would begin in Rome. His visit to Rome was kept secret partly out of fear of the papal government and the danger that it might suppress his activities, and not merely because of Jewish opposition, as Sasportas thought. Nathan's circumventing the papal palace was a type of magical action meant to bring about the destruction of "sinful Rome." His whole purpose in coming to that city was surely connected with the talmudic statement that the Messiah sits at the gates of Rome among the poor sufferers.[99] It would not be unreasonable to imagine some consternation among the local Jewish leadership.

Some sources also indicate deep concern within the Church on the part of those who viewed the Sabbatian movement as the appearance of an Antichrist. Commotion and unrest were, indeed, felt within the Vatican, and Pope Alexander VII actually sent messengers to Jerusalem to investigate certain reports he had received.[100] Yet in the face of all this evidence of unrest within Roman Jewry, our sources pertaining to Zahalon are silent. Scholem's comment about this period is particularly instructive. The factor which attracts our attention more than any other, he

---

[98] Jacob Sasportas (1610–1698), a rabbi originally from Morocco, later living in Hamburg, Amsterdam, and Leghorn, was the articulate spokesman for a small number of "infidels" who rejected Sabbatai Zevi's claims in the face of what Scholem describes as "a mounting wave of messianic terrorism" (*Kabbalah*, p. 260). Sasportas corresponded with a number of other skeptics (Samuel Aboab of Venice among them) who shared his views but were very cautious about revealing them to "believers," who were in the majority. In 1669, Sasportas put together his letters to other opponents of the movement, carefully editing them, under the title *Zizat Nobel Zevi* ("The Fading Flower of Zevi"), complete text based on MS. copy of A. Z. Schwartz, ed. I. Tishby (Jerusalem, 1954).

[99] Sanh. 98a.

[100] Scholem, *Shabbatai Zevi ve-ha-Tenu'ah ha-Shabbeta'it bi-Mei Hayyav* (Tel Aviv, 1957), pp. 394–395. (This is the original Hebrew version, later translated and expanded into the work first referred to in n. 73.)

noted, is the silence as to what was happening at that very time in Rome.[101]

Perhaps, however, this is especially understandable in the light of the fact that there, in the center of the Catholic world, the greatest danger existed from possible overconfidence concerning the coming of the Messiah, or the hint of some resistance to papal rule on the part of the local Jewish population eager to believe that the "end of days" was at hand. Responsible leadership within the Jewish community had to exercise caution. Personal feelings had to be set aside. Some scandals had occurred, and some individuals had already been imprisoned.[102] The attempt to muzzle all disturbing reverberations had met with failure in Venice. The rabbinical pronouncement of the second of *Tammuz* (July 4), 1666, had proven that there must be another way of dealing with Sabbatian matters by the organized Jewish community.[103] Quite obviously, the appearance of Sabbatai Raphael in that same year had already led the Jewish leadership in Rome to conclude that silence was the best vehicle for handling the dizzying procession of events. That policy must have been all the more essential now following Nathan's mystical acts. Sabbatian preaching was, as Scholem explained, "going underground."[104] Hence, it became more subtle and difficult to counteract.

Of central importance to us in attempting to understand the motivation behind the expanded version of the preacher's manual from its small prototypic version in 1660 to its complete form in the *Or*,[105] is the evidence we have of bizarre sermons with forced, weird conclusions now delivered in the wake of the Sabbatian

---

[101] *Ibid.*, p. 396 (English version, p. 484).

[102] *Ibid.*, p. 397.

[103] Scholem, *Sabbatai Ṣevi*, p. 508. The rabbis attempted to prohibit all discussions of Sabbatei Ẓevi with non-Jews as well as among Jews.

[104] *Ibid.*, p. 770.

[105] See below, Chap. 13.

apostasy.[106] As Scholem expresses it, preachers who attempted to justify the now-defiled Messiah unveiled material which until then had never appeared in normative Jewish thought. They produced sermons "from biblical verses and fragments of verses, from rabbinic sayings whose implicit possibilities nobody had noticed before, from paradoxical expressions in kabbalistic literature, and from the oddest corners of Jewish literature, . . . the like of which had never been seen in Jewish theology."[107]

---

[106] Surely there must have been much homiletic excess even before the advent of Sabbatai Ẓevi and his apostasy. M. Mortara in his *Mazkeret Ḥakhmei Italyah* (Padua, 1886), p. 63, mentions R. Nathan Shapira, who preached a series of some twenty-four sermons which were proto-Sabbatian in nature. Mortara described these *derashot* as indicating that their writer "shared the fantastic illusions of some of his contemporaries regarding the imminent advent of redemption." Similarly, preachers had joined the foray earlier in fighting on the opposite side of the issue. R. Joseph HaLevi of Leghorn lashed out in his sermons against the extremist tendency of many Sabbatians to prefer self-mortification in various ascetic practices in place of repenting and seeking to improve their interpersonal relations through strengthening their character. Speaking against Nathan of Gaza, he wrote, "He had written that an unbeliever, though he had *Torah* and good works, could not be saved. . . . This heresy was believed by everybody as if it were the Law of Moses. And I openly preached against it and said that lack of faith (in the Messiah) did not matter, and that the main thing was *Torah* and good works" (quoted from Jacob Sasportas, *Ẓiẓat Nobel Ẓevi*, [Jerusalem, 1954], p. 170). See Scholem, *Sabbatai Ṣevi*, p. 488. Compare *Or*, Chap. 10:4, ll. 678–689, for similar thoughts on the purpose of preaching. See below, pp. 46 and 60.

[107] Scholem, "Miẓvah ha-Ba'ah ba-Averah," in *Keneset*, II (1937), 360, translated in *The Messianic Idea in Judaism* (New York, 1971), as "Redemption through Sin," pp. 96–97. The Sabbatian sermons, according to Scholem, contained calls for repentance, words of gratitude for the privilege granted to that generation of experiencing the fulfillment of what previous generations of Jews had yearned for, and various mathematical attempts using *Gematria* to provide scriptural justification for the years 1665 to 1667 with the momentous events occurring in them, as well as for the names of Sabbatai and Nathan. "None of the many sermons preached at the time will be found in the homiletic literature printed subsequently. The homilies, which several preachers collected during the year 1666, later prudently disappeared." Some sermons have been preserved, Scholem adds, by being quoted in polemical writings of the "infidels," or, in rare cases, in their original form (*Sabbatai Ṣevi*, p 440, and see below in n. 72 on the text of the *Or*, on *Gematria*).

One example of such preaching was that of the ardent kabbalist and physician, an enthusiastic believer in the Sabbatian faith, R. Joseph Hamiz, originally from Venice.[108] Hamiẓ preached a sermon after the apostasy urging the faithful not to despair, for the Messiah and his prophet, Nathan of Gaza, were in the last difficult process of bringing about the final *tiqqun.* Hamiz praised Nathan's mystical acts performed in Rome in 1668, when he threw a scroll into the Tiber River and predicted the fall of Rome within one year. The prophet, Hamiz argued, faced "an unprecedented danger, and surely he was protected by angels because he could not otherwise have escaped the mouth of the lion in a natural way ... for he had to descend to the depth of the *qelippot* and cast himself thither, so as to fulfill 'Thou shalt tread upon the lion and the adder, upon the young lion and the serpent shalt thou trample' (Ps. 91:13), as he no doubt did on that occasion."[109]

If anything could have been *be-dohaq,* or "forced," a form of preaching Zahalon explicitly warned against,[110] surely the concept that a redeemer who meant to aid in *saving* his people could be doing so while actually *betraying* them and his religion, was an exceedingly dangerous influence on the Jewish faith. "Once the first step was taken on this slippery road anything was possible ... Sabbatian apostasy ... was essentially destructive of all

---

[108] Scholem, *Sabbatai Ṣevi,* pp. 744–745. Moses Zacuto continued the work of Ḥamiẓ in writing a commentary on the *Zohar, Yode'ei Binah.* Cf. Scholem, *Kabbalah* (Jerusalem, 1974), p. 450.

[109] *Ibid.,* p. 774, n. 225, refers to the whole sermon in Isaiah Tishby, "Te'udot al Natan ha-Azzati be-Kitvei R. Yosef Hamiz," in *Sefunot,* I (1956), 112–117.

[110] Zahalon himself makes this point in three different places in the *Or:* ll. 361–362 (Chap. 2:8), ll. 603–604 (Chap. 7:6), and ll. 636–638 (Chap. 9:1). His cautions to avoid, in the course of a sermon, anything which might leave theological doubts in the minds of one's hearers and plant within them a *shemeẓ pisul,* "a particle of suspicion that what he is saying is not according to accepted opinions," and his quotation from M. Avot 1:11 (urging scholars to be careful with their words), would seem to be further efforts to guide *darshanim* away from Sabbatian, and other, forms of heterodoxy. See *Or,* Chap. 2:11, ll. 393–403, and notes 65 and 72 on the text of the *Or.*

values."[111] It was only depraved theology that could teach that while prophets or saints performed good deeds through raising holy sparks from the depths of the *qelippah,* and at the same time kept safely free from the dangers of becoming entangled in the *qelippah,* the Messiah himself performs his descent into the netherworld "to do His work—strange is His work! And to perform His task—astounding is His task!" (Isa. 28:21).[112]

In the antinomian world of Sabbatian preaching, out-of-the-way aggadic sayings of the *Talmud* became pivotal in the light of the apostasy. "David wished to worship idols" (Sanh. 107a) and "A transgression performed with good intention is better than a precept performed with evil intention" (Nazir 23b), two sayings with very limited or even questionable applicability, now became common choices of Sabbatian preachers seeking to justify the bizarre actions of their heretical leader.[113]

The ultimate effect of the Sabbatian sermons could best be gauged by their application in the realm of behavior, for example, sexual morality. Nathan of Gaza had taught in his interpretation of how the Tree of Life had taken the place of the Tree of Knowledge that the biblical laws against incest, the restraints within Judaism on sexual immorality, may become eventually no longer binding. One famous *darshan* who preached at the end of the seventeenth century, R. Elijah b. Kalonymos, quoted from "the kabbalists" who maintained that, based on the *Talmud* in Erubin 100b, incest and adultery were forbidden only after Eve had been cursed for her sin, implying that with the new order brought by the Messiah, once again these prohibitions would be absent.[114] In the

[111] Scholem, *Sabbatai Ṣevi,* p. 799.

[112] *Ibid.,* p. 801. According to the new Jewish Publication Society translation (Philadelphia, 1978), the reference here is to the Lord, who, instead of giving His people victory as in other instances, will punish them for their wrongdoing.

[113] *Ibid.,* p. 805.

[114] *Adderet Eliyahu* (Frankfurt/Oder, 1694), fol. 93c, as quoted in Scholem, p. 811. Elijah b. Kalonymos had attributed to early kabbalists what he had found in the works of Nathan of Gaza and his pupils. This is Scholem's conclusion, pp. 810–811, n. 323. See Ḥ. Wirszubski, "Ha-Teologia ha-Shabbeta'it shel Natan ha-Azzati," *Keneset,* VIII (1944), 210–244.

topsy-turvy world of the Sabbatians, it was quite natural to make use, too, of the *parah adumah,* or red heifer, mentioned in *Numbers* 19, and its symbolism, for the rabbis had explained the mystical purification as that which "makes the pure impure and impure pure."[115] This, too, served as a further justification for antinomian thinking, for it provided the rationalization for a Messiah who saves the world but at the same time transgresses Jewish law.[116]

We cannot fully document the Sabbatian preachers and their homiletic perversities in detail. We do, of course, know of the presence of Sabbatai Raphael in Rome in 1666, from which he had gone to Venice, where he learned of the conversion of Sabbatai Zevi. According to Scholem, Sabbatai Raphael was the first of a long series of Sabbatian *Ba'alei Shem,* or "missionaries," who wandered up and down Europe promoting Sabbatian propaganda mixed with "practical *Kabbalah.*"[117] As we have indicated, Nathan of Gaza's presence in Rome in 1668 was kept secret, although his theological ideas might have received some attention then or later as a result of his closeness to Sabbatai Zevi.[118] Besides these major figures in the movement, and the circulation and popularity which their interpretations may have had, numerous other preachers, as we have shown, imparted to Sabbatian believers a sense of homiletic legitimacy.[119]

Such *darshanim,* we can be sure, disseminated teachings which constituted a threat to established, normative Jewish doctrines. A self-respecting *darshan* living in Rome at this time must have been appalled by the liberties and distortions taken by such influential figures. If the Sabbatian distortions of texts and religious teachings did not always fit clearly into the category of "preaching,"

---

[115] Scholem, *Sabbatai Sevi,* p. 808.

[116] H. Wirszubski, "Ha-Idi'ologia ha-Shabbeta'it shel Hamarat ha-Mashiaḥ lefi Natan ha-Azzati ve-Igeret *Magen Avraham,*" *Zion,* III (1938), 215–245.

[117] Scholem, *Sabbatai Sevi,* p. 783.

[118] Scholem, *Major Trends in Jewish Mysticism* (New York, 1954), p. 419, n. 48, for references to Nathan's epistles on the reasons for apostasy, and other references from pp. 419–422.

[119] See above, pp. 42–44.

obviously a community-minded, concerned *darshan* such as Jacob Zahalon could not ignore their potential danger. How very plainly such bizarre teachings diverged from his concept of *darshanut* is obvious from his description of the purpose of the sermon: "to reconcile the people with the Almighty, that they should perform good deeds and that all who have sinned should repent."[120] Further, the constant prayer which Zahalon in the *Or,* in the same section, counseled preachers to utter, was an unequivocal plea for divine aid in bringing Jews to observe the traditional paths in tangible ways:

> May my words fall on attentive ears. May those who hear me not turn aside my words, reproofs, and admonitions from their hearts, but may they accept them and always be careful to do them and not to veer to the right or the left . . . let my portion be with those righteous individuals to whom it is said, "preach, Rabbi, preach, for to you, it is appropriate to preach" (Sanh. 100a), for "you preach well and practice well" (Ḥag. 14b).[121]

Publishing a preacher's manual around 1660, when the first outline of the *Or* existed, would have been an important contribution to rabbinic scholarship, as it would have been at any time.

---

[120] *Or,* ll. 685–686 (Chap. 10:4). Of course, it should be understood that the preacher-congregant relationship, along with the very institution of the sermon as a means of communication, might have been subtly undermined for nearly a century by the continued conversionist sermons which Jews were required to hear in their own synagogues. This practice, instituted by a papal bull in 1584, must have given added urgency for good, constructive, and inspiring *derashot.* Consider the fanatic fervor of Francisco de Torres' advice to inquisitors in 1555(!), demanding that such preaching be done not merely in the houses of catechumens, for new converts, but in the synagogues themselves: "Why do you not force them [the Jews] to hear the Word of God, since you have been given the power to do so? Why do you not compel them, either by expulsion, or by disproving [Judaism] in the synagogues on the basis of the Law itself, so that they wish to convert?" (De Torres, *De Sola Lectione,* p. 159, as quoted in Stow, CTPJP, p. 215). On the practice as it was actually instituted, see above, pp. 13–14 and n. 20.

[121] *Margaliot Tovot,* 3b–4a, *Or,* ll. 687–689.

However, after the Sabbatian apostasy in 1666 and the distorted and even dangerous preaching which followed in its wake, the publication of the *Or* must have assumed an urgency which made its eventual revision, expansion,[122] and circulation a supremely important service to the Jewish people of its day, and especially for anyone who took the profession of delivering the *derashah* as seriously as did Jacob Zahalon.

We might mention that in spite of his apparent opposition to the Sabbatian movement and its outcome after the apostasy, Zahalon was among the conservative kabbalists who had looked forward to a far more satisfactory fulfillment of their mystical expectations. R. Sabbatai Baer of Palestine, whose name and whose work, *Be'er Eseq* (Venice, 1674), are mentioned on the page preceding the title page of the *Morashah Qehilat Ya'aqov* manuscript, had written a *haskamah* for that work, dated the same year.[123] We may assume that Zahalon would never have requested such a recommendation concerning one of his works from a scholar with whose religious point of view he was not in sympathy. Baer, who had been traveling in Italy in the spring of 1666, was asked elsewhere whether *Hazot,* or Midnight Devotions, should now be abandoned in the light of the good news concerning Sabbatai Zevi. He referred to the Jewish tradition that one who claims to be the Messiah must first prove himself by certain appropriate signs. "So far we have seen none of the signs. Why then should we cease to mourn for the exile of the *Shekhinah* (or make other changes in the laws)?"[124]

Another kindred spirit with whose name and work that of Zahalon is associated was R. Moses Zacuto of Venice. He, too, was a kabbalist who yearned for more satisfying signs of redemption. He quotes a responsum written by Zahalon in his writings,

---

[122] See below, Chap. 13, especially n. 257.

[123] See above, n. 75.

[124] *Be'er Eseq,* responsum no. 29, quoted in Scholem, *Sabbatai Sevi,* pp. 503–504. See below, pp. 88–89 on Israel Foa's views.

disagreeing with our author and taking a more stringent position on a halakhic matter.[125] Zacuto went out of his way to praise those German Jewish communities that continued to keep the traditional fasts in 1666, probably implying that the many Italian Jews who had intentionally feasted on the seventeenth of *Tammuz* and the ninth of *Av* in that year and in 1667 had surely gone astray.[126] These men, Baer and Zacuto, were at least two of the important scholars of the time who would appear to have shared Zahalon's point of view toward Sabbatianism. The eager anticipation and hopefulness which are indicated by the two dates printed in the 1665 edition of the *Margaliot Tovot*[127] mark Zahalon as one who might have had a deep sympathy with the movement. However, the absence of any references to the messianic figure after that time in his writings, the general silence of the rabbinical leadership in Rome (of which he was an important, if not central, figure), and his counsel in the *Or* to avoid "forced" treatment of texts and to focus on the meaningful, humane goal of preaching—all of these factors point to Zahalon's disillusionment.

That our author ceased to hope for an immediate end to the

---

[125] Neppi-Ghirondi, pp. 129, 131, referring to responsum 36 in *Teshuvot ha-Ramaz*. See also Scholem, "Le-She'elat Yaḥasam shel Rabbanei Yisro'el el ha-Shabbeta'ut," *Ẓion* XIII–XIV (1948–1949), 47–62. Zacuto had become very hostile to the movement following the apostasy, though earlier he had had secret contact with Sabbatai Ẓevi. Elsewhere Scholem notes that Zacuto also opposed the giving up of *Ḥaẓot* and other customs. Another interesting aspect of his biography for our purposes is that he served for a while in Venice as a *darshan* under Azariah Picho, a central figure in the history of Italian *derashot*, and, as we hope to document in the future, an important influence on Zahalon. See Scholem, *Kabbalah* (Jerusalem, 1974), pp. 449–451, and below, p. 85.

[126] Scholem, *Sabbatai Ṣevi*, p. 769. Zahalon's inclusion in the *Margaliot Tovot* of poetic prayers, such as *Yedid Nefesh*, emanating from the kabbalistic community of Safed would indicate the depth of his own mystical leanings. See above, n. 85. He must have wanted very much to believe in the mystical messiah at the outset of the movement.

[127] See above, notes 89 and 90. Leibowitz ascribes these allusions in the dates, especially the one on the title page, to the influence of de' Piattelli, who was "almost certainly . . . one of the believers," and not to Zahalon.

"abundant hardships" of *Galut*[128] would not have distinguished him from numerous other learned men of his day. However, Zahalon's response to the movement was unique, because his disillusionment and recognition of the spiritual and moral damage it threatened to cause as a result of irresponsible preaching among both the believers and the nonbelievers served as an essential motivating force in his efforts to publish the *Or.* It is our contention that Jacob Zahalon's expansion and revision of the *Or,* and his efforts to have it approved by high Catholic officials, even up to the last year of his life, in order to clear the way for its eventual publication, may in a large part be traced to his concern to combat the effects of Sabbatianism in Italian Jewish life through strengthening the efforts of its *darshanim.*

7. Zahalon's Contact with Giulio Bartolocci

> [Zahalon] showed me a large portion of [his] works and asked me to express my opinions about them.
> (Giulio Bartolocci, *Bibliotheca magna rabbinica,* III, 854)

From the year of the *haskamah*[129] until Zahalon's move to Ferrara, we are unable to document any facts about the author's life other than that his manuscript of the *Or* was brought to the attention of Giulio Bartolocci, the Catholic Hebrew scholar and author of a comprehensive four-volume work on the history of rabbinic

---

[128] *Or,* 1. 196. Lest one imagine that Zahalon's theological response to the bleakness of his times was at all one of despair, it should be noted that in his "prayer for [sufficient] sustenance," he expresses a remarkably objective and sane world-view: "'You did not withhold manna from them' (Neh. 9:20), for even on the day that Israel made the [golden] calf, You gave them the manna [to eat], for You are a merciful and gracious God, and You have known that 'the devisings of man's mind are evil from [his] youth' (Gen. 8:21), and You do not want to destroy Your world because of [the actions of] fools" (*Margaliot Tovot,* 10b; see above, p. 37).

[129] See below, Chap. 14.

writings.[130] Bartolocci gave his "clearance" to the *Or* with these words, which he wrote in Latin at the top of the page preceding the title page on the Casanatense manuscript:

> I, the undersigned, have seen the book composed by Rabbi Jacob Zahalon of Rome, a philosopher and professor of medicine, and it is an index to the subjects in alphabetical order of what is found in the work known as *Yalqut,* and (these indexed subjects) are spread about in it (i.e., the *Yalqut* itself, not alphabetically, but) in different places. Rome, 15 April 1675. I am, D. Giulio Bartolocci.[131]

Bartolocci wrote a similarly approving statement on that same date on the manuscript of *Ohalei Ya'aqov.*[132] *Ohalei Ya'aqov, Ozar ha-Hakhmot,* Part 2, was the original name given to the *Ozar*

---

[130] Bartolocci held several important positions which made his signature extremely influential. He was the *Scriptor Hebraicus* at the Vatican library. He had also been appointed a consul to the Congregation of the Index, served as superior of Cistercian houses in Brisighella and Rome, presided at their general chapter, and was visitor for the Roman province. In 1651, he became professor of Hebrew languages and rabbinic literature at the Collegium Neophytorum (for Jewish converts) in Rome. His chief work was the *Bibliotheca magna rabbinica des scriptoribus et scriptis hebraicis,* published in four volumes in 1675, 1678, 1683, and 1693. Cf. *New Catholic Encyclopedia,* II (Washington, 1967), 137, and E.J., IV, 265.

[131] See picture opposite p. 92. This is according to the translation of M. Benayahu in *Haskamah u-Reshut bi-Defusei Venezia,* p. 354. See also photo, p. 153. Although Zahalon's medical degree was described as *Doctoris Philosophiae ac Medicinae,* or *Artium ac Medicinae* (see above, p. 20), we must assume that the words *Medicine Professone* indicated a complimentary description of Zahalon by Bartolocci himself, as nothing is recorded about any academic appointment which the author of the *Or* received. Comp. above, n. 11 on Jacob Mantino, who was appointed professor of medicine at the University of Rome.

[132] Vatican MS. 466. There are slight variations in the titles of the medical work from the 1683 Venice edition. The note written by Bartolocci appears on the other side of the folio on the title page, which reads: *Sefer Ohalei Ya'aqov, Ozar ha-Hokhmot, Heleq 2, Hokhmat ha-Refuah,* and then indicates that it is "divided into twelve books." Bartolocci's note does not appear in the printed edition of the *Ozar.*

ha-Ḥayyim, the twelve-part medical work later published in Venice in 1683.[133] The obvious intent of Bartolocci's description on the manuscript was to permit the authorities to remove any obstacle in the path of publishing the *Or.*

It would seem that Bartolocci had more than a purely scholarly interest in Zahalon's work. From his biographical comments about our author in the *Bibliotheca magna rabbinica,* he appears to have been personally acquainted with Zahalon, judging from the Catholic scholar's explanation for the Zahalon family's moving from Rome to Ferrara. In 1683, the date of publication of the third volume of the *Bibliotheca,* in which Zahalon and his works are described at some length (covering nearly two full pages, or 144 lines), Bartolocci wrote that Zahalon had left Rome for Ferrara "four or five years ago," i.e., in 1678 or 1679, for two reasons: (a) to avoid being the object of his opponents' envy, and (b) to be closer to the center of Hebrew publishing, Venice. [134] Bartolocci lists seven works by Zahalon which were, at the time of the publication of the Catholic Hebraist's volume, in the possession of our author. Concerning all of these written works, Bartolocci comments: "He (Zahalon) showed me a large portion of these works and asked me to express my opinions about them. I praised the man's diligence, and (I also expressed praise for) most of his scholarly works. Shortly afterwards, he left Rome together with his family . . ."[135] One senses that there is more than a detached scholarly interest in Zahalon on the part of the Catholic writer. Bartolocci appears to express concern and personal interest in the compositions and welfare of his Jewish colleague.

Another account, much later than that of Bartolocci, holds

---

[133] See below, Chap. 9.

[134] III, 854.

[135] *Ibid.* Cf. above, n. 32, for Bartolocci's pejorative comment about learning among Jews. This tone does not appear in his later remarks about Zahalon; Bartolocci lists the five works mentioned in the introduction to the *Margaliot Tovot* (see above, pp. 32–37), a compendium of the work of Thomas Aquinas (see below, p. 72, especially n. 229), and the *Oẓar.*

that Zahalon remained a *Morenu,* or rabbi, in Rome until 1680. Then, according to Vogelstein and Rieger, he "received an invitation to Ferrara, which he accepted. In 1682, he was already the rabbi of that community. From here he began his (serious) rabbinical and *halakhah* work."[136]

8. The Jewish Community of Ferrara When Zahalon Arrived

The Honorable Renowned Physician, Devoted Preacher to His People in Rome in the Holy Congregation in Israel of Cataloni and Aragonesa . . . *for Twenty-Seven Years and Afterwards in the Holy Congregation in Israel of Ferrara* [italics added].
(From the title page of the Casanatense MS. of *Or ha-Darshanim*; italicized words added in marginal note and later deleted)

The Jewish population of Ferrara was only one-third that of Rome, but the stature of the Jewish community at the time of the arrival of the Zahalons between 1678 and 1680[137] was equally significant. In the middle of the seventeenth century there were some 600 Jewish souls in Ferrara, a high proportion of the total population of the little city. A century later there were less than 250 Jews living there. Yet the northern Italian city was one of the most outstanding communities in the country for Jewish scholarship.[138] Although Jewish settlement there went back to the eleventh century, and important scholars were living there in the thirteenth century, at the time of the Spanish expulsion in 1492 Ferrara became one of the most vital Jewish communities in all Italy.[139]

In the second quarter of the sixteenth century there were two communities in the country which more than any others had signi-

---

[136] II, 269, apparently basing this on Bartolocci, I, 33, which seems to be an error, and Isaac Lampronti, *Paḥad Yiẓḥaq* (Venice, 1750).

[137] See above, n. 48.

[138] Roth, *History of the Jews of Italy,* p. 333.

[139] *Ibid.,* p. 179.

ficant numbers of Marranos who were now openly professing Judaism, Ancona and Ferrara.[140] When Ancona ceased to exist as a Jewish center in 1556, Ferrara stood out above all. Amatus Lusitanus, the renowned ex-Marrano physician who had also been at one time a papal physician, taught medicine at the University of Ferrara.[141] In 1556, the duke of that city exempted a Jewish academy from all tolls, claiming that the school would be a great asset to both Jews and non-Jews within the community. "No more eloquent testimony to the completeness of the emancipation of Jewish studies" could have existed, Roth comments.[142]

Gracia Mendes, aunt and mother-in-law of the Duke of Naxos, "the most adored Jewish woman of that or any other age," had lived in Ferrara for a time, during which she first reverted from her Marrano status to practice Judaism openly.[143] Yet by 1581, as a result of the persistence of the Inquisition, the Marrano colony there had been broken up.

The Jewish community of Ferrara had gone a long way in organizing itself and surrounding communities for the benefit of protecting and preserving Jewish life. There had been a *Va'ad Klali,* or General Council, in Ferrara in 1554, that was frequently cited for its progress in communal legislation.[144] Just prior to the establishment of the ghetto in Ferrara in 1624, there were about ten synagogues, the same number as existed in Rome and in Mantua.[145] The famous Leon da Modena had preached in Ferrara every Sabbath for three years at the community's invitation.[146]

---

[140] *Ibid.,* p. 187. Moses A. Shulvass, *The Jews in the World of the Renaissance* (Chicago, 1973), p. 21.

[141] Roth, p. 202. In the *Oẓar* introduction Zahalon cites the seventy-seven principles of medical conduct of Lusitanus, some of which, as we note below, pp. 58–60, have interesting parallels to our author's advice to *darshanim* in the *Or.* On Lusitanus, see Friedenwald, I, 332–380.

[142] P. 214.

[143] *Ibid.,* pp. 215, 314.

[144] Shulvass, p. 90.

[145] *Ibid.,* p. 74.

[146] *Ibid.,*p. 343. Cf. n. 47 above.

אוצר החיים

על מלאכת הרפואה הוא חלק ג' מספר אוצר החכמות אשר
חבר הרופא כובהק דורש טוב לעמו כמוהר"ר
יעקב בכמוהר"ר **יצחק צהלון** זצ"ל
נחלק לי"ג ספרים

ספר א' על שמירת הבריאות
ספר ב' על כל מיני קדחות ורפואתם
ספר ג' על רפקים ובעי רגלים והלשון
ספר ד' על כל מיני ארסיים וסמי מות שבצומחים מתכות ובעלי חיים ורפואתם
כללית ופרטית
ספר ח' על אותית וסכות החולאים
ספר ו' על סגולות רפואות פשוטות וטורכבות
ספר ז' על חולאים פרטיים שבראש ואברים שבו ורפואתם
ספר ח על חולאים שבחזה ואברים שבקרובו ורפואתם
ספר ט' על חולאים שבקרב ואכרים שם ורפואתם
ספר י' על חולאים חיצונים קידוגיאה בלקז ורפואתם
כפר יא על חולאים פרטיים שבנשים ורפואתם
ספר יב על חולאים פרטיים שבקטנים ורפואתם
ספר יג דרושים רותניים על חולאי הנפש רובים לחולאים גופניים הנ"ל

בויניציאה

כשנת וכפשי **תגיל** כס'

IN VENETIA, M.DC.LXXXIII.
Nella Stamparia Vendramina,
Con Licenza de' Superiori

Title page of *Ozar ha-Ḥayyim*, Venice, 1683

Jewish learning was highly regarded in Ferrara, and Jewish instruction was required until the age of thirteen for those educated privately, and until sixteen for children educated in the communal free school.[147] By the early eighteenth century, not long after the death of Jacob Zahalon, 328 Jewish families in Ferrara had to support 72 charity cases. Nevertheless, says Baron, "they were still better off than their coreligionists of the papal capital."[148] One can well imagine that the improved economic conditions coupled with the climate more conducive to creative Jewish scholarship—aside from the motives cited by Bartolocci[149]—might have served to induce Jacob Zahalon to leave Rome for Ferrara.

9. 1683—The Publication of the *Oẓar* and Its Significance

> May it be Thy will, O Lord my God and God of my fathers, to endow me with good understanding . . . so that I may discern and diagnose the physical ailments thoroughly and correctly in all cases that come to me.
>
> ("Prayer for Physicians," *Margaliot Tovot*," pp. 5b–6a)

The final steps in the preparation for publication of the *Oẓar ha-Ḥayyyim,* or "The Treasure of Life," which was meant to provide practical medical advice to physicians as well as to laymen in emergencies when physicians were unavailable, must have occurred in Ferrara.[150] Whether any revisions or editing occurred

---

[147] Roth, p. 363. See Louis Finkelstein, *Jewish Self-Government in the Middle Ages* (New York, 1964), pp. 92, 304–306.

[148] Baron, XIV, 90–91.

[149] See above, n. 134.

[150] In the introduction to the *Oẓar,* p. 2a, Zahalon gives five reasons for his having written the work: (1) as a guide for a community in which, although there is no physician, there is at least a scholar who will be able to look into this book, to understand symptoms and treatments, and to provide some help to the sick; (2) for a community which has its own doctor during such a time that he is away from the city and unable to return; (3) for physicians themselves to be aware of

in that city we cannot know, as apparently a copy of the finished work was shown to Bartolocci already in 1675, as we have indicated.[151]

The *Oẓar* is the first medical work to be originally written and published in Hebrew and dealing with all phases of medicine and only with medical matters.[152] It was published by Vendramin, a Christian publishing house, and the printer of the work, who signed his name at the end of the volume, was a certain Jacob ben Abraham Aboab, who had been in this trade in Venice since 1669.[153] While the work appeared during a period of decline in the illustrious Hebrew publishing tradition of Italy, it represents a typographical achievement which is at once both lovely and dignified. Much is contained in the 189 folio pages with rather small print comprising a mixture of Rashi script and block letters.

The volume is divided into thirteen chapters, according to the title page and the introduction, dealing with such subjects as general health care; fevers and their cures; pulse, heartbeat, urine, and the tongue; various poisons from plants, metals, and animals and their cures; signs and causes of illnesses; simple and complex prescriptions; specific diseases of the head and limbs; chest diseases and their cures; stomach ailments and their cures; various

the most highly recommended treatments in the event of some disagreement among them; (4) as an aid to doctors to find "a *Shulḥan Arukh,* a prepared table before them, without different opinions . . . for I indicated those cures which are most correct and agreed upon and tested"; and (5) as an aid to the indigent sick who are not able to pay the doctors and who seek to find a simple cure to heal themselves. On 2b, at the end of the introduction, he advises: Physicians "should not accept a fee from the indigent, from relatives, and from friends who are as close as brothers." See below, pp. 63–64.

[151] See above, n. 135.

[152] Leibowitz, "R. Ya'aqov Zahalon Ish Roma u-Fizmono le-Shabbat Ḥanukkah mi-Shnat 1687," p. 173. Leibowitz points out that a translation of the medical work of Avicenna into Hebrew appeared in Naples in 1491–1492.

[153] Not to be confused with the rabbi of Venice, who died in 1727, or the other Jacob Aboab, who was one of the earliest Jewish immigrants to New York, arriving in 1654, probably from the Netherlands. *Jewish Encyclopedia,* I (New York, 1915), 75.

external surgical procedures and their healing processes; gynecological ailments and their cures; pediatric diseases and their cures; and psychiatric ailments which parallel physical conditions. Although this last subject, which was meant to constitute the thirteenth chapter, was indicated, as we have said, on the title page and in the introduction, it was never published, and the decision was apparently made very late, while the earlier part of the work was in the process of being published. Apparently, a lack of funds prevented its being completed in print.

We have already discussed the references in the book on pages 21a and 21b to the plague in Rome in 1656 and 1657.[154] They are regarded as an important contribution to the history of epidemiology, a valuable document regarding communal organization and various means of quarantine in use at the time. They provide important details about the medical and economic assistance provided by the Jewish community, as well as by the government authorities in Rome during the emergency.[155] We have referred to an account by one of Zahalon's contemporaries, Cardinal Gastaldi, appointed by the pope to oversee all matters related to the plague.[156] While Gastaldi wrote from the vantage point of a church or government official, Zahalon emphasized the specifically medical and human sides of the tragedy in his observations from within the Roman ghetto.

The *Oẓar,* which is written after the manner of rabbinic responsa with questions and answers, is noteworthy for its descriptions of some of the latest medical findings. Quinine is mentioned as a cure for malaria, a very new remedy in Zahalon's day, not written about formally until 1781.[157] Citrus juices are advised as treatment for scurvy some seventy years before the discovery by Lind, and

---

[154] Above, Chap. 3.

[155] Leibowitz, "R. Ya'aqov Zahalon Ish Roma," p. 173. Baron, *The Jewish Community,* II, 329–330. See above, p. 27.

[156] *Ibid.,* pp. 174 f. See above, n. 52.

[157] Leibowitz, "Jacob Zahalon, a Hebrew Medical Author," p. 434.

long before the vitamin found in the juices had been isolated. Other descriptions of the symptoms of fevers appear to be far in advance of their formal discovery.[158] Because Zahalon's work was meant to be a practical guide for laymen as well as physicians, he does not attempt to fashion terms in Hebrew, but rather, so as to be understood immediately without difficulty, in most cases he gives the Italian names for diseases in Hebrew transliteration. These names are printed in large square letters, while the rest of the book is printed in the Rashi letters.

It is interesting to locate the parallels between some of the medical information and advice offered in this work and the counsel which Zahalon gives to *darshanim* in the *Or*. On a more obvious level, there is in the *Ozar* a question concerning the nature of wine and whether it makes one dry or moist. The answer given is that wine is warm and dry and produces "joy and strengthens the vital spirits, aiding in the digestive process."[159] Now our author devotes an entire chapter of the *Or*, Chapter 12, to the care which a *darshan* ought to give to his health. There he notes that preachers should drink a little fine, unadulterated wine before delivering their sermon, as it "tends to induce a pleasant mood and also strengthens the voice and the body organs."[160] During the post-delivery period, Zahalon also recommends rest and a little fine wine or chicken soup to the *darshan*.[161] In the *Ozar* he advises such

---

[158] *Ibid.,* p. 433. Leibowitz has many other comments on Zahalon's classifications of diseases and listing of symptoms. He is especially impressed, too, by Zahalon's reference to "fever dwelling in the parts" of the body, which is, he maintains, a reference to the dawn of tissue pathology, almost a century before Morgagni's published work on the subject in 1761, *De sedibus morborum.* Zahalon distinguishsed this fever from that caused by "contamination of the blood." For a rather thorough bibliography of medical writings about the *Ozar* and Zahalon as a physician, see Leibowitz, "R. Ya'aqov Zahalon Ish Roma u-Fizmono le-Shabbat Ḥanukkah mi-Shnat 1687," pp. 180–181.

[159] *Ozar*, p. 3b.
[160] *Or*, ll. 722–724.
[161] Ll. 726–728.

soup as helpful in "strengthening the bowels, relieving stiffness in the limbs,[162] and heaviness in the rheum."[163]

Numerous similarities between Zahalon the physician and Zahalon the *darshan* emerge when we examine the seventy-seven principles of medical conduct of Lusitanus cited with approval by our author on the second page of his introduction to the *Ozar*. Note some of the superficial parallels on certain points:

Lusitanus, quoted in *Ozar*	Parallels in *Or*
1. a physician shall be God-fearing[164]	10:4. when one wishes to begin preaching, he should pray with

[162] *Ve-liftoah otem ha-eivarim.*

[163] P. 78a, *ve-neged gasut ha-leihut.* A further parallel is that in the *Ozar*, p. 6a, and the *Or*, l. 719 (Chap. 12:2) he urges avoiding harsh lentils.

[164] On the following page, at the end of the introduction to the *Ozar*, the author advises physicians: "And before he prescribes a cure, he should seek God's help in instructing him what will be proper in this instance." Further, at the very end of his introduction, the author says, "let the physician say at least once a week the Prayer for Physicians whch I have composed in the *Margaliot Tovot,* printed in Venice, 1665 . . ." In the *Or*, ll. 687–689, he advises preachers to say the "appropriate Prayer for Preachers" which he has written in his *Margaliot Tovot* (see above, n. 86), but he does not suggest how often it should be said. Some interesting aspects of the Prayer for Physicians include: his request for divine help in making the correct diagnosis of illnesses as well as in choosing proper drugs or treatments to cure them, his prayer that he not hasten the death "by even one second" of seriously ill patients who come to him, that he not be blamed or suspected by the family and friends of a patient who dies of having caused his death, that he be a force for bringing about repentance in one who is ill and whom God is chastising or testing. Especially does he pray that the Lord will strengthen his memory when he visits a patient, and that He will cause the right medical book to have been studied by him or that He will cause him to have been present when his colleagues happened to be discussing the specific cure for the illness he is called upon to treat—all of this on the assumption that God is the ultimate source of healing, and that He causes it to come about that physicians learn of the correct treatments. He prays that Satan or the wicked not influence him to use drugs for wrong purposes, and that in his treatment of women patients he be perfectly chaste in his thoughts. He asks God, too, to show him kindness by causing patients who are curable to seek him out, and by preventing those who are incurable from coming to him for treatment.

all his heart and soul that He
will aid him . . .[165]

7. he shall not be haughty or
snobbish

13:3. he should pray that he not
become conceited . . .[166]

10. let him accept reproof from
a superior willingly and
graciously

10:2. whenever he is reproving
the people, he should indicate
to them that he is at the same
time chastising himself.[167]

14. he should acquire for himself a few excellent medical
reference works

2:3. he should have access to
many books, for no one can be
a scholar without the aid of
many good books.[168]

22. he shall not burden himself
with technical terminology
of the different diseases and
their cures

2:8. never trouble the people
with overly complex explanations . . .[169]
7:4. speak without excess verbiage . . . utter no words which
are not straightforward . . .[170]

29. he should make use of both
experience and theory

3:3. if one's explanation of a
subject be complex, he ought to
elucidate it with some illustration.[171]

30. he should be diligent and

2:5. he should not be too long in

[165] Ll. 677–680.
[166] Ll. 745–746.
[167] Ll. 654–655.
[168] Ll. 331–333.
[169] Ll. 361–363.
[170] Ll. 588–589.
[171] Ll. 459–460.

speedy in his acts without
any indolence in the hour of
a patient's need

giving the explanation[172]
3:1. one should not prolong the
sermon in order not to burden
the congregation[173]

32. his main purpose (*ha-
takhlit*) shall be the healing
of the patient

10:1. the purpose (*takhlit*) and
intention of the preacher shall
be the improvement of the
people . . .[174]

35. at times it is necessary to
cheer up the patient with
soft, kind words

2:7. when you sense that the
people are tiring from listening,
you should relate some pleasant
incident . . . to give them something pleasurable[175]

50. he should take cognizance
of the patient's tempera-
ment in determining
whether he can bear a
strong purgative
51. he shall . . . take into consideration the patient's
habits
60. let him observe the strength
of the patient and particularly his mental condition

3:1. one should consider and
weigh carefully the time, the
subject, the place, and the
preacher. If the weather is hot,
one should be brief . . . if the
hour is close to mealtime, one
should be concise . . . if the
content of one's sermon arouses
anxiety, one should speak briefly . . . if the place is narrow and
the people standing together
uncomfortably crowded, one
should give a short sermon[176]

172 L. 344.
173 Ll. 431–432.
174 Ll. 649–650.
175 Ll. 355–357.
176 Ll. 430–445 passim.

This physician-rabbi, who counseled doctors and *darshanim* to be sensitive to the limitations and circumstances of those whom they were treating or teaching, also called for great professionalism in both fields of expertise. In his introduction to the *Oẓar,* Zahalon explains that we have already seen that the "authorities ruled that no one should practice medicine unless he had been granted permission after suitable examination and then found knowledgeable and worthy."[177] Similarly, he adds:

> It is possible to explain the fact that [the ancients deliberately] hid the Book of Remedies but did not burn it, because [at the same time] wisdom and understanding ceased to flourish, and those who would know how to use the book properly dwindled in number. There could have been [great] danger in the [book's being misused]. For this reason it was hidden from the masses, and only those with understanding and ability to grasp the book and its language were permitted to study it. So it is that it has been said that "The best of the physicians are fit for *Gehinnom*" (M. Kid. 4:13), which is explained by Rashi as referring to that type of physician who does not pursue his profession with reverence, who is indolent, or who does not try hard enough to find a cure for his patient. Rather he simply relies on his general learning [and recollection], not stopping to think that forgetfulness is very common, and new kinds of illnesses come on the scene which our forebears did not know about . . .[178]

These allusions to the prevalence of malpractice and a lack of professionalism and sufficient dedication on the part of physicians perhaps help to supply some additional motivation for Zahalon's writing the *Oẓar.* Although one could likewise argue that the whole of the *Or,* including both the index to the *Yalqut* as well as the manual, were aimed at increasing the degree of professionalism on the part of *darshanim,* all of the ninth chapter of that work, on

---

[177] Introduction, first page, left side.

[178] *Ibid.* In the introduction to the *Or,* l. 197, there is also concern for forgetfulness and its effect on preachers.

what one should do before going up to preach, is quite specific on that subject:

> After he has composed his sermon . . . he should look it over very carefully to be sure it has a well-ordered quality (Chap. 9:1).[179]

> He should practice delivering his sermon in a small, quiet place with learned and perceptive friends before he delivers it publicly . . . (9:2).[180]

> He should take care before he delivers his sermon publicly to review all the verses and sayings and not to rely solely on his memory (9:4).[181]

There are further parallels to the preacher and his situation found in the *Oẓar* in the author's reference to the *Olat Shabbat* of R. Joel Ibn Shu-aib (Venice, 1577).[182] Zahalon quotes from that work the four qualities which physicians must possess: (a) they must be men of dignified bearing, gracious, inspiring confidence, reverent, from good families; (b) they must be wise and well versed in the medical arts; (c) they must be widely familiar and experienced within the profession; and (d) they must have a *leshon limmudim* (Isa. 50:4), or learned tongue, which can softly set the patient at ease, or at times state the required regimen the patient is to follow forcefully, "as a king commands his people within his government."[183] One might well say that the entire purpose of the *Or* was to develop that "learned tongue" which our author specifically prays for at the very end of the preacher's manual, and which

---

[179] *Or*, ll. 623–626.

[180] *Ibid.*, ll. 629–631.

[181] *Ibid.*, ll. 640–642.

[182] See below, p. 84.

[183] Introduction, second page, right column, and third page, right column. For the same expression concerning a king, see *Or*, l. 542. Also cf. below, n. 263, and n. 54 on the text of the *Or*, on the *Olat Shabbat*.

he gives thanks for in the Prayer for Preachers.[184] So, too, did the outward appearance, or *form,* of the sermon have to be pleasant and worthy of respect, even as the doctor had to have the appropriate "bedside manner" and a bearing that would command respect. That a *derashah* must have an attractive style was a constant theme of the *Or.*[185]

From all that has been said concerning Zahalon's focusing attention on the particular patient and his needs both psychologically as well as medically, it should be obvious that the *Oẓar* testifies to the humanity of its author. That Zahalon urges his readers to be so attuned to the feelings of sick people gives us deep insight into the character of our physician-rabbi. "At times (the doctor) should specify some of the reasons (for his medications or regimens prescribed) in order that patients should not despair from (the length) of the healing process, but let him not be too harsh that he cause anxiety to the sick person, rather leave the matter somewhat in doubt, albeit with goodly reassurance at the same time."[186] "And (the physician) should not accept payment on the Festivals or on Sabbaths,"[187] Zahalon adds, reminding his colleagues that the practice of medicine does not set aside those Jewish observances that we can still keep in spite of the necessity of healing at all times of need. In conclusion, consider the breadth of concern and sensitivity of a man who could write this:

> And if (the physician) sees that his friend (whom he is treating) wishes to give him some fee on a regular basis in order that he

[184] *Or,* ll. 752–753, and *Margaliot Tovot,* 4a.

[185] This may be found at least twenty-five times throughout the work. It is Zahalon's concern that one should have an attractive subject (Chap. 1:1), interpretations (*ibid.*), nuances (*ibid.*), pleasing stories (2:7), commentaries (2:8), biblical verses (2:13), an attractive order of the sermon (4:1), pleasant inventiveness (4:5), words (5:5), and that he should generally preach and practice in a way pleasing to his Creator and mankind (10:4).

[186] *Oẓar,* introduction, third page, right side.

[187] *Ibid.,* left side.

should not be obligated to give him an expensive gift, or so that he should not feel embarrassed to call him (when he needs the physician), he may accept the fee, even though a doctor visiting the sick is performing a *miẓvah* . . .[188]

Among other accomplishments in Ferrara, Jacob Zahalon also responded to a number of questions of *halakhah* raised by a certain Michael Yaḥya of Lugo,[189] gave a *haskamah* to another scholar,[190] and decided a talmudic question in the year 1689.[191] Further, during his years in Ferrara, the entire Jewish community was miraculously saved from a terrible fire which broke out in the ghetto. Providentially, a torrential rain fell, quenching the fire, all of which occurred on the eve of *Shabbat Ḥanukkah,* 1687. Lampronti records that event in his *Paḥad Yiẓḥaq* explaining that "in the city of Ferrara it is customary to fast on the eve of *Ḥanukkah* because we were saved on that night in the year 5448 from the fire which was in the bakery near the street of the Jews."[192]

---

[188] *Ibid.* That one as concerned for human sensitivities as Zahalon should have had an influence beyond his time and country of origin, is understandable. Professor Shraga Abramson mentions one such example in his "Defusei *Musar Haskel ve-Toldot Adam* le-R. Yeḥezkel Feivel," in *Sinai, LXXXII* (Tishri—Kislev, 1973), 107, where in the midst of a discussion of the teachings of Maimonides on the *Mishneh Torah* and the *Moreh Nevukhim,* R. Ezekiel Feivel speaks of "a beautiful explanation of caring for one's health from Chapter 4 of *Hilkhot De'ot* the like of which I have not found in Hebrew elsewhere with such complete explanation to this very day." Abramson points out that this explanation was taken by Feivel from the *Oẓar* by Jacob Zahalon, and duly acknowledged. The reference to our author is from the *Musar Haskel* (Dyhernfurth, 1790), *Leshon Ḥakhamim,* Chap. 4, *Hilkhot De'ot,* 1 ff. Abramson notes that this was a new way of explaining Maimonides, by citing a physician to support his writings.

[189] Vogelstein and Rieger, II, 269, n. 7, ascribing this to *Paḥad Yiẓḥaq* (Venice, 1750), *Bet,* p. 36a.

[190] *Ibid.,* n. 8, *Paḥad Yiẓḥaq, Samech,* p. 136a.

[191] *Ibid.,* n. 9, *Paḥad Yiẓḥaq, s.v. Oqer,* p. 80a.

[192] *Ibid., s.v. Ḥanukkah,* quoted by Leibowitz in "R. Ya'aqov Zahalon Ish Roma," p. 175.   [193] *Ibid.,* pp. 176—177. On pp. 178—179, Leibowitz explains that another fire on 23 Av 1794, prompted some changes in the original poem of Zahalon, and another event in 1840 led to further changes in the *piyyut* to fit that

Zahalon composed a moving *piyyut* in that same year to commemorate the saving of the Jewish community. The poem, which Leibowitz has published, reveals tender feelings and concern for the infants and children caught in the conflagration, and a recapturing of the state of panic and momentary hopelessness of the situation.[193]

In Ferrara, Zahalon established himself as "one of the three most remarkable men of his generation in terms of his wisdom," as testified by R. Nathaniel ben Aaron Segre.[194] Some of Zahalon's responsa are included in the latter's work, *Afar Ya'aqov*. Other *teshuvot* are cited in the responsa of R. Moses b. Mordecai Zacuto

---

tragedy. Davidson, *Oẓar ha-Shirah ve-ha-Piyyut*, III, 645, cites the poem as authored by Mordecai Zahalon because of the adaptations to the 1794 catastrophe. Although Mordecai died in 1749, he was closer to the 1794 fire than his father. Yiẓḥaq Baruch Ha-Levi, in *Kavod Levanon*, I (1874–1875), 17, in an article, "Al Meshorarei Yisro'el she-Hayu ba-Ir Ferrara," also attributed the *piyyut* to Mordecai Zahalon. Leibowitz explains how the error may have come about and closely compares the different versions. There appear to be three manuscript collections of *piyyutim* in which works by Zahalon appear: (a) *Qiẓur Zemirot Yisro'el*, written down by Phinehas Hai Anau (Piattelli) in 1705, in the possession of Leibowitz. The *piyyut* in this collection, acquired by Leibowitz from a private family in Venice, in 1935 (see p. 175 in his article), beginning with the line *Hagot Pela'ot Amqu Gadalu*, has been published in full by him. (b) *Seder Qiẓur Zemirot Yisro'el ke-Minhag Qehal Qadosh Sefaradim*. It is found in the British Museum, Or. 10437, Gaster 437, and is dated Ferrara, 1770, with a question mark following. It is no. 7799 in the Hebrew University microfilm collection. Most of the *piyyutim* are attributed to Israel Najara, and the one by "Rav Zahalon" is found on pp. 9a and 9b. It is written for the fire of 5448 and begins also with the same words as the *piyyut* in the Leibowitz collection. (c) *Seder Qiẓur Zemirot Yisro'el ke-Minhag Q"Q Sefaradim*. Found in Leeds, England, in the Roth collection, no. 23, and dated Ferrara, 1792. It is no. 15255 in the Hebrew University microfilm collection. Most of the poems are by Israel Najara, and one on p. 6b begins with the same line as those cited above, and is attributed to Zahalon concerning the same conflagration in Ferrara. On Najara, see above, n. 85.

[194] Cited in Neppi-Ghirondi, p. 131. The reference to the *Afar Ya'aqov* is to responsum no. 65.

(d. Mantua, 1671).[195] We have already referred to the relationship between Zahalon and Zacuto in terms of their attitude toward Sabbatianism.[196] Likewise, Zahalon's opinions are cited in three places in the *Paḥad Yiẓḥaq.*[197]

Jacob Zahalon died in Ferrara on September 18, 1693, corresponding to the seventeenth of *Elul.*[198] According to Leibowitz, it is impossible to locate the grave of Jacob Zahalon today because in 1775 the Church ordered all tombstones in Ferrara destroyed.[199] As if that were not enough posthumous harm to have been done to our author, the Italian Fascists destroyed the local synagogue in Ferrara on September 24, 1941, and apparently the library of the *Talmud Torah,* where a number of Zahalon's manuscripts were stored, was destroyed.[200] Fortunately, however, copies of several of Zahalon's unpublished works which were found only in the Ferrara *Talmud Torah* are available in microfilm.[201]

10. Mordecai Zahalon, Son of Jacob, and His Works

Especially I pray, Lord of all hosts above and below, that I shall be

---

[195] *Ibid.,* see above, n. 125 on *Zacuto.*

[196] See above, pp. 47–48.

[197] Boaz Cohen, "Mazkeret Meḥabrei ha-Teshuvot be-Sefer *Paḥad Yiẓḥaq,*" in *Sefer Likhvod Professor Marx* (New York, 1943), p. 51, no. 83. These are under the heading of *Ben,* p. 36a; *Sefer Torah,* pp. 135–136; and *Oqer Dirato,* pp. 78–80.

[198] Jonathan Christoph Wolf, *Bibliotheca Hebraea,* III (Hamburg, 1715), 509. According to Wolf, the date of Zahalon's death is given by his son Mordecai in a published work dated 1717. Whether Zahalon's death at the age of sixty-three prevented him from having the words of his "Prayer for Parents Concerning Their Children," that one be privileged to see one's own great-grandchildren, answered in his *own* life, we cannot know for sure, though it seems very unlikely. His son Mordecai, however, did achieve considerable longevity (see *Margaliot Tovot,* 8a; also above, p. 37, and below, p. 68).

[199] "Jacob Zahalon, a Hebrew Medical Author," p. 432.

[200] In a letter received by this writer from the secretary of the Communità Israelitica in Ferrara and dated June 15, 1970, it is noted that ". . . nostra biblioteca non abbiamo ciò che desidera poichè gran parte di essa è stata distrutta durante l'ultima guerra" ("our library does not have the [MSS.] you desire since the greater part [of the library] was destroyed during the last war").

[201] See below, pp. 69–70, and above, n. 79.

worthy of fathering children and be privileged to see grandchildren. May my children achieve all that I have accomplished and many times over.

("Prayer for One Who Preaches Publicly," *Margaliot Tovot,* p. 4b)

We might note here that Zahalon's son, Mordecai, succeeded his father in Ferrara, achieving renown as the head of the Talmudic Academy there.[202] He was also a physician and a poet.[203] Mordecai was the author of the *Megillat Naharot* (Venice, 1707), which describes the miraculous rescue of the Jewish community of Ferrara from the flood that occurred in that year. Landshuth records that in the Sefardic synagogue in that city on *Shabbat Ḥanukkah* it is customary to recite a poem written by Mordecai Zahalon concerning another local miracle, the saving of the Jewish population from a fire which broke out in the bakery near the ghetto in the year 1700.[204] It may be that this poem was incorrectly ascribed to Mordecai, and is rather a revised version of the *piyyut* his father originally wrote for the conflagration in Ferrara in 1687.[205] Three of the poetic works of Mordecai were chanted in the Fanisi synagogue, one on *Shavuot,* one on *Hoshanah Rabbah,* and one on another occasion.[206]

Mordecai Zahalon's decisions in *halakhah* are recorded in several places. He is cited no less than eleven times in the *Paḥad Yiẓḥak.*[207] He is also referred to by R. Samson Morpurgo in the

[202] Vogelstein and Rieger, II, 270.

[203] L. Landshuth, *Amudei ha-Avodah* (Berlin, 1857), p. 199.

[204] *Ibid.*

[205] See above, n. 193, where Leibowitz maintains that others had confused a *piyyut* of 1794 as if it were originally written by Mordecai. The same could apply to the bakery fire mentioned by Landshuth as coming only thirteen years after the catastrophe in 1687 which Jacob Zahalon responded to with his *piyyut.* Yet, considering the frequency of fires within the crowded quarters of the ghetto, it is not impossible that Landshuth is referring to an entirely separate poem by Mordecai.

[206] Landshuth, p. 199. We cannot locate this place. It may be the name of a specific synagogue in Ferrara.

[207] Boaz Cohen, p. 53, no. 123.

Shemesh Zedakah in four places.[208] Raphael Meldola also mentions one of the younger Zahalon's decisions in his *Mayyim Rabim.*[209]

Mordecai wrote a polemical work concerning the Priestly Blessing entitled *Meẓiẓ u'Meliẓ* (Venice, 1715), in which he defended a certain Nehemiah ben Baruch ha-Kohen against Lampronti.[210] Landshuth adds that Mordecai "bitterly attacked those wicked ones who tended to establish religious decisions on shaky grounds, and all of them feared him."[211]

Mordecai Zahalon lived to be at least eighty, passing away while he was still at the helm of the *Talmud Torah* of Ferrara on November 30, 1749.[212] He was succeeded in that office by Isaac Lampronti, who later became the teacher of the grandson of the author of the *Or,* named for his grandfather, Jacob Zahalon. According to Lampronti, this descendant of our author was one of his three most outstanding pupils.[213]

[208] *Yoreh De'ah* 16; *Eben ha-Ezer* 3; *Ḥoshen Mishpat* 20, 32. Cf. Landshuth, p. 199.

[209] *Ibid., Yoreh De'ah* 7.

[210] Isaiah Sonne, "Avnei Binyan le-Qorot ha-Yehudim," in *Ḥoreb,* VI (1941), 80–81. Mordecai Zahalon was involved in an unusually heated controversy involving the rabbis of Ferrara. It started in 1715 with the publication by Isaac Lampronti of a periodical in which some of the halakhic rulings of his pupils were found. One such ruling was that of Phinehas Hai Anau, who stated that the Priestly Blessing should be pronounced according to the Ashkenazi custom of stressing the last syllable of each word. This was in opposition to the view of Nehemiah ha-Kohen and his followers, that emphasis should be on the penultimate syllable. Nehemiah considered himself insulted by this ruling, seeking out Zahalon's aid against Anau. Zahalon had refused to recognize Lampronti as the chief rabbi of Ferrara, and now in *Meẓiẓ u'Meliẓ* openly attacked Lampronti and all of the rabbis who had sided with him regarding Anau's decision.

[211] Landshuth, p. 199.

[212] *Ibid.* Vogelstein and Rieger, II, 270, say Mordecai Zahalon died in 1748.

[213] Yiẓḥaq Baruch ha-Levi of Ferrara, *Sefer Toldot Yiẓḥaq Lampronti* (Lyck, 1871), p. 3a. I am indebted to Dr. Abraham David of Jerusalem for this reference.

11. Zahalon's Other Unpublished Works

> Great is the reward of him who performs a service for the commu-
> nity through publishing books which are great in quantity as
> well as in quality, as the Almighty has taught me to do.
>
> (*Or ha-Darshanim*, ll. 232–234)

We have evidence of another work written by Jacob Zahalon in
1686 or 1688 in Ferrara. It is known as the *Zohola ve-Rina*, a
commentary on the *Song of Songs, Qoheleth,* and *Daniel.*[214] A copy
of it exists today in microfilm from the Ferrara *Talmud Torah*
collection.[215] The subtitle reads, "Sermons and Explanations of the
Song of Songs Composed by the Physician and Preacher . . . in the
year 1686." About ten pages from the end of the manuscript, there
is a note on the upper margin which indicates that some of the
sermons were delivered during Passover, 1688. Two pages later the
date 1688 is again referred to in the margin. We might surmise that
the work was completed in some earlier form by the earlier date,
and added to and brought to a final completed form by the later
date.

We shall deal later with a note written by Zahalon himself
(apparently) in the Casanatense manuscript in a revision which
was added and then meant to be deleted,[216] that his work *Zohola
ve-Rina* "on the *Song of Songs* and *Qoheleth* and *Daniel*" was
among some of the works he wrote in which he was specifically
guided by the principles he enunciated in the *Or.*[217]

---

[214] See below, n. 249.

[215] No. 48 in that collection. It is no. 2428 in Hebrew University microfilm collection. Vogelstein and Rieger, II, 269.

[216] See *Or*, ll. 216–226.

[217] *Or*, ll. 215–217. Although Vogelstein and Rieger only mention the commentary on *Song of Songs*, and indicate a separate one known as *Qehilat Ya'aqov*
on the book of *Qoheleth*, the actual MS. contains a section on *Sukkot*, about eight
pages from the end, which may include sermons on *Qoheleth*. Vogelstein and
Rieger also indicate a separate work on the book of *Daniel, Derushim al Daniel,*
though Zahalon in the *Or* in the lines cited includes his work on *Daniel* as part of
Zohala ve-Rina. See below, p. 78.

One remaining unpublished work by Jacob Zahalon is the *Shuvu Elai,*[218] sermons on the recitation of the *Shema* and its accompanying blessings.[219] This work includes some very beautiful poetic *vidduyim,* or confessionals.[220] There is one long confessional devoted to transgressions of the positive commandments in the Bible,[221] another on the negative biblical commandments,[222] and a

[218] This title is found in Zech. 1:3 and Mal. 3:7.

[219] Listed as no. 14 in the Ferrara *Talmud Torah* collection. It is numbered 2391 in the Hebrew University microfilm collection. See above, n. 29.

[220] The lettering of this section of the MS., including the confessionals and the prayer, is unusually large, carefully written in block letters, as if it was being prepared for recitation by several people looking on together, or for presentation, or for some other special purpose.

[221] This begins with two words in very large letters at the top of the page, *Adonai Sefatai,* "O Lord, my lips . . ." the first words of Ps. 51:17. There are no numbers on these MS. pages. The first confessional appears to follow the order of the 248 positive commandments according to the listing of Maimonides. See Charles B. Chavel, *The Commandments: Sefer ha-Mizvot of Maimonides,* translated with notes (New York, 1967). The opening section is in carefully voweled poetry for fifteen lines before Zahalon begins the actual confessional, each sentence of which begins, "Woe is me that . . ." Zahalon presents many of the confessions in a particularly dramatic way, e.g., "Woe is me that I honored You with my mouth, but I was far away from You in my heart . . . Woe is me that when I bound Your *tefillin* on my head, I did not purify my body, my soul, and my feelings, and what good was it in my recalling Your commandments through the fringes on the corners of my garment? . . . Woe is me, for how can I deserve the blessing of the Priests, for in my hearing the cry of the poor and the needy in their pleas, I did not respond compassionately? . . . Woe is me that on *Yom Kippur . . .* in the hours of the fast I sought out pleasant diversions, and I sat among those who were being frivolous . . ." He refers, too, to the sins of eating and sating oneself and neglecting to say the grace after meals, allowing his hair to grow long not in fulfillment of the commandment of the Nazirite but rather to be attractive to his wife, having eaten meat which had been prepared by a *Shohet* whose knife had not been properly sharpened or who had not thoroughly removed the blood from the meat, finding it difficult to dwell in the *Sukkah* for the full seven days, for not having bought his own *Etrog* even though he expended much on foods which were luxuries. Some of the confessionals are especially indicative of a sensitive person, as "Woe is me, for though I betrothed my wife according to the law of Moses and the tribes of the Lord, afterwards I looked at her as if she were a cap-

third on violations of rabbinic commandments.[223] Lastly, there is a special prayer for forgiveness.[224]

The last unpublished work that we are aware of is the *Sefer Oẓar ha-Shamayyim al Ḥokhma Elohit ve-Limmudit,* or "The Book of the Treasure of Heaven on Theological and Learned Wisdom." This manuscript, not dated in any way, is found in the Budapest-Kaufman collection, numbered 293.[225] Like the *Or* and the *Oẓar ha-Ḥayyim,* this work has thirteen chapters.[226] The subject matter of this work includes consideration of angels, evil

tive woman now in captivity," or, "Woe is me that instead of causing my wife to rejoice for a full year after marrying her, I aggravated her and vexed her constantly . . ." It would be of considerable interest in the future to compare the *vidduyim* of Zahalon within the framework of *viddui* literature in general.

[222] The negative commandments, though listed seemingly in the order arranged by Maimonides, are not treated with the poetic and imaginative style that Zahalon used on the positive commandments. They seem to be merely listed, also in the large block letters as the earlier confessionals.

[223] In this section, after an opening prayer, the author personifies each principal part of the body, having each make its own extensive confessional. He includes among these the heart, the eyes, the ears, the tongue, the mouth, the feet, the hands, and the sexual organs (the last for wrongs committed in the act of sexual intercourse). Samples of the sins mentioned include: "My ear has been closed to hearing words of *Torah* . . . I have closed my ear to the cry of the poor . . . my tongue has not been the first to greet another person . . . talks too much . . . has not been scrupulous in saying blessings . . ." The various sins leveled against the parts of the body are phrased in poetry.

[224] This is a very long and plaintive prayer, making ample use of biblical verses, put in poetic form in parts which are carefully vowelled, covering most of twelve MS. pages. It is arranged in alphabetical form, with each section beginning with another letter of the Hebrew alphabet. Toward the end of the prayer he adds, "and remember the merit of Isaac, my father, who prayed for me most of his days [as a result of which] I did not stumble in wrongdoing . . ." I am indebted to Rabbi Jacob Brumer for his aid with this difficult passage.

[225] No. 14715 in the Hebrew University microfilm collection.

[226] The thirteenth chapter, not mentioned on the title page, is referred to, and then crossed out, on p. 40 of the MS. There seems to be some special significance to the use of the number thirteen. See above, pp. 55–56, and below, pp. 79–80 and n. 261, where *Tena'ei ha-Darshan* has thirteen chapters. The thirteen attributes of God are one obvious source for the importance of this number. See also

spirits, Adam and Eve and their creation, the body and the soul, reward and punishment, resurrection of the dead and the hereafter, and numerous other philosophical and theological matters. The other manuscripts have been referred to in various sources, but no copy of these appears extant today. One is *Milḥamot Ya'aqov* ("The Wars of Jacob"), a polemic work, mentioned in Vogelstein and Rieger[227] and in Neppi-Ghirondi.[228] The other is an ethical work, on the good qualities in mankind as well as the harmful ones, an abbreviation of all the books of St. Thomas Aquinas "in pure and poetic Hebrew,"[229] apparently seen by Bartolocci because of his description of it but not listed in any manuscript collection.

12. *Or ha-Darshanim,* Its Original Form and Purpose

It [i.e., the *Or ha-Darshanim*] is a virtual necessity for preachers, as is well known to anyone who researches and takes pains with his sermons. How very much of his time is needed just to find even one

---

Tosafot, Ber. 20a, s.v. *Telasar metivta,* and J. Bergmann, "Die rumden und hyperbolischen Zahlen in der Agada," *Monatsschrift fur geschichte und wissenschaft dés Judentums,* LXXXII (1938), 361–376. I am indebted to Professor David Weiss Halivni for these references.

[227] II, 269.

[228] Pp. 129–131, no. 11.

[229] Bartolocci, III, 852; see Wolf, I, 600 f. Steinschneider, in his *Die Hebraeische Uebersetzungen des Mittelalters* (Berlin, 1893), p. 483, par. 295, lists Hebrew translations of Thomas Aquinas. He refers to the work by Jellinek, *Thomas von Aquino in der juedischen lituratur* (Leipzig, 1853). Steinschneider indicates that, according to Jellinek, Zahalon had prepared a compendium, or abstract, of the *Summa contra gentiles.* Yet there is no mention of any existing MS. of this work. In his *Jewish Literature* (London, 1857), Steinschneider describes this as "a compendium of the *Summa* of Thomas Aquinas, written by Jacob Zahalon but never printed," p. 231. Bartolocci indicates that Zahalon showed him this and other works (see above, n. 135). That Zahalon wrote on Thomas Aquinas at all bears further attention.

rabbinic saying, and before long an entire day is gone.
(Israel Foa, *Haskamah* to the Casanatense MS. of *Or ha-Darshanim*, p. 2)

The title of the *Or* had originally been given to a well-arranged index and compendium of the rabbinic sayings found in the *Yalqut Shimoni*. This text was composed, the author writes, in his "youth at a time when he began to speak publicly every Sabbath, even daily."[230] It represented an effort by the young preacher to list all of the topics of this *Midrash* alphabetically in a readily usable form. This he did for two reasons:

. . . that this would be a brief summary of the entire *Yalqut*; and in order that the preacher should be able to understand from the rabbinic saying written here in the reference whether or not it is relevant to his subject before he bothers to search out the quotation in the *Yalqut* proper.[231]

Zahalon called his work a *mareh maqom*, an index, or reference work, claiming that it would indicate, after the manner of the early editions of the *Yalqut*, the original source of each *Midrash*, *Ein Yisro'el*,[232] *Rabbot*,[233] *Yelamdennu*,[234] *Pirqei Rabbi Eliezer*, *Sifra*, *Sifrei*, and others.[235] The "light," or enlightenment, which he

---

[230] Cas. MS., l. 84, has the word *be-na'aruti* ("in my youth," or "as a youth") crossed out, and *be-vaharuti* ("in my young manhood," or "as a young man") written by the author over it. The MS. of JTS and the Oxford MS. have *bena'aruti* with no change indicated, apparently having been copied before the author eventually changed the text. See below, p. 75 and n. 238 on *bahur* and its age range.

[231] Ll. 159–162.

[232] More popularly known as *Ein Ya'aqov*. See n. 28 to the translation of the *Or*.

[233] An abbreviation for *Midrash Rabbah*.

[234] Another name for *Midrash Tanhuma*.

[235] Ll. 149–152. The 1687 Frankfurt a. M. ed. of the *Yalqut* lists: *Sifra, Sifrei, Mekhilta, Rabbot, Tanhuma, Mishnah, Gemara*, and *Aggadah*. On the title page it

sought to provide for *darshanim* like himself was in his having alphabetized all of the sayings according to their subject matter, thereby drastically reducing the work load of the average preacher in having to search out a certain saying or an applicable *Midrash*. It was this accomplishment by Zahalon which Rabbi Israel Foa, the emissary from Jerusalem who wrote a *haskamah,* or statement of recommendation, for Zahalon's work in 1672, praised so highly:

> It was truly an act of his devotion to have produced this work and provided such enlightenment, for it is a virtual necessity for *darshanim,* as is well known to anyone who researches and takes pains [in the writing of] his sermons. How very much time is necessary even to locate one rabbinic saying, and before long an entire day is gone. [Furthermore,] even after all the effort and trouble [one might take to find a rabbinic source,] he [still] might not [be able] to locate it.[236]

adds that it has brought a *mareh maqom* of sayings and verses and pages as found in the *Yalqut* printed in Livorno, 1657. Zahalon would have had to use an earlier edition, as he was at work on the index already by 1651. Evidence from the Cas. MS. of the index itself points to the Salonika editions as Zahalon's sources. His frequent use of the term of reference *qunteres* (literally, "booklet"), followed by a number designating one of the *remazim,* or allusions, could only refer to the Venice or Salonika editions. However, his use of the term *qunteres aharon* ("last booklet"), as for instance on pp. 56, 57, 77, 82, 86, 91, 113, 138, among others, proves conclusively that he was using the Salonika editions, *Prophets* and *Hagiographa* (1521) and *Pentateuch* (1526). As E.J., XVI, 709, notes, referring to the Salonika text, "to this edition a *qunteres aharon* (addendum) was added (at the end of Part 1) containing 256 *remazim* of *aggadot* of the *Jerusalem Talmud,* with deviations from the present order of the tractates and 55 *remazim* from the *Midrash Yelammedenu* on the *Pentateuch* to all of which cross-references occur in the main work. This addendum was omitted from all subsequent editions." Professor Shraga Abramson has been extremely helpful to me in examining the MS. of the index and calling these and other facts to my attention. A. Jellinek, in his *Qunteres Virmiza u-Qehal Vina* (Vienna, 1880), lists the *Qol Ya'aqov* (also called *Or ha-Darshanim*) as one of a number of unpublished indexes of rabbinic works, indicating that it is the same work cited in the intro. to the *Margaliot Tovot* and that it is found in MS. in the Biblioteca Casanatense in Rome, p. 17, n. 72a. I am indebted to Professor Avraham Holtz for this reference.

[236] Cas. MS., second page of *haskamah.*

Yet Zahalon reveals a second and earlier motive for having composed the index to the *Yalqut,* a concern which he as a young preacher obviously felt keenly:

> I wrote it as a young man (*be-vaḥaruti*) at the time when I began to preach publicly every Sabbath and even daily in order to *ease my burden* in having to search out sermonic material appropriate to each weekly *Torah* portion.[237]

In other words, one of the chief motivations for his undertaking such an ambitious task was both personal and very practical.

Now from Zahalon's own emendation of the above-quoted text from the word *be-na'aruti* ("in my boyhood"), we may infer that he began his work on the index to the *Yalqut* even earlier than 1651, when he would have been twenty-one years old. Conceivably, he might have started cataloguing the sayings of the *Yalqut* while in his late teens. However, by the time our author had moved to Ferrara, having completed twenty-seven years of service as preacher and in various other communal capacities on behalf of Roman Jewry, he was a man of considerable stature both as rabbi and as physician. By then he had already written many important works and was preparing his text for the printer. It might not have appeared dignified to indicate that the *Or,* which was now being presented for publication when the author was fifty or sixty years old, had been begun at such an early age! The period of *baḥarut* would not only indicate a time of greater maturity as a starting-point. It could also be a term appropriate as an umbrella under which to describe not only the period of earliest composition but also the later periods of expanding the text, editing earlier material, and putting the *Or* into something closer to its present form.[238]

---

[237] Ll. 84–89, italics added.

[238] M. Benayahu, in his *Sefer Toldot ha-Ari* (Jerusalem, 1967), p. 176, no. 2, points out sources contemporary with or slightly earlier than Zahalon, including Leone da Modena's works, which made use of the term *baḥur* to indicate a man up to the age of thirty-five or forty. Or course, the term would be appropriate as well for one of twenty.

From the well-ordered and useful form in which he rendered the *Yalqut* we have clear evidence of Zahalon's organizational and intellectual abilities. Though one cannot consider it an original work, he was clearly unusually talented and energetic to have accomplished such an impressive task as a rather young man.[239] It is no wonder that he so admired Maimonides for his brilliance in carefully ordering all of Jewish law.[240] Considering the voluminous nature of the *mareh maqom,* numbering some 501 manuscript pages, we would not be exaggerating to argue that he must have fulfilled his role as *darshan* most conscientiously.[241]

Undoubtedly, other studies competed for the time of the young *darshan,* such as his premedical and medical learning. Yet the work of the index was begun as an aid to his own sermonic work, and publishing the text seems to have been an afterthought. Zahalon makes light of the whole endeavor:

> God himself knows that I have not written this work for the sake of personal glory, for the honor of my family, or for any such selfish motive. On the contrary, the book represents more sheer drudgery than it does real insight. It is not meant for those scholars who are able to envisage the entire *Yalqut* as if in one glance . . . but for one such as myself.[242]

13. The Earliest Indications of the Preacher's Manual

[We should] not be like those who expatiate at great length in

---

[239] The fact that the index is mentioned in a completed work by Joab ben Baruch de' Piattelli in his introduction to the *Margaliot Tovot* (Venice, 1665) indicates that our author had effectively catalogued the *Yalqut* by the age of thirty-five. (Although de' Piattelli refers to the work by the title *Qol Ya'aqov,* it is clear that he means by that title what Zahalon later called *Or ha-Darshanim.* See below, n. 283 and cf. p. 87.)

[240] Ll. 127–135.

[241] There are, in addition to the Cas. MS., two other copies, or two parts of one copy, of the index extant in the JTS collection. See below, n. 291.

[242] Ll. 190–196.

sermons which do not relate to the issues of the times, and [only as an] after[thought] append a few words about the matter [which is on people's minds].

(*Or ha-Darshanim,* ll. 300–302)

May none of my words or sermons be burdensome to Your people, but rather may they be regarded with special affection, even loved from beginning to end.

("Prayer for One Who Preaches Publicly," *Margaliot Tovot,* p. 5a)

By the year 1660, we know that Zahalon had already prepared the basic plan for his preacher's manual, which was later incorporated into the *Or* as part of the introduction,[243] overshadowing it considerably as far as historical significance is concerned. It is this small manual of rules relating to the effective preaching of sermons with which we are chiefly concerned. As part of the introduction to his homiletic work on the first part of the *Mishneh Torah* of Maimonides, the *Morashah Qehilat Ya'aqov,*[244] dated 1660, Zahalon included a prototype of what he was later to expand upon in his advice to *darshanim.*[245] He explained why he included these rules of good preaching there:

[243] *Or,* l. 25, of the Cas. MS., the author's instructions (which we have not translated in our English text) "to print with the Lord's help first the introduction to the *Yalqut* and afterwards the precautions for preachers," seem to indicate two strata in the *Or.* First, the index to the *Yalqut* had been completed. Then, later, the author composed the preacher's manual. Here we see his decision to *insert* the manual *into* the already existent index. L. 204 clearly indicates that the manual was an *addition,* or afterthought. Cf. ll. 425–429, Chap. 2:14, found only in the Cas. MS., wedged into a space between chapters, contains a reference to the *Yalqut,* an obvious attempt to establish continuity between the two sections.

[244] The title is a quotation from Deut. 33:4.

[245] British Museum, MS. Or. 10044, and London-Gaster 157. Like so many of Zahalon's works this was never published. The MS. is dated with the use of the Hebrew word *Yismah* ("he will rejoice"), which adds up in the numerical value of the Hebrew letters to 5420, or 1660. There is a notation on the page preceding the title page that a *haskamah* has been written by R. Sabbatai Baer, author of the *Be'er Eseq* (Venice, 1674), and a Ḥiyya Dayyan. See above, n. 75. Also, cf. n. 79.

In order to provide greater usefulness for these sermons which I have composed at the beginning of every *halakhah,* I have attempted to indicate how preachers might utilize these guidelines in the composition of their sermons. Therefore, I have placed these rules at the beginning of this compilation of sermons inasmuch as these same rules have actually motivated me to compose new and clearly organized sermons enthusiastically.[246]

Expanding on this theme in the *Or* some years later, he says:

Now inasmuch as the purpose of this book is to smooth the way for preachers, enlightening their path as they go about composing their sermons, I decided to add to it a supplement. This addition, great in quality though small in quantity, will teach young men some valuable guidelines for the composition and public delivery of sermons. Because until now there has not been a guidebook which would show them the necessary steps in preparing and delivering an effective sermon, they are excessively burdened with fashioning and improving their sermons. They must take much time and abundant practice in learning the ways of the art of homiletics. With the limited knowledge that I have acquired during the years that I have preached publicly, I have learned the various approaches and techniques needed in this field. I have written them at the beginning of this work. I have been personally guided by these rules . . .[247]

Zahalon specifies that these rules have aided him in his preaching, the fruits of which were incorporated into his *Titen Emet le-Ya'aqov,*[248] on the weekly biblical portions, and *Zohola ve-Rina,*[249] on *Song of Songs, Qoheleth,* and *Daniel.* Even more revealing

---

[246] P. 5a.

[247] *Or,* ll. 204–214. At some future time it is my hope to study some of Zahalon's other works, *derashot* in particular, to see if he himself followed his guidelines in the *Or* in composing his own writings.

[248] The title is a quotation from Mic. 7:20.

[249] The title, which is a play on the author's last name, is similar to Isa. 12:6 or 54:1. The words are the same as a line in the Sabbath liturgy. See Zeligman Baer, *Avodat Yisro'el* (Redelheim, 1868), p. 212.

about the time during which the manual was written, Zahalon tells us:

> This supplementary work has been at my side in the composition of nearly five hundred sermons alone, from those I composed in my *Morashah Qehilat Ya'aqov* on the books of *Mada, Ahavah,* and *Zemanim* of Maimonides . . . and my *Qzar ha-Ḥokhmot* and *Shnei Me'ðrot Teshuvah* . . .[250]

Two of these works are mentioned in the introduction to the *Margaliot Tovot,* published in 1665, as already extant. Joab ben Baruch de' Piattelli, who wrote the introductory section of Zahalon's first published work,[251] refers to a number of other works of the author in manuscript form, among which are *Titen Emet le-Ya'aqov* and *Morashah Qehilat Ya'aqov.*[252] The existence of the first of these two works today is uncertain,[253] and the second remains in manuscript in the British Museum.[254] We have referred to this latter work as a prototype of the preacher's manual, as it appears to be an early stage of the writing of the work as we have it today in the three manuscripts available throughout the world, at the Jewish Theological Seminary, the Bodleian Library at Oxford, and the Biblioteca Casanatense in Rome.[255] The prototype in the *Morashah Qehilat Ya'aqov* deals with the same subject matter as the *Or.* It also consists of thirteen chapters like the *Or,* although

[250] *Or,* ll. 217–222.

[251] De' Piattelli was affiliated with the rabbinate in Rome in some official capacity, according to Vogelstein and Rieger, II, 273. He served as a teacher of young children within the community. He was an assistant also to R. Joshua Menagen. Joab seems to have been active generally, too, in assisting Zahalon in his scholarly and educational endeavors. Aside from writing the introduction to the *Margaliot Tovot,* de' Piattelli wrote the preface to the *Morashah Qehilat Ya'aqov.* Also, see above n. 74, n. 90, and n. 127.

[252] P. 2.

[253] See above, p. 34.

[254] See n. 75.

[255] Described below, n. 291 and Chap. 5, d, and above, n. 41.

there are some differences in order and titles.[256] Whereas the prototype contains three manuscript pages, the *Or,* at least the Casanatense manuscript, contains six and one-half folio pages in the section constituting the preacher's manual.[257]

Oẓar ha-Ḥokmot is an inclusive title that Zahalon used to encompass several works, one of which is the *Oẓar* we have already discussed.[258] Another was also referred to earlier.[259] As to the last work referred to in the quotation from the *Or, Shnei Me'orot Teshuvah,* we have not been able to locate this in any manuscript collection.

Regarding Zahalon's statement in the introduction to the *Or* that "until now there has not been a guidebook which would show them (young preachers) the necessary steps in preparing and delivering an effective sermon,"[260] some comment is in order.

---

[256] See above, n. 226.

[257] *Morashah Qehilat Ya'aqov,* p. 5a, contains the principles for every *darshan* to use in order to be an effective and pleasing preacher and teacher. The work, which represents an explanation of the laws of Maimonides, is preceded by these lessons in good preaching techniques. This MS. has in its Chap. 1 only fifteen lines with no subheadings, whereas the Cas. MS. has in its first chapter thirty-five lines, among which are six subheadings. Chap. 2 of this MS. has twenty-nine lines with no subheadings, whereas the Cas. MS. has seventy-one lines in its second chapter, among which are fourteen subheadings. Chap. 3 of this MS. has eight lines and no subheadings, whereas Chap. 3 of the Cas. MS. has twenty lines, among which are three subheadings. The chapter titles are basically the same, with these variations: Chap. 6 of the prototype has the title of Chap. 9 of the Cas. MS. Chap. 7 of the prototype has the title of Chap. 6 of the Cas. MS. Chap. 8 of the prototype has this title: *Aikh Yitnaheg bi-Devarov,* "Concerning One's Use of Words," a slight variation from the title of Chap. 7 of the Cas. MS., *Aikh Yitnaheg be-Ma'amar Devarav,* "Concerning One's Manner of Speaking." Chap. 9 of the prototype has the title of Chap. 8 of Cas. MS. Chap. 12 of the prototype has the title of Chap. 13 of Cas. MS. Chap. 13 of the prototype has the title of Chap. 12 of Cas. MS. In these instances of a changing of titles, obviously the subject matter is similarly changed.

[258] See above, Chap. 9.

[259] See above, p. 71. Cf. also n. 132, where the inclusive title is *Sefer Ohalei Ya'aqov, Oẓar ha-Ḥokhmot.*

[260] Ll. 207–208.

Although there appear to be numerous references to what consti-
tutes effective preaching in the works of many of Zahalon's predecessors, we have not been able to locate an actual comprehensive manual for preachers published before the *Or*.[261]

[261] *Ein ha-Qorei* of Joseph Ibn Shem Tov, mentioned in Zunz in his *Ha-
Derashot be-Yisro'el* (see above, n. 65) as fifteenth-century general rules for
preachers (p. 196 and on p. 519, n. 60, as "a MS. in two chapters") is *the earliest*
homiletic handbook known. I obviously erred in my article "A Rabbi-Physician's Prescription for Effective Sermons: The Earliest Hebrew Preaching Manual," in *Judaism*, XXVIII, 1 (1979), 109–113. Yet none of the earlier works are so
thoroughgoing as the *Or* in providing detailed guidance for the preacher.
Written after 1455, this MS. is found in the National Library in Paris (Heb.
325), Oxford (Bodleian 2052 [Michael collection 350]), Jews' College library in
London (Montefiore 61), as well as elsewhere. Jellinek had published the introduction of the MS. in his *Kunteres ha-Mafte'aḥ* (Vienna, 1881), pp. 30–32. Shem
Tov notes what Zahalon was later to follow implicitly, that "just as in the medical
profession there is theory and practice, so is the case in this [preaching] profession" (see above, p. 59). The author, a Spanish philosopher, wrote his MS. on the
basic rules for the art of preaching. E.J., VIII, 1197, calls it "probably the only
work of its kind in the literature of the Middle Ages . . . rich in quotations from
Muslim and Christian sources."
Zunz also refers to "different guidebooks and indexes" to aid preachers which
were composed from the sixteenth century on. In a note to this text, Zunz specifies nine works, one of which is the *Or* of Jacob Zahalon (p. 199 and p. 522, n. 3,
and p. 526, n. 59). Of the remaining works cited, only three preceded the approxi-
mate date of the *Or*, and, therefore, might have had some influence on our
author: (1) *Hitnazlut le-Darshanim*, or *Ktav Hitnazlut le-Darshanim*, of David
Darshan (Lublin, 1574); (2) *Toldot Aharon* of Aaron of Pesaro (Venice, 1591); (3)
Beit Leḥem Yehudah of Leone da Modena (Venice, 1625), cf. below, n. 290. Only
the first of these three works can be called a preacher's manual, though it apparently had none of the didactic structure of the *Or*. The other two works are
indexes on the order of Zahalon's index to the *Yalqut* (see above, pp. 72–76).
Ktav Hitnazlut le-Darshanim has been translated and annotated by Dr.
Hayim Goren Perelmuter and is published together with David Darshan's *Shir
ha-Ma'alot le-David* (Cracow, 1571) under the title of *"Shir ha-Ma'alot le'David"*
[Song of the Steps] and *"Ktav Hitnazzelut l'Darshanim* [In Defense of Preachers]
by David Darshan in 1984. I am extremely grateful to Dr. Perlmuter for sharing
with me his valuable work and insights, as well as information about the only two
copies of *Ktav Hitnazzelut* extant until now. One, which he has used for his forth-

A much earlier work, which translates the principles of rhetoric
formulated by the ancient Greeks into Hebrew, appears to have

coming work, is in the British Museum (see van Straalen, *Catalogue of Hebrew
Books in the British Museum* [London, 1894], p. 61), and one copy was in the
Vienna Gemeindebibliothek, but, according to information from the late
Gershom Scholem received by Dr. Perelmutter, was taken by the Russians after
having been abandoned by the Nazis in 1945, and probably is in the Leningrad
Library. David Darshan's book reflects some of the same concerns found in the
Or about a century before Zahalon. David ben Manasseh Darshan, a rabbi living
in Cracow, recognized that the institution of preaching was at a crossroads and
that it, together with its practitioners, was being severely criticized unfairly (par.
4). Therefore, he reasoned, an objective understanding, and, beyond that, even
some defense of *darshanim*, their profession, goals, and techniques, was in order.
"The purpose of *derashot* is to give strong admonitions to the masses . . . in order
to encourage that which is fine [in human character] and discourage what is
ugly." To explain that properly, and to counteract the increasing dissatisfaction
with sermons, David wrote his work. He attempts to elicit the sympathies of his
readers on behalf of his colleagues. The devices which preachers employ, such as
exaggeration, the use of additional biblical quotations or *Midrashim*, the injection
of wit or colorful illustrations, and roundabout explanations of a verse, are "to
make the *derashah* significant to one's listeners, whose natural impatience" does
not permit one merely to cite a verse as a support or to offer simple explanations
without making them *significant* explanations (par. 6). Ultimately, David
believed that sermons served an extremely essential social and religious purpose
in actually transmitting the Jewish tradition to the people. With the same concern
which was later to preoccupy Zahalon, Darshan justified the skills of preachers as
necessary "for awakening the drowsy" (par. 5) not only physically but spiritually
as well (*ibid.*). Of interest for our purposes is the fact that this Polish rabbi spent
some time in Italy, wandering through many communities in 1556 (*Shir
ha'Ma'alot*, p. 8a). Ben-Sasson in his *Hagut ve-Hanhagah* (Jerusalem, 1959)
describes how David in his manual also included at least four rabbinic sayings for
each weekly *Torah* portion which preachers might use for their sermons during
four consecutive years (p. 54).

In addition to the sixteenth- and seventeenth-century works cited by Zunz as
homiletic guidebooks, three texts should be noted:

(1) *Mateh Yehudah* of Leone da Modena, mentioned in his *Beit Leḥem
Yehudah* in the introduction (p. 2b) as a work which he wrote on "how to
compose a well-ordered sermon." We have not been able to locate this MS.

(2) *Tena'ei ha-Darshan* of Moses ben Samuel ben Bassa of Blanes, a MS. written by a *darshan* who preached in Florence and Sienna and a rather comprehen-

numerous direct or indirect reverberations in the *Or.* Judah
Messer Leon helped to popularize the rules for effective speaking

sive manual for preachers. Reuben Bonfil, in his excellent work, *Ha-Rabbanut
be-Italia bi-Tekufat ha-Renaissance* (Jerusalem, 1979) mentions two MSS.: (a)
Columbia University x893T 15Q, and (b) Livorno *Talmud Torah* 34. We have
examined the Columbia MS., dated 1627, the title of which means "Qualifications
for the [Good] Preacher." It has seventy-nine folio pages in Italian cursive script.
In his introduction Ben Bassa lists thirteen (a number which, according to Dr.
Isaac Mendelsohn, who catalogued the Hebrew MS. collection, the author had a
special fondness for) reasons for having written this work (see above, n. 226). The
fourth of these reasons is that, while he has seen "many *darshanim,* modern as
well as ancient, who have composed *derashot* filled with wisdom and knowledge,
whoever will follow them and seek to understand their greatness [will be unable
to do so as the *darshanim*] did not concentrate on explaining in a book the conditions for being an [effective] *darshan* and the requirements for the [good] sermon." Therefore, Ben Bassa decided to compose such a manual concerning
qualifications for the accomplished preacher and rules for writing his *derash* (p.
13). He lists the bad qualities which preachers should avoid, and the good attributes they should acquire. Among the latter, highest on the list, and because the
principal task of the accomplished *darshan* is to reprove his people, he must have
"a different kind of wisdom as well, a special sensitivity . . . and that is to be able
to admonish in such a way that people will accept what he tells them . . ." (pp.
19b–20a). In addition, he must have "a tongue capable of saying great things,"
"be precise and sharp," "be a person of *derekh erez*" [i.e., good manners in relating to people]; and be able to talk clearly about the concepts of our faith regarding important matters, and to speak profoundly in a very comprehensible and
inspiring way (pp. 20a–24a). Ben Bassa describes how he and a distinguished
scholar and physician, Raphael Modiliani, who also used to preach on the Sabbath in Sienna, made an agreement between themselves to give constructive criticism on each other's sermons (p. 15a). On pp. 32b–52b of his work, Ben Bassa
explains the special strengths of some of the leaders of Israel whom he considers
darshanim, Noah, Abraham, Isaac, Jacob, Judah, Moses, Aaron, Joshua, Caleb,
Phineas, David, and Solomon. In the last section of *Tena'ei ha-Darshan,* he gives
examples of how to develop sermons.

(3) *Qol Ya'aqov* of Jacob ben Kalonymus ha-Levi, a pupil of Menahem
Azariah de Fano (d. 1623) and Benzion Sarfati, a manual for preachers, primarily
a subject index meant as an aid for *darshanim* in the difficult process of choosing
topics for their sermons. Bonfil describes this work (pp. 192–193, 202) and notes
that the only MS. is in the Columbia University Collection x893J151Q. I have
examined this MS. It is dated as "seventeenth century" and has 553 folio pages in

of Cicero and Quintilian in Jewish circles through his *Nofet Ẓufim* (Mantua, before 1480).[262] R. Joel Ibn Shu-aib included in his *Olat Shabbat* (Venice, 1577) five rules for effective speaking in explaining the rabbinic statement in *Song of Songs Rabbah,* which itself represents a very early bit of counsel on effective preaching in the time of the *Talmud.*[263] Similarly, R. Judah Moscato, in his *Nefuẓot*

Italian cursive script. An alphabetical listing of subjects, it appears incomplete with blank spaces left, sometimes in large amounts, on many pages as if to allow for later additions. In his introduction the author relates that for many years it was his practice to preach on *Sukkot,* as well as to deliver eulogies for a number of brilliant rabbinic leaders. He says that he "has seen the tears [sic] and the drudgery of those who are engaged in the preaching profession, especially their struggle to find appropriate new and valuable subjects to preach about, whether related to the weekly *Torah* portion, on the festival, in praise of some commandment or attribute," etc. "At times [the *darshan*] will find an attractive subject without any biblical verse, rabbinic sayings, illustrations, and the like, [leaving him] many troubles [in composing the rest of the sermon . . .] For this [problem] I set myself to arrange an interpretation of different subjects suitable for the person desirous of building from them valuable *derashot*" (intro. to *Qol Ya'aqov*). Kalonymus has arranged his MS. with subject headings from pages 33 to 485. Folio pages 486 to 530 contain quotations from the Bible, *Talmud,* and *Midrash.*

Of all these seven homiletic guidebooks or indexes which preceded the *Or, Ktav Hitnaẓlut le-Darshanim* and *Tena'ei ha-Darshan* seem to come closest to what Zahalon did. Yet the focus of David Darshan's work is on explaining various types of sermons and techniques to laymen, rather than on providing preachers with comprehensive instructions concerning how to compose and deliver *derashot.* Ben Bassa's work, on the other hand, deals with matters for the preacher, but, specifically, requirements for him and his profession rather than for the dynamics of preaching. *Mateh Yehudah* may have approached Zahalon's careful advice, but until we can locate that work we shall never know. In the meantime, the *Or* remains the most complete early example of a manual designed to aid *darshanim* in their craft.

[262] Because of the numerous possible parallels to the *Nofet Ẓufim* in the text of the *Or,* we have included our comments below, in our notes to the text, n. 14.

[263] *Song R.* 4:11, 1, quoted in *Olat Shabbat,* introduction. See below, n. 54 on text of *Or.* Moscato also deals with this *Midrash* in Ser. 12, 33b (Warsaw edition, 1871). Israel Bettan, in his *Studies in Jewish Preaching* (Cincinnati, 1939), analyzes the preaching methods of Picho, Moscato, and others who preceded Zahalon. Especially helpful are his chapter on early preaching in the synagogue, a

Yehudah (Venice, 1588), makes innumerable valuable suggestions for attractive and well-organized homilies, although his words to preachers are scattered throughout his sermonic work.[264] Azariah Picho, in his *Binah le-Ittim* (Venice, 1648), also has plentiful suggestions throughout his work on delivering sermons of admonishment to a congregation in the least offensive and most acceptable manner, as well as many ideas on making the most of the vital presence of the *darshan* in delivering the words of *Torah* enthusiastically. Picho's homiletic advice, too, is spread all through his published sermons.[265]

Yet Zahalon's statement concerning the absence of a single available guidebook on advice to preachers appears completely accurate. While it is our intention to deal in detail at a later time with the specific influences on the writing of the *Or*—and there are innumerable possible traces within his manual of terms or suggestions given by earlier *darshanim* in Italy, especially some of those mentioned above—we shall content ourselves here with having merely alluded to some of these men and their general concern with dynamic, well-articulated, and attractive preaching. One could even speculate on the influence of other non-Italian preachers on our author, such as R. Isaac Arama, whose *Aqedat Yizhaq* (Venice, 1573) is cited by Zahalon as exemplary in includ-

---

chapter on the sermons of Jacob Anatoli (Naples, 1194–1256), a chapter on the sermons of Isaac Arama (Spain, 1420–Naples, 1494), the sermons of Ephraim Luntshitz (ca. 1550–1619, Prague). Isaac Barzilay, in his *Between Reason and Faith: Anti-Rationalism in Italian Jewish Thought 1250–1650* (The Hague, 1967), has some valuable chapters on Picho and Moscato. Hayyim Hillel Ben-Sasson, *Hagut ve-Hanhagah* (Jerusalem, 1959), is extremely valuable in understanding the techniques and styles of European *darshanim,* especially the social, communal, and economic effects of what they preached or did not preach. He devotes much space to a thorough understanding of the force of Luntshitz's preaching, as well as to the manner in which Luntshitz and others treated texts. Ben-Sasson draws a keen distinction between the impressive innovations of preachers who sought to dazzle their listeners and those whose actual goal was social improvement.

[264] See below, notes 14 and 79 on the *Or.*

[265] See below, notes 97 and 103 on the *Or.*

ing sermons on subjects "at once novel, attractive, containing an element of surprise, and yet perfectly true," and from whom "we ought to learn."[266] Yet that kind of scholarly detective work, involving what Professor Harry A. Wolfson elsewhere described as the historico-critical method of research,[267] will have to be taken up at a later time. We have, nevertheless, in our notes to the text of the *Or,* cited many parallels between Zahalon and earlier sources which might have influenced his thinking and writing.

From all that we have been able to piece together, we might conclude regarding the origins of the writing of the preacher's manual that:

1. By 1660, the date of the British Museum manuscript of *Morashah Qehilat Ya'aqov,* our author had formulated his preaching philosophy, articulated the rules of good *darshanut,* and intended to share all he had learned concerning composing and delivering excellent sermons with younger colleagues.
2. The author's reference to that knowledge acquired over "the years that I preached publicly"[268] probably refers to the years from 1651, when he began to preach in an official capacity,[269] or

---

[266] *Or,* ll. 273–279.

[267] *The Philosophy of Spinoza* (Cambridge, 1948), p. vii, "the presupposition that in any text treated by [the historico-critical method] there is a sort of dual authorship—an explicit author, who expresses himself in certain conventional symbols and patterns, and an implicit author, whose unuttered thoughts furnish us with the full significance of those symbols and patterns." In his *Philo: Foundations of Religious Philosophy in Judaism, Christianity, and Islam* (Cambridge, 1948), I, 106–107, Wolfson calls this the "hypothetico-deductive method of text study," which he explains as "the assumption that every philosopher in the main course of the history of philosophy either reproduces former philosophers or interprets them or criticizes them . . . the uttered words of philosophers . . . are nothing but floating buoys which signal the presence of submerged unuttered thoughts." What Wolfson applies to philosophy study can also be applied to the words and thoughts of Zahalon.

[268] *Or,* l. 211.

[269] See n. 48 above.

earlier, when he might have preached without the title of *morenu*, until approximately 1660, the date of the *Morashah Qehilat Ya'aqov*, containing the prototype of the manual.

3. Zahalon later expanded the prototype, adding many more details and examples. Surely he had the benefit of further reflection and material accumulated over additional years of preaching. Perhaps the manual was complete in its expanded form before R. Israel Foa of Jerusalem visited Rome and appended his *haskamah*, or preface, consisting of praise and recommendation for the author of the *Or*, in 1672.[270]

4. Undoubtedly, Zahalon considered the manual in a completed and presentable state when he solicited the imprimatur of Giulio Bartolocci in 1675.

5. In the Casanatense manuscript there is also evidence that the manual was further edited, and its name changed back to *Or ha-Darshanim*, from *Qol Ya'aqov*, after the Zahalon family moved to Ferrara, sometime after 1680. This is attested to by the reference to the move from Rome to Ferrara on the title page.[271]

Whatever the precise date of the completion of the preacher's manual, we can be certain about Zahalon's life-long preoccupation with effective preaching. We know that from his early twenties, by 1651 or before, he had spent long, tedious hours compiling his personal index to the *Yalqut Shimoni*. This interest in good sermon composition was refined still further with his articulation of the proper procedures that go into constructing a *derashah* and delivering it effectively. During his career in Rome, and even after his appointment in Ferrara at least twenty-seven years later, Zahalon had been preoccupied with the matter of homiletic dynamics, aside from his other major interests. As Vogelstein and Rieger rightly noted, Zahalon was one of the first

---

[270] Abraham Yaari, *Sheluḥei Ereẓ Yisro'el* (Jerusalem, 1951), pp. 291–292, n. 136.

[271] *Or*, l. 19, "and afterwards in Ferrara." See below, n. 283.

in Italy to recognize the true religious value of *darshanut* in the synagogue service.[272]

14. The *Haskamah* of Israel Foa to the *Or* in 1672

Inasmuch as we are privileged to [be able to hold] this great book in our hands [let us say] as is its name, so is it, [literally,] *Or ha-Darshanim* [*A Light for Preachers*].
(Israel Foa, *Haskamah* to the Casanatense MS. of the *Or ha-Darshanim*, p. 1)

The next date that we have been able to pinpoint in the development of the *Or* is 1672, the date of an autographed *haskamah*, or letter of recommendation, appended to the front of the Casanatense manuscript of the *Or*. It was written in a difficult Sefardic script by R. Israel Foa, an emissary from Jerusalem who, we know from other sources, visited several communities, including Rome, in 1672.[273] The two-page *haskamah* has on the top margin of the first page the following notation, in the same handwriting that is used in other parts of the manuscript to make corrections and provide directions to the printer: "Praise and commendation concerning the compositions and books which R. Jacob Zahalon, may God protect and preserve him, has written, from the scholar of Jerusalem, our teacher and rabbi, Israel Foa, may God preserve him." On the same margin, to the right of that descriptive phrase, in the corner, one finds written in the same script: "This should not be printed here." Through this page and the following page of the *haskamah* a vertical line has been carefully drawn through the center, indicating that the pages should be omitted by the

---

[272] II, 268. Their comment concerning Zahalon in Italy is somewhat similar to Ben-Sasson's description of David Darshan in sixteenth-century Poland. Darshan defended the various techniques used by preachers to reach and hold their listeners exactly because of the practical social and religious role which he believed *derashot* had within the society (*Hagut ve-Hanhagah*, p. 43).

[273] See above, n. 270.

printer.[274] Before speculating as to Zahalon's reasons for choosing to omit these words of praise from a respected colleague, we should understand something about the life of Foa and what he observed about our author.

Israel Foa, a native of Italy and a scion of a famous Italian Jewish family, left his birthplace to settle in Jerusalem, where he became one of its noteworthy scholars. He undertook a mission in 1672 on behalf of the scholars of Jerusalem, traveling by way of Egypt, where he also attempted to rally support for his cause. During this stay in Egypt, Foa wrote to R. Ḥayyim Beneviste in Izmir that he was being sent to the cities of Frankia (i.e., the countries of Western Europe), that he was, meanwhile, sitting and studying in Egypt, hoping that he might be able to draw upon the generosity of the community. From Egypt he wrote, "Perhaps I shall go to Livorno, for my intention is to publish some of my decisions and sermons, the writing of which requires much more time to complete."[275] Yaari tells us that Foa's intention to publish never materialized, and it is even possible that he died during this mission. How poignant that some of his only surviving written words were said in praise of a fellow preacher and scholar.

Of interest to us is a responsum of Israel Foa found in manuscript in the British Museum. In it he answers a certain Catholic priest in Turin concerning the length of the Diaspora. Yaari points out that we can assume that this responsum was written during Foa's mission to Italy, when there was increased interest in the length of the *galut* after the disappointment of the Sabbatian movement.[276] Here then is a third contemporary of Zahalon's, in addition to Zacuto and Baer whom we have mentioned above,[277] who reflected the Sabbatian events and, particularly, their subsequent end in disillusionment. Baer and Foa each wrote *haskamot* for our author, and in the course of examining his writings must

---

[274] See below, Appendices A n. 1 and B, n. 1.
[275] Yaari, p. 291.
[276] *Ibid.*, n. 140, on MS. Brit. Mus. 27108 Add. p. 173b.
[277] See pp. 47–48.

have had opportunity to exchange ideas and reflections with him on the events of their day.

Was the year 1672, when Israel Foa wrote his *haskamah* to the *Or,* the completion date of the revised preacher's manual? It may be that still further revisions were made even after that time, as we have noted that the same handwriting used to provide directions not to print the *haskamah* was also used throughout the manuscript to introduce additions and make corrections. Yet we must assume, too, that the very fact that Zahalon originally included the *haskamah* together with the manuscript of the *Or* indicates that he was putting together a completed work, and that he had shown Foa the work in a state of relative completion (as opposed to the prototype version of 1660) in order to solicit his comments.

Thus, the *Or,* which now appears to have reached a stage of readiness for publication, was originally begun before 1651 as an index to the *Yalqut.*[278] The introductory chapters of the *Or,* giving advice and counsel to preachers, first appeared in very abbreviated form by themselves and apart from the index to the *Yalqut* in 1660, in the introduction to the *Morashah Qehilat Ya'aqov,* a homiletic work on the *Mishneh Torah.*[279] Now, in the year 1672, according to our hypothesis, the expanded preacher's manual and the extensive index to the *Yalqut Shimoni* are both in a final form being prepared for publication.

Foa was especially impressed with the index to the *Yalqut* and the amount of aid it would provide for preachers. He does not refer to the manual. What we learn about Zahalon from the *haskamah* was that (1) he was regarded as a *matmid,* or extraordinarily diligent scholar, (2) he was considered extremely versatile in the vast amount of learning he evidenced personally and from his works, (3) he was widely honored by his colleagues and students for his brilliance, and (4) he possessed a good sense of humor, or at least had an extremely pleasant personality. To this

---

[278] See above, Chap. 12.

[279] See above, pp. 76–79, 86–87.

last point, one should add Foa's observation: "If it were possible to write some cheerful words about this holy man, the author who is very good humored in this world [and deserves to be cheerful,] in the next [world, I would say,] as is his name (Zahalon), so is he for 'rejoicing (*ẓohola*) and joy' (Est. 8:15)." Clearly, Foa thought that the similarity between the Hebrew root *ẓ-h-l,* "to shout with joy," and the author's name was more than purely coincidental.

Why then did Zahalon choose to omit these complimentary words written by his colleague from Palestine? One can only speculate. Zahalon seems to have been a rather modest man. Towards the end of his introduction to the *Or,* he states that "the Almighty is my witness that 'I have not composed this work for my own glorification, nor even for the glory of my family' (B. M. 59a), not for any such self-seeking motive. On the contrary, this book represents more sheer drudgery than it does insight."[280] Perhaps Foa's flowery words of praise appeared to violate Zahalon's concern to provide a service for fellow *darshanim* and to do so in the most direct and unaffected manner. One could also speculate that Zahalon, who was a practicing physician and had written philosophic texts and was familiar with the nuances of satisfying the Catholic readers who would have to pass on a work before its publication, wanted to prepare his work in as austere and scientific a form as possible, which the generous and perhaps less-sophisticated comments of his effusive colleague from Jerusalem would have militated against.

15. The Ban Placed on the *Or* and Possible Explanation for It

> This book may never be printed in any form, nor may it be returned to anyone claiming ownership of it.

---

[280] Ll. 190–193. Da Modena, not known for his humility, had used somewhat similar words in his introduction to his *Beit Leḥem Yehudah* (Venice, 1625): "This is *melakhah* (work) and not *ḥokhmah* (wisdom)," p. 2b, which may have been a stylistic disclaimer.

Censors' notations on Cas. Ms. of *Or ha-Darshanim*

(from the 1694 inscription on the manuscript of the *Or ha-Darshanim* in the Biblioteca Casanatense in Rome by the Holy Office)

Jacob Zahalon appears to have made an additional effort to obtain permission for the publication of the *Or*. Below the explanatory note of Bartolocci on the page preceding the title page, which we have referred to above,[281] we find this imprimatur, also in Latin:

> The name of this Hebrew work is *Zikhron Ya'aqov*,[282] that is, A Memorial of Jacob,[283] composed by Rabbi Jacob Zahalon. I have seen and read the work in its entirety, from beginning to end. It is an index of subjects to the ancient rabbinic sayings which are included in the work of the *Yalqut*[282] which is, in fact, a collection, a large commentary to all of the Scriptures. The fact is that I have found nothing in this work which is contrary to the Catholic faith. Therefore, I believe that it may be published if it is acceptable to the father, the honored Inquisitor of Ferrara. 30 January 1693. Valerius Botticinus from the Holy Office, reader of Hebrew books.[284]

[281] See above, Chap. 7.

[282] These titles are written in Hebrew letters.

[283] Where the name *Zikhron Ya'aqov* originates is not clear. Actually, a careful study of the title page of the Casanatense MS. reveals that the original name for the work was meant to be *Or ha-Darshanim*. That name was then deleted, and *Qol Ya'aqov* ("The Voice of Jacob") was written in at the top of the left side of the title page. See above, Chap. 5, d. Apparently, the ultimate decision of the author was to delete the name *Qol Ya'aqov* and to place small vertical lines over the deleted original name, *Or ha-Darshanim*, indicating that that name, after all, was to be retained. This still does not explain *Zikhron Ya'aqov*. Although at the time Botticinus wrote on the MS. Zahalon was still alive, it would almost seem that the title may have been changed to *Zikhron Ya'aqov* after his death and inserted into Botticinus's words as a pious gesture in memory of Zahalon. Yet who might have done it we cannot imagine.

[284] See picture, opposite page. There is a photo of this inscription and the one below in Benayahu, *Haskamah u-Reshut bi-Defusei Veniẓia*, p. 153.

In the meantime, before the work could be published, Zahalon died the following September. Yet the *Or* was not destined to be printed. On a page preceding the page with the notations by Bartolocci and Botticinus, there are two additional Latin inscriptions. Seemingly this page was added for the purpose of cataloguing the manuscript. The first inscription is dated about fourteen months after the death of our author and reads: "10 November 1694. Instruction is herewith given that this book may never be printed in any form, nor may it be returned to anyone claiming ownership of it. Instead, it shall remain in the chancellory of the Holy Office."[284] Last among the descriptive passages concerning the *Or* is one dated over fifty years later:

1745

from the Holy Office

R. Jacob Zahalon, a Roman physician, alphabetical index of the words found in the *Yalqut*. Composed in the handwriting of the author, never printed, with the opinions of the censors in manuscript and the decision of the Supreme Holy Tribunal. It is an index of all the *Yalqut,* which includes all of the Hebrew Scriptures.

This is the description of the work by the Biblioteca Casanatense in Rome, where the autographic manuscript remains today. That library, which was at the time of its founding second to the Vatican Library in size and value of manuscripts and volumes, was named for Cardinal Girolamo Casanate, appointed by Innocent XII as Librarian of the Holy Church in 1693, the year of Zahalon's death. It was first opened to the public in 1701. The presence of the *Or* manuscript there may be explained by the special papal dispensation which permitted heretical works to be kept there for the purpose of being consulted by a group of six Dominican theologians chosen from six different countries, England, France, Germany, Italy, Poland, and Spain. These scholars were commis-

sioned by the Casanate endowment to teach and defend the faith
with the writings of Thomas Aquinas.[285]

What objections did the Holy Office find to the *Or* in 1694,
especially in the light of the approval which the same agency had
given one year earlier, in January 1693? At the time of his death,
Zahalon must have believed that all final obstacles had been
removed from the path leading to publication. Yet we know from
the history of the censorship of Hebrew books that attempts by
Jewish authors to cite scholarly authorities such as Bartolocci or
Reuchlin were not always helpful in convincing the Holy Office.[286]
Further, we do know that, whatever conclusions Botticinus had
come to in 1693, the *Yalqut Shimoni* (first published in 1521) was
added to the index of forbidden books after its publication in
Livorno in 1650.[287] It was not the only *Midrash* to have been
condemned. The *Ein Ya'aqov,* sometimes referred to as *Ein
Yisro'el,* was also on the list.[288] According to Benayahu, the opposition to the *Or* was not to the preacher's-manual section but to its
later and principal section, the index to the *Yalqut,* which was a
work mentioned in the list of those works requiring some form of
expurgation.[289] Berliner explains that on March 12, 1703, the Holy

[285] *New Catholic Encyclopedia,* III (Washington, 1967), 175. The present librarian of the Biblioteca Casanatense was extremely helpful to this writer in making
a microfilm copy of the MS. of the *Or,* including the entire index to the *Yalqut,*
readily available.

[286] William Popper, *The Censorship of Hebrew Books* (New York, 1899), p.
119.

[287] *Ibid.,* p. 110, n. 419. See Heinrich Reusch, *Der Index der verbotenen Bücher,*
II (Bonn, 1883–1885), 148 ff.

[288] Zahalon refers to this work as one of the sources for the index section of the
Or, l. 151.

[289] *Haskamah u-Reshut bi-Defusei Veniẓia,* p. 213 and notes. Cf. Popper, pp.
82–83, where the rules of expurgation, eighteen in all, are given. For example, the
word "idolatry" must be replaced by the phrase "worshippers of stars and
planets," *akkum.* The word "apostate" must be effaced and *akkum* written in its
place. Any passage referring to the messianic hope, claiming that the Messiah is
yet to come to be, or any similar idea, must be removed. Any passage which mentions such a principle of the Jewish faith as "the law is eternal," which was con-

Office officially ruled against the *Ein Ya'aqov* because of its containing allegories and metaphysical illustrations from the *Talmud* which had been completely banned. The *Yalqut* is listed among those books which cannot ever be corrected and were, therefore, to be absolutely banned.[290]

It is interesting to speculate on how the *Or* was copied by an English scholar and eventually found its way to the Adler collection, now housed at the Jewish Theological Seminary.[291] The

sidered in opposition to the Catholic faith, must be effaced. Cf. explanatory note on *akkum* in I. Schorsch, *Jewish Reactions to German Anti-Semitism, 1870–1914* (New York, 1972), p. 240. See also Baron, XIV, 55.

[290] A. Berliner, *Ketavim* (Jerusalem, 1949), pp. 35–36. Other works were the *Ikkarim* of Joseph Albo, *Emeq ha-Melekh* (on the *Zohar*), and *Yalkut Reuveni*. E.J., V, 278, notes that the last edition of the *Index librorum prohibitorum* in 1948 still included *Yalqut Shimoni* and *Yalqut Reuveni*. It mentions their kabbalistic interpretations of the Bible as an apparent cause among others. *Ein Yisro'el* (*Ein Ya'aqov*), published with *Sefer Beit Lehem Yehudah* by Leone da Modena and banned in 1693 and again in 1694, is also on the 1948 list. We have tried unsuccessfully to locate a MS. combining the *Ein Yisro'el* with the index of da Modena in the hope of finding a notation and date similar to those appearing on the *Or* from the Holy Office in 1694.

[291] JTS R 1339, placed in R 84a in the JTS MS. collection. Part of a small book containing a lamentation on the death of the king of England, *piyyutim,* wise sayings, admonishments, riddles, inscriptions for tombstones, etc. Along with these assorted writings included by the young da Costa Athias is the preacher's manual of the *Or,* along with the words of introduction to the index of the *Yalqut.* This MS. is also listed as Adler 2247, accession no. 01942. The MS. measures 13.6 by 7.5 cm. and has thirteen to eighteen lines per page, thirty-two pages. In addition to this Zahalon MS., the Seminary has three other works entitled *Or ha-Darshanim.* (1) No. 161, an index to the *Yalqut Shimoni,* essentially the same as the Cas. MS., except that this contains only 276 pages out of what was originally 520, and that the preacher's manual is not found here, although the author expresses his prayer that "Jews will make use of my work that my soul may live on, as great is the reward of he who performs a service for the community through publishing books . . ." (Cf. *Or,* ll. 230–234). According to Rabbi Judah Brumer, the Italian rabbinic style of writing here resembles that of our author in the Cas. MS. This measures 13.5 by 20.5 cm. and has twenty-seven to thirty lines on each page. It is from the Sulzberger collection, accession no. 03428. (2) No. 162, a continuation of 161. The original pagination goes up to p. 474, but

young man who copied the manuscript in the year 1717, Solomon ben Isaac da Costa Athias,[292] had to have learned of the remarkable thirteen-chapter preacher's manual from someone who had seen it before him. Judging from all we know about the location of the manuscript of the manual together with the index to the *Yalqut,* only one copy existed in the world, and that appears to have been in the possession of the author himself. Could it have been that one of the Dominicans associated with the Casanate endowment, perhaps the theologian from England who was part of the commission investigating heretical works mentioned earlier,[293] was so impressed with the advice to preachers that he arranged to have that section copied? Surely reproducing a copy of the preacher's manual did not in any way violate the scruples of the Holy Office, which apparently had objections only to the index to the *Yalqut* itself.

Of course, other theories are also possible, perhaps even more probable. Zahalon was eager to share his work with other

only 247 pages are found here. Also from the Sulzberger collection, it is listed as accession no. 03429. (3) No. 84, the introduction to the index, written in London in the ninteenth century, a copy of the 1733 Bodleian MS. mentioned above, Chap. 5, d, made by a Hirsch Edelman. It is no. 1256 in the Adler collection.

[292] See n. to *Or,* l. 751 of Hebrew text. Although da Costa was only twenty-seven at the time, he became very well known as the founder of the Hebrew collection of the British Museum. Before he presented the Museum with three manuscripts and 179 printed volumes in 1759, it had only one Hebrew book in its collection. Da Costa's gift did not include any of Zahalon's works. Apparently he retained his copy of the *Or* among other works which he copied in his attractive and careful style both in Hebrew and Latin letters. He seems to have had some interest in Sabbatian works, which he copied for his own use, from which Hyamson concluded that da Costa "was not altogether untouched by the Sabbatian heresy." Da Costa's work as a scribe was only an avocation. He was by profession a broker, and extremely successful in his field, also known for his charitable works in the non-Jewish as well as the Jewish community. Perhaps he refers to himself as a *baḥur* at the end of the MS. partly because he was unmarried at the time, whereas four months later he was married (see "Solomon da Costa and the British Museum" by Albert M. Hyamson, in *Occident and Orient* in honor of Moses Gaster [London, 1936], pp. 260–266, and on *baḥur,* above, n. 238).

[293] See above, p. 93.

scholars. He had shown it to Bartolocci. Israel Foa had examined it. Undoubtedly, others traveling through Rome or Ferrara had been privileged to read the work. We can easily imagine that one of these visitors to the eminent rabbi-physician might have received permission to make a copy for himself, and even to bring back that copy to England. We may never know the exact route taken by the manuscript of the *Or*. Regarding the 1733 Bodleian manuscript from Oxford we have even less information, not even the name of the copyist.[294]

Considering the large number of unpublished manuscripts by Jacob Zahalon that are still extant, as well as the works which have been completely lost, bringing the preacher's manual of the *Or* to the attention of modern *darshanim,* scholars, and interested readers takes on some added significance. Zahalon's repeated efforts to clear the way for its widespread dissemination were clearly unavailing. Yet perhaps in some way the present work might be seen as a tribute to Rabbi Dr. Jacob Zahalon in the form of a living memorial, in which at least one of the unpublished works in which he invested considerable effort and deliberation in attempting to crystallize the guiding principles of his years of experience as a *darshan,* will now at least receive some serious attention from his colleagues of a later age.

[294] See above, Chap. 5, d, and n. 291.

II. Translation of the *Or ha-Darshanim*

BLESSED IS THE LORD[1]

THE BOOK OF *QOL YA'AQOV*,[2] ["THE VOICE OF JACOB"]
PART I, ON THE *TORAH*
A BOOK KNOWN AS *OR HA-DARSHANĨM*,[3] ["A LIGHT FOR PREACHERS"]

A GUIDE [INDEXED] BY CROSS-REFERENCES OF ALL MATTERS AND SUBJECTS

5

[1] Translation of the Hebrew letters *B' H'*. In the Casanatense MS., which is an autographic MS., and is, therefore, our principal source for this translation, the author surrounds the letters *B"H* with a box.

[2] Literally, "The Voice of Jacob," possibly a reference to Gen. 27:22. This entire line, "The Book of *QOL YA'AQOV*," has been deleted by the author or someone else. We cannot know the reason for his preferring the other title, *Or ha-Darshanim*, over this, but it is interesting to speculate that Zahalon might have thought that the verse in full, "The voice is the voice of Jacob, but the hands, are the hands of Esau," could have been in some way objectionable to the Holy Office of the Church, inasmuch as Esau was frequently used as a reference to Rome. E.g., in the *Yalqut* itself, I, 115, 69a, this verse is explained as: "'The hands are the hands of Esau'—this is the kingdom of Rome that destroyed our Temple and burned our Sanctuary and exiled us from our land." Cf. *Or*, ll. 411–417, where reference to Church (?) has been retained.

[3] For additional explanation of the different names of the treatise, see Intro., n. 283.

WITHIN KNOWN [RABBINIC] SAYINGS[4]
FOUND IN THE *YALKUT SHIMONI* IN DIFFERENT
FORMS
VALUABLE TO BOTH YOUNG MEN AS WELL AS
ELDERS
10 IN REDUCING THE BURDEN [OF PREACHING] FOR
MEN OF UNDERSTANDING
And Further to Kindle before Them Lights
On Writing Sermons [to Provide] Insights[5]
Attractively Written and with Sayings [Clear]
On Composing *Derashot* Precious [to Hear][6]
15 WRITTEN BY THE HONORABLE RENOWNED
PHYSICIAN
DEVOTED PREACHER TO HIS PEOPLE[7] IN ROME IN

---

[4] This line has been deleted. Where we indicate that the *author* made corrections, it is also possible that someone else may have done so. The word *ne'emonim*, which we have translated "known," could also be translated as "reliable" or "faithful." It seems to indicate that the author has traced the rabbinic sayings to their original sources.

[5] We have attempted to convey the poetic quality of these lines in English as the author wrote them in Hebrew.

[6] This line and the one above it have been deleted by the author. They had both been written in poetic form with rhymed endings. Seven lines in the title page (ll. 4–10) end with the syllable *nim*, while four lines (ll. 11–14) end with the syllable *rōt*.

[7] Zahalon has deleted this entire phrase. It is a direct quotation from Est. 10:3, where it refers to Mordecai, and means literally "seeking the good of his people." The word *doresh* in biblical Hebrew, "to seek out," later took on the additional meaning of "to preach," or give a *derashah*. The term *Midrash*, from the same root, means "to seek out" the hidden meaning of a text, as opposed to the *peshat*, which is the "spread out, plain," or obvious meaning of a text. As W. Braude and I. Kapstein explain, "what Midrash seeks out is the secret chambers of *Torah*, or the mysteries of *Torah*" (*Pesikta de-Rab Kahana, R. Kahana's Compilation of Discourses for Sabbaths and Festal Days* [Philadelphia, 1975], p. ix). In Ezra 7:10, the root has the meaning of to "explain" or "teach" about the *Torah*. Already in the *Mishnah*, *doresh* becomes a discourse or brief lesson on the *Torah*. E.g., M. Sot. 5:2, where R. Aqiba "expounds" on the meaning of a verse in Lev. See L. Zunz in his *Ha-Derashot be-Yisro'el* (Jerusalem, 1954), pp. 21–31. *Midrashim*, Zunz demonstrates, were very early *derashot*.

THE HOLY CONGREGATION IN ISRAEL OF CATALONI AND ARAGONESA, MAY THEIR ROCK PRESERVE THEM[8] FOR TWENTY-SEVEN YEARS AND AFTERWARDS IN THE

Rashi, in his commentary on the role of Aaron as his brother's spokesman, draws our attention to another aspect of preaching which was very essential to Zahalon in the *Or,* namely, the preacher as one who delivers *tokheḥa,* or reproof (see *Or,* Chap. 10:2–3). On the verse in Ex. 7:1, where Moses is told that his brother Aaron will be his prophet, Rashi explains: "[Understand this] as the Targum does, *viz.,* your interpreter. And similarly, the term *nevu'ah* [or prophecy, indicates that] a man who publicly proclaims and imparts to the people words of reproof . . . which in the vernacular [i.e., Old French] is called *predicar* [preacher]." Concerning the specific words used by Zahalon for "preacher," *doresh* and *darshan* both appear frequently in the *Or.* Our author prefers *drush* for "sermon," occasionally *drash.* In three places he uses *derashah,* ll. 12, 210, and 313. In the plural it is always *derashot* except for one instance of *drashim* (l. 425).

Aside from giving sermons with the purpose of reproving the people, some rabbis were renowned for delivering interpretations of the Bible which served to instruct and delight their congregations. When a famous *darshan* such as R. Johanan came to town, all the people would run to the place where he was delivering his *derashah* in order to have the privilege of seeing and hearing him (T.J., Hor. 3:7, 48b). Where generally one was not to run on the Sabbath, it was permitted and even encouraged to do so when one's object was to hear a sermon (Ber. 6b). The *Mishnah* includes a provision in the laws of *eruv,* allowing a person to attach a condition to the *eruv* he is making for the Sabbath, permitting him to walk an extended distance to the east or to the west in order to hear a Sage coming from one of those directions and delivering a *derashah* on that Sabbath (M. Er. 3:5). While a mourner is forbidden many things during the week of mourning, including reading the *Torah* and *Prophets,* if many people need him to interpret the *Torah* homiletically, as Rashi explains, he is allowed to do so (M.K. 21a). In fact, the *Talmud* even cites instances from the lives of renowned scholars who, in spite of the loss of precious loved ones, went and expounded, or preached, in the *Beit ha-Midrash (ibid.).* J. Heineman, in his *Derashot be-Ẓibbur bi-Tequfat ha-Talmud* (Jerusalem, 1970), cites Lam. R., Intro. 17, to prove that the masses of the Jewish people during Roman and Hellenistic times preferred the *derashot* in the synagogues to the performances and competitions in the theatres and circuses, p. 9.

[8] Translation of Hebrew *Y' Z'.* The entire phrase, "in Rome in the holy congregations of Cataloni and Aragonesa," was originally deleted by Zahalon, and then later retained.

HOLY CONGREGATION IN ISRAEL IN FERRARA,[9]
OUR HONORED MASTER AND TEACHER,[10]
20 JACOB, SON OF OUR HONORED MASTER AND
TEACHER,[10] ISAAC ZAHALON,
MAY THE MEMORY OF THE RIGHTEOUS AND HOLY
BE FOR A BLESSING[11]
[HERE ARE BOTH] NEW [INSIGHTS] AS WELL AS[12]
OLD
FOR THE SAKE OF THE CREATOR, May He Bring us
Relief.[13]

25 THE INTRODUCTION OF THE AUTHOR, OUR HON-
ORED MASTER AND TEACHER, JACOB, THE SON OF
OUR HONORED MASTER AND TEACHER, ISAAC
ZAHALON, MAY THE MEMORY OF THE RIGHTEOUS
BE FOR A BLESSING.

It is the way of scholars in various fields of learning to
utilize their ability [fully] in finding a short and easy way to
30 express all forms of wisdom so as to remove or ease as much as
possible any burden or difficulty from those who delve deeply
into some field of learning. It is an accepted and well-known
teaching of our Sages, of blessed memory, that "a man should
always teach his pupils in [the most] direct manner" (Pes. 3b).
35 Similarly, they say, "the Scripture spoke of the usual practice"
(M. B.K. 5:7), and "the *Torah* spoke according to the [ordi-

---

[9] "For twenty-seven years and afterwards in Ferrara" is a marginal note written by the author, and meant to be deleted. It is very difficult to read.

[10] Translation of the abbreviated Hebrew honorific, *K' M' H' R' R'*.

[11] Translation of the Hebrew abbreviation *Z' Ẓ' V' Q' L,*.

[12] The theme of preaching on *new* ideas, insights, or experiences is very central
to Zahalon's counsel to *darshanim*. See *Or*, ll. 257–258, 306, 329–330, 347–348,
380, and 505–510. Also see my textual notes 14 and 63. All references to notes
below, or on the text of the *Or,* are to the *English translation* of the text unless
otherwise specified.

[13] The original words on the MS. title page have been carefully deleted and
these words written in, in smaller letters, above them.

nary] language of mankind" (Ber. 31b). And what [exactly] is being said here? It teaches us the importance of brevity, clarity,[14] and the use of parables in easing the burden of those

. [14] The Hebrew word here, *be-zaḥut,* meaning "with clarity" or "eloquently," is a term used in rhetoric. Moscato, referring to the first-century Roman rhetorician Quintilian, quotes from the classical author's book on rhetoric, Part XI, in describing those "who speak *ba-zaḥut,* or eloquently, in their combining pleasantness in their words with a fine use of bodily gestures, variations in their voice, or facial expressions . . . according to the teachings of Marcus Cicero . . . on bodily rhetoric" (*Nefuzot Yehudah* [Venice, 1588] Ser. 17, 45a). Also in the *Or,* l. 527, Zahalon urges preachers to begin their *derashot* with *devarim zaḥim,* or "eloquent words." It is very likely that in their use of *zaḥut* and other technical terms from the art of rhetoric, both Moscato and Zahalon were influenced by Judah ben Yeḥiel Messer Leon's *Nofet Zufim* (Mantua, before 1480). In the fourth chapter of his work, Messer Leon lists five qualities which are appropriate for an effective speaker: *hamza'a* (inventiveness or imagination), *seder* (order), *zaḥut* (eloquence or clarity), *zekhira* (an appeal to the *memory* of one's listeners, so that they will not forget one's message), and *remiza* (use of gestures with one's voice and body) (Jellinek ed. [Vienna, 1863], p. 13.) Zahalon uses the first three of these rhetorical terms as they are, and he makes use of the last two in his suggestions to preachers, though without the specific technical terms. *Hamza'a* is mentioned in the *Or,* l. 506 and l. 517, as an important ingredient in the introduction of the sermon. *Seder* is the subject of an entire chapter, Chap. 4. Especially striking in similarity is Zahalon's use of the same example in his discussion of *seder* as that used by Messer Leon. In Chap. 11 of the *Nofet Zufim,* on the importance of *seder,* speakers are urged to bring their strongest proofs at the beginning and end of their talks (p. 36). Weak or ordinary ones should be placed in the middle. The *Or,* ll. 477–478 and ll. 486–487, makes the same point.

We have already mentioned Zahalon's use of *zaḥut.* Concerning *zekhira,* Messer Leon devotes his Chap. 13 to ways of making an impression on listeners. Zahalon in ll. 700–705 advises preachers how to leave a vivid impression on the memories of their congregations. Messer Leon quotes Cicero on varying one's voice, that it should be alternately strong, normal, and soft (p. 45), and imitating in one's speaking the subject one is trying to convey, speaking plaintively when we are talking about asking for mercy, or appearing angry when one is condemning. Zahalon likewise suggests that the preacher speak plaintively when quoting the words of a servant (l. 545), or in an authoritarian manner when quoting a king (l. 540), and he, too, advises speaking softly (l. 532), naturally (l. 533), and strongly (l. 556). In his Chap. 12 on *remiza* Messer Leon quotes Cicero's division of gestures into two parts, visual movements (through the body), and auditory gestures (with the voice). Zahalon in his Chaps. 6 and 8 deals with the same sub-

who seek to acquire wisdom through delving into a matter

jects. Aside from similarities in these five basic areas, the *Or* parallels the *Nofet Zufim* in three other emphases: concern for overcoming the fatigue of listeners through attractive, new, and humorous material, warnings about too many parts in the speech or sermon, and citation of the same biblical proof text for good rhetoric as for effective preaching. Messer Leon speaks of the listeners becoming *nilah* (tired, exhausted), p. 21, and Zahalon describes listener fatigue with the same term, l. 454. The *Nofet Zufim* notes that the way to remove such weariness from one's audience is to economize on words, p. 23, and the *Or* devotes all of Chap. 3 to that subject. Messer Leon describes speaking in a fashion which is, according to Cicero, *mekoar* (ugly), p. 19, while Zahalon compares a type of sermon to an unattractive (*kiura*) woman, l. 271. Messer Leon devotes an entire chapter to the indirect introduction, following his Chap. 6 on ordinary introductions. He includes in his description of opening a talk in a "hidden" or less obvious way, various attention-getting devices, such as humor, changing one's style of speaking (if one is used to talking in a Sefardic way, he speaks in his introduction in the Ashkenazic manner, or vice versa), some dramatic effect (stammering or deliberately mispronouncing or distorting an expression), or purposely saying something which could be understood in two different ways (pp. 22–23). Zahalon in his chapter on the introduction of the sermon points out that the *darshan* should have enough nuance and imagination in his opening to make it appear that he is speaking about something far removed from his actual subject. Then, after thus winning people's attention, he draws the connection between his introduction and his theme (ll. 516–519, see below, n. 78). Messer Leon's stress on including new things in one's speech (pp. 23, 45) is obviously an important rule for Zahalon, who advises using material which is unfamiliar to one's listeners. See above, n. 12. The *Or* also counsels humor or a change of style to awaken people who are drowsing (ll. 355–360).

Messer Leon, citing Quintilian, warns against too many parts in one's speech, p. 23, and Zahalon cautions similarly, ll. 280–284. Finally, after citing Quintilian on the purpose of the rhetorician, Messer Leon explains that this advice is found in Isa. 50:4, on the *leshon limmudim* ("trained tongue") which gives "timely words to the weary," pp. 6–7. Zahalon cites the same verse in the *Or*, ll. 753–754, in his Prayer for Preachers, p. 169, and in the *Ozar* (see above, Intro., p. 62), where he counsels physicians. These are only some, but by no means all, of the parallels between the Mantuan and Roman texts on speaking.

The combination of *zahut* and *mashal* ("parable, example, or metaphor") in the *Or*, ll. 37–38, has at least two parallels in Bahya's *Hovot ha-Levavot*, which Zahalon obviously studied thoroughly in order to write his *Margaliot Tovot* on that work. Because our author placed so much emphasis upon the use of *meshalim* (*Or*, ll. 38, 44, 148, 460, and also cf. *ma'aseh*, ll. 356, 388, 405, 408, 409, 461,

through serious study.[15] Even the prophets, may they rest in peace, had to be concerned about this. As Maimonides, 40 of blessed memory, said in his *Hilkhot Yesodei ha-Torah,*[16] prophecy was revealed to each one according to his virtue, and the style of one prophet is not the same as that of another. This one [received his prophecy] with utter clarity, another [received his prophecy] in a parable, while another through images and another through visions, each one according to his [special] virtue or strength.[17] So, too, did our Sages interpret 45 the verse "The voice of the Lord is power" (Ps. 29:4). [The *Midrash* reads this verse as if it were "The voice of the Lord is in the power."] "*His* power" is not said, but [rather] "*in* the power," in the power [or strength] of each and every single person (Ex. R. 29:1).[18] Now who in our estimation is greater than Moses our teacher, may he rest in peace, the teacher of prophets, about whom it is written, "Not so with my servant Moses; he is trusted throughout my household. With him I speak mouth to mouth, plainly and not in riddles, and he 50 beholds the likeness of the Lord" (Num. 12:7–8)? With all this honor accorded to Moses it is yet written, "The Lord called to Moses, and spoke to him" (Lev. 1:1). In *Midrash Sifra* it is taught, and Rashi, of blessed memory, quotes at the beginning

491) the references in Baḥya's text are especially worth noting. At one point the instinct in man advises him to learn unusual *meshalim* and to frequent the classes of *anshei ha-ẓaḥut* ("rhetoricians") (Ibn Tibbon trans., A. Ẓifroni ed. [Tel Aviv, 1959], pp. 364–365). Again Baḥya describes how one might use all *ẓaḥuto* ("his eloquence") along with his talent in poetry, prose, and *mashal* to thank his ruler, i.e., God (p. 469). Also, a somewhat pejorative use of *ẓaḥut* alone is found in his referring to *ẓaḥut devarav* (his unusual words) that might come in a letter from the king, which would deserve our fullest attention and respect (p. 462). Cf. below, notes 34 and 110.

[15] Zahalon introduces here a theme which he will later make much use of in his manual for preachers. See above, n. 14, on *meshalim* for references.

[16] Cf. M. Hyamson, *The Book of Knowledge* (Jerusalem, 1965), pp. 42b–43b.

[17] This is not a direct quotation from *Hilkhot Yesodei ha-Torah,* but generally refers to Chap. 7.

[18] Also found in Yal. Ps. 709.

of [his commentary on] *Leviticus*, "and he called to Moses, and
55 He spoke to him." "The voice of God went on and reached his
ears [only], but all of the other Israelites did not hear it. One
might think that for the pauses there was also such a call.
However, Scripture states ['The Lord *called* to Moses] and He
spoke [to him],' to teach that before 'speaking' there was 'calling' [only in the complete sections of the *Torah,*] but
not at the pauses [or subsections]. What purpose then did the
60 [biblical] pauses [or subsections] serve? To give Moses an
interval for reflection between one section and another and
between one subject and another. All the more so [is it impor-
tant] for an ordinary person who learns from another ordinary
person." It is possible that Scripture alluded to this subject [in
the words of Isaiah], "Hark! one calls: 'Clear ye in the wilderness the way of the Lord. Make plain in the desert a highway
for our God" (40:3). Aside from what I have already explained
65 in my commentary on the books of *Isaiah*,[19] one may say "one
calls" concerns the *Torah,* which was given in the wilderness,
and as our Rabbis, of blessed memory, have written on "and
from the wilderness [*Midbar*] to Mattanah" (Num. 21:18,
quoted in Erub. 54a).[20] It may also be said that the *Torah* is
called *Midbar* from the word *dibbur* [speech] because most of
our speaking will be about *Torah,* as it said, "and
you shall speak of them" (Deut. 6:7), and mere idle talk is not
70 intended. [Further, when Scripture] says, "Clear ye the way of
the Lord" (Isa. 40:3), its meaning is: You are the teachers and
those who speak the *Torah* of the Lord and who explain what
He requires to the masses. You must, therefore, do everything
within your power to remove any [possible] confusion and to

[19] This work, referred to in the introduction to the *Margaliot Tovot* (Venice,
1665), is called *Yeshu'ot Ya'aqov.* It was also a commentary on those biblical
verses which might be used by teachers in a blasphemous way. See Intro., Chap.
5, b.
[20] The comparison of the *Torah* to a *mattanah,* or "gift," is also found in Ned.
55a, Num. R. 19:26, and *She'iltot, Nasa* 121.

rectify [anything which has been made] unclear [in transmission, thereby] removing every stumbling block and obstacle 75 from it. [You who are the teachers and the spokesmen for *Torah* must also strive] to clear [and smooth out] its paths for those who will traverse [its ways] in their search for truth through their own [channels of] perception. "The rugged shall be made level, and the rough places a plain" (*ibid.,* 40:4). This is [what is meant by the words] "make plain [in the desert a highway for our God]" (*ibid.* v. 3). Remove any difficulty from it, [any obstacle which might prevent us] from traversing it [and establish the *Torah*] in a pleasant and easy style. Then all may be able to follow this path [of *Torah*] and walk in 80 the ways of knowledge and service of our God.

Therefore, I who "am a worm, and no man" (Ps. 22:7) have composed this book and called it *Qol Ya'aqov, Or ha-Darshanim* [*The Voice of Jacob, A Light for Preachers*] to help young men [who are learning to preach]. I composed it as a young man[21] at a time when I began to speak publicly "every 85 Sabbath" (Isa. 66:23) and even daily.[22] In order to relieve my own burden of work in searching for homiletical subjects relating to each weekly *Torah* portion, I resolved, Rise up! "Go your way by the footsteps of the flock and feed your kids, 90 beside the shepherds' tents" (Song 1:8). This is what our prede-

[21] On the meaning of this text in terms of Zahalon's age when he composed the *Or,* see Intro., pp. 73–75.

[22] The verse in Isa. reads, "From one new moon to another and from one Sabbath to another." Zahalon changed this to read, "from one Sabbath to another and from one day to another." The reference to preaching on ordinary weekdays may be found in Leone da Modena's *Riti,* which refers to preaching as "done every Sabbath day, and at all the chief Festivals, for the most part, and only then: unless there be some Funeral Sermon to be made, at the death of any Person of Note, which useth to be done upon any of the Week daies, or working daies, according as the Occasion requireth," found in *Historia de gli riti hebraici* (Venice, 1638), trans. by Edmund Chilmead (London, 1650), entitled *The History of the Rites, Customes, and Manner of Life, of the Present Jews, throughout the World,* p. 61. For more details, see below, n. 39.

cessors have instructed us, to remove the stones from the dry
land, to make a path for our God. They have eased our burden
of traveling on a trail [which they have blazed]. Now I have
95 heeded the voice of my teachers when I crossed the "mighty
waters" (Ex. 15:10) of the sea of the book of the *Yalqut*. I have
carefully weighed each [rabbinic] saying according to the
subjects for which it may be useful in preaching.
Then I have noted it in the index in two or three places, or
more, depending upon the subjects referred to in the saying.
100 Thus, when I shall want to compose a sermon on a particular
topic, I shall be able to find easily all the sayings which have
been written in the *Yalqut* on that topic. Besides this, I shall
also [be able to] make use of this compilation [and reference
work] to study the entire *Yalqut* in abbreviated form, for I have
105 written down most of each saying with utmost brevity. I have
avoided writing out the biblical proof texts and other [extrane-
ous] words in order to be succinct.
      Furthermore, it has been my intention to arrange the
rabbinic sayings in some [kind of] order by subjects, for the
author of the *Yalqut* already wrote them down according to
110 their appearance in [biblical] verses. My effort to put the
subjects in order is aimed at making the *Yalqut* complete from
every point of view. This matter of order is extremely essential,
as we have found that the greatest of prophets gladly accepted
the advice of his father-in-law, Jethro, who suggested a proper
115 order and suitable manner by which most of the students
would be able to judge the people. If it had not been
for that ordered [manner of judging], both he and they would
have become confused. As it is said, "So Moses hearkened to
the voice of his father-in-law, and did all that he had said"
(Ex. 18:24).
      Even the philosophers extolled the [value of] order in all
120 matters. Aristotle in his book *On the Heavens*[23] and in his

---

[23] This seems to be the *De Caelo*, but we cannot locate the reference.

Physics, VIII, 15,[24] and in his *Logic,* VI,[25] praised order in all things because, from the fact that there is order within existent things, wise men have found a proof for the existence and unity of God.

Likewise, you will find that the author of the *Guide* [*of the Perplexed*] in I, 34, indicates among the five obstacles [which 125 prevent us from learning difficult matters properly] that "it is not [fitting in teaching] to begin with what is most difficult and obscure for the understanding."[26] Consider, if you will, the magnificent [quality of] order with which Maimonides has arranged his *Code of Laws.* Aside from the profound wisdom with which he has arrived at all of the legal decisions of the *Gemara* and the *Tosafot, Sifra, Sifrei,* and *Mekhilta,* he also 130 brilliantly attempted to arrange the laws in an attractive, completely proper order in which [one can find] all of the rulings of any one subject together under one heading. [He was able to do this] in spite of the fact that the laws are scattered throughout the *Gemara.* [He organized his *Code* in 135 this way] because the quality of order is not only appropriate and proper, but also [absolutely] necessary in all matters.

[24] Actually Book VIII, 16, in the text with which Zahalon was familiar, namely, that of Averroes. It reads, "Sed nihil omnino naturale aut currens cursu naturali est sine ordine, natura enim est causa ordinis in omni, in quo est." Averroes, *Long Commentary on Physics,* VIII, 15, in *Aristotelis opera cum Averrois commentariis* (Venice, 1562–1594, repr. Frankfurt a. M. 1962), 348 M. This corresponds to the English trans. of the *Physics,* ed. Richard McKeon, VIII (New York, 1941), 358, 11–13: "But that which is produced or directed by nature can never be anything disorderly: for nature is everywhere the cause of order." I am indebted to Dr. Arthur Hyman for helping me locate this source of Zahalon's text of Aristotle.

[25] I have not been able to find this.

[26] Pines ed. (Chicago, 1969), pp. 73 ff. Maimonides explains the other obstacles as the insufficiency of the minds of all men at the early stages of their learning, the lengthy nature of preliminaries, limitations in the natural dispositions of individuals, and the fact that people are preoccupied with their bodily needs.

I have written [on the importance of order] in the introduction to my *Morashah Qehilat Ya'akov*[27] concerning Maimonides, of blessed memory. So, too, did King Solomon, may he
rest in peace, compose three books in a remarkably well-
140 ordered style. Is it not obvious that all of [those] matters necessary for one's personal conduct and concerning the love of the
Lord are found in *Song of Songs,* those things relating to the
conduct of one's home he included in *Proverbs,* and those considerations necessary for the governing of the state he wrote in
the book of *Ecclesiastes?* Thus did our Sages, of blessed
145 memory, say in [*Tractate*] *Erubin* (21b): "Ulla said in the name
of Rabbi Eleazar, the *Torah* was at first like a basket which had
no handles, and, when Solomon came, he affixed handles to it,
as it is written, 'Yea, he pondered, and sought out, and set in
order many proverbs' (Eccles. 12:9)."

In this reference work you will find all of the [rabbinic]
sayings that are in the rest of the works of our Sages, of blessed
150 memory, *Ein Yisro'el* [*Ein Ya'aqov*],[28] [*Midrash*] *Rabbah,*
Yelammedenu [*Midrash Tanḥuma*], *Pirqei de-Rabbi Eliezer,*
Sifra, Sifrei, and others, for the editor of the *Yalqut,* who
quoted the [rabbinic] saying, also refers to the source [of the
quotation].

---

[27] This work, dated 1660, is found in MS. form in the British Museum. It
contains in its introduction a prototype of the preacher's manual, which Zahalon
later expanded extensively in the *Or ha-Darshanim.* See Intro., Chap. 13 and
Chap. 5, a. The specific reference to order in the *Morashah Qehilat Ya'aqov* may
be on p. 8 within the prototype, in the section entitled "The Order of the
Sermon."

[28] According to H. L. Strack, *Introduction to the Talmud and Midrash* (trans.
of 5th ed. of Berlin, 1920, New York, 1959), p. 167, this work originally called *Ein
Ya'aqov,* by Jacob b. Solomon ibn Habib of Zamora, Spain, was first published in
Salonika in 1516, and in Venice in 1546–1547. It appeared under the title of *Bet
Yisro'el* in Venice in 1566. It was published with the title *Ein Yisro'el* in Prosnitz
in 1603 and in Venice in 1625, in two folio volumes, Cat. Bodl. no. 5518, which
edition Zahalon might have used.

[Let me explain] that I did not abbreviate too much, merely
referring briefly to a [rabbinic] statement, as other reference 155
works have done.[29] Instead, I [deliberately] dealt at length with
[rabbinic] sayings for two reasons: (a) for [the reason] that I
have given above, [namely,] in order that this would be a brief
summary of the entire *Yalqut;* and (b) in order that the 160
preacher should be able to understand from the [rabbinic]
saying written here [in the reference] whether or not it is relevant to his subject before he bothers to search out [the quotation in the *Yalqut* proper].

I prepared [this work in] two parts, one on the *Torah,* and
one on the *Prophets* and *Writings.* [Further,] I [deliberately]
did not assemble [all of the material] into one volume [alone]
in order that it should not appear too difficult for the reader.[30] 165
[If the entire work were to have been in one volume, then the

---

[29] By comparison, da Modena in the introduction to his *Beit Leḥem Yehudah*
(Venice, 1625) described how he prepared that index to the *Ein Yisro'el* (*Ein
Ya'aqov*) as a result of his personal experience preaching in Venice and in other
Italian communities. He meant it to be a "set table for whoever might seek to
compose a sermon . . . to find every rabbinic saying (*ma'amar*) on that subject
(*nose*)," p. 2b. Da Modena's reference work showed where the sayings of the *Ein
Yisro'el* were to be found in the *Talmud,* but quoted them in abbreviated
form, forcing the *darshan* to go to the sources for the complete text. In contrast,
Zahalon composed his work on the *Yalqut* without giving the sources in the *Talmud,* yet quoting the entire rabbinic sayings to spare the preacher the work of
having to look them up. Obviously, as a result of these different objectives, the
size of da Modena's index is but a fraction of that of Zahalon. On the title page of
his *Beit Leḥem Yehudah,* da Modena claimed that his work followed the pattern
of another index work, *Zikhron Torat Moshe* (Constantinople, 1553, 1554), of
Moses b. Joseph Figo, a reference work on sayings from the *Talmud,* Maimonides' *Moreh Nevukhim,* Albo's *Iqqarim,* and Arama's *Aqedat Yizḥaq,* among
others.

[30] Cf. Intro., n. 291. It is clear from the two sections of the JTS MSS. of the *Or,*
nos. 161 and 162. However, the Cas. MS. is described as in one volume.
Cf. Intro., n. 41. Yet from this writer's examination of the microfilm of that MS.,
it seems clear that a second volume begins after folio p. 123.

reader] would see in front of him a vast array of [rabbinic] sayings under one heading and would be overwhelmed [by the prospect of having to peruse so large a quantity of sayings in order to find exactly what he was looking for]. Instead, [I arranged the reference work in two separate parts so that the reader] could make use of whatever he might find in Part I, and, if he wishes to search further—or he did not find what he was looking for in Part I—he may search for it in Part II.

170   Now do not be surprised if you find a certain [rabbinic] saying which is [already] included in Part I repeated in Part II, for the editor of the *Yalqut* himself must have repeated that saying. Also, a saying which deals with many subjects [would be referred to accordingly] under different headings, in order that one might [surely] find that saying [under the specific] subject needed by the person who is preaching.

175   Similarly, I have included [different] sayings which deal with the same subject under different headings as, for example, *adamah* [earth], *erez* [land], and *afar* [dust]. I did not assemble [all of the similar sayings] under any one of these headings, for at times there is a [rabbinic] saying which belongs [specifically] under the rubric *adamah*, and not under that of *afar*. The opposite is also [true, namely, that I have frequently combined different subjects under one heading, and examples will prove

180 this]. This, too, facilitates one's finding a saying under one rubric, and not having to think of another word [or heading, under which it may be found].

Because the *Yalqut* was published in different editions [which are at variance with each other,] I composed this [reference] work through the use of an old edition.[31] The newer

185 editions are not completely homologous with the older ones. Therefore, I have indicated and made reference to the *chapters*

[31] See Intro., n. 235. Zahalon must have used the Salonika ed., of 1521 and 1526.

as [the chapters] are the same in all of the versions. If you [happen to] have an old edition of the *Yalqut,* and the chapter is indicated there, then you will [be able to] find what you are looking for unmistakably.

The Almighty is my witness that "I have not composed this 190 [work] for my own glorification, nor even for the glory of my family" (Tan. 20a), nor for any such self-seeking motive (cf. M. Avot 4:5). [On the contrary,] this book [represents] more [sheer] drudgery than it does insight.[32] [This work is] not meant for those who are able "to survey in one glance" (R.H. 18a) the entire *Yalqut* and are thus not in need of this reference work. For them all of the subject matter of the *Yalqut* is 195 [immediately] available [to their mind's eye].

However, for a person such as myself, abundant hardships of our [present] time[33] have [,on the one hand,] diminished our [intellectual] abilities, and [,on the other hand,] increased our forgetfulness [concerning sources]—as a result of our many transgressions (cf. Ezra 9:6)![34] Therefore, I have "made handles for my basket" (Erub. 21b)[35] in order that one may hold on to them, thereby making use [of this reference work] for the service of the Lord, may His name be blessed.

Further, I hope to fulfill that which is said, [Who is] "he who does righteousness at all times" (Ps. 106:3)? This refers to 200

[32] Cf. above, n. 280, in Intro.

[33] This could be a veiled reference to persecution by Church authorities, or possibly to the undermining of the Jewish community brought about by the effects of Sabbatianism. See Intro., Chaps. 1 and 6. Another, more open reference is found below, ll. 415–416.

[34] Bahya in his *Hovot ha-Levavot* cites his "fear of forgetfulness" concerning all that he had learned and accumulated in his mind about the duties of the heart, along with the "very limited help from [his] contemporaries" in recalling the material, among the reasons for his having written his work (Ibn Tibbon trans., A. Zifroni ed. [Tel Aviv, 1959], Intro., p. 87). Cf. notes 14 and 110.

[35] Cf. above, the text of the *Or,* ll. 147–149.

him who writes books and lends them to others (Yal. II, 864, 477b).

Now inasmuch as the purpose of this book is to smooth the way for preachers, enlightening their path as they go about composing their sermons, I decided to add to it a supplement.
205 [This addition,] great in quality though small in quantity, will teach young men some valuable guidelines for the composition and public delivery of sermons. [Because until now] there has not been a guidebook which would show them [the necessary steps in preparing and delivering an.effective sermon], they are excessively burdened with fashioning and improving their sermons.[36] They must take much time and abundant practice
210 in learning the ways of the art of homiletics.

With the limited knowledge which I have acquired during the years that I have preached publicly, I have learned [the various] approaches and techniques needed in this field. I have written them at the beginning of this work. I have been personally guided by these [rules] in my *Titen Emet le-Ya'aqov*,[37] which is [a collection of] sermons on the [weekly] portions, and
215 also in my *Zohola ve-Rina*,[38] [which is a commentary] on *Song of Songs, Ecclesiastes,* and *Daniel.* [I have also followed these rules in] my book of sermons for the Sabbaths written in Italian.[39] Truly, this supplementary work has been at my side

[36] See Intro., n. 261.
[37] See Intro., Chap. 5, c, and n. 248.
[38] See Intro., p. 69, and n. 249.

[39] We cannot be certain what volume of sermons the author intends. Da Modena adds many details regarding sermons, especially the paucity of Hebrew quotations in them: "There are at this time very few . . . that are able to discourse perfectly in the Hebrew . . . nor yet in Chaldee [Aramaic] . . . because they all generally learn, and are brought up in the Language of the Countries, where they are born: So that, in Italy, they speak Italian: in Germany, Dutch: in the Eastern Parts, and in Barbary [North Africa], they speak the Language of the Turks, and Moors; and so of the rest." He goes on to note that Jews who have left Germany for Poland, Hungary, and Russia have made "High-Dutch," which is now Yiddish, their mother-tongue, while Jews leaving Spain for the Levant speak Ladino, which he calls "Spanish." He adds, "But in Italy they use both the one, and the

in the composition of nearly five hundred sermons alone, from
those I composed in my *Morashah Qehilat Ya'aqov*[27] on the 220
books of *Mada, Ahavah,* and *Zemanim* of Maimonides, of
blessed memory, and my *Ozar ha-Ḥokhmot,*[40] [The Treasure of
Wisdom,"] and the book *Shnei Me'orot ha-Teshuvah,*[41] ["Two
Lights of Repentance,"] a penance for every single sin, and
sermons on the Psalm "when Nathan the prophet
came to him" (Ps. 57:2) on repentance and a penance, [or
remedy, for the violation] of every error.[42] May the Holy One, 225

other; according to the place, from whence the Fathers are descended. So that the
Common people every where conform themselves to the Language of the
Nations, where they inhabit; onely mixing now and then a broken Hebrew word,
or two, in their discourse one with another: although the Learneder sort among
them are somewhat more perfect in the Language of the Scripture, and have it, as
it were, by heart." He describes their preaching as in "the Language of the
Countrie," along with quotations from Scripture and rabbinic sources which are
later interpreted in "the Vulgar Tongue." "Their manner of Preaching . . . is
thus: the Whole Congregation sitting quietly in the School [synagogue], He that
hath a Mind to Preach, (which is easily granted to any that desire it,) either putting on the . . . Taleth, or else going, without it, up to the Wooden Alter, or
Table . . . begins his Speech there, repeating some Verse or other, out of the Lesson for the day, and this is called *Nose,* that is to say, the Text, or Subject,
whereof he intends to treat: adding after it some Sentence out of the Wisemen, or
Rabbins; and this is called *Ma'amar:* and so making a kind of Preface, and pro-
posing some certain Subject, suitable to the sense of the aforesaid Passage out of
the Lesson for the Day, he proceeds on to his Sermon . . . every man as he is
able, both for the Style, and Method: which is very different, among the several
Nations" (*Riti,* pp. 56–61). Cf. above, notes 22 and 29, on other descriptions by
da Modena of preaching in his day. Concerning the language of sermons, see
below, notes 80, 92, and 114.

[40] See Intro., note 132, Chap. 9, and p. 79.

[41] See Intro., p. 79. We have found no other reference to this work, except that
found below in the MS. in the author's note, ll. 227–229, "It is not necessary to
mention these (referring to ll. 215–226, 'And also in my *Zohola ve-Rina,* which is
a commentary on *Song of Songs* . . .') as I have already referred to them in the
introduction to the book *Shnei Me'orot ha-Gedolim al ha-Teshuvah."*

[42] The text is not clear here. I am indebted to Dr. I. Marcus for this rendition.
Cf. his *Piety and Society, the Jewish Pietists of Medieval Germany* (Leiden, 1981),
pp. 144–145, on penitential terminologies. The terms *tiqqun kol avon* (l. 223) and

praised be He, deal kindly with me that these works should [eventually] be published. Amen. Finished and completed, praised be the Lord Creator of the universe![43]

230   May it be the will of our God in heaven that He reward me with His lovingkindness with the help of God by having the people of Israel make use of this book of mine, that it may sustain my soul in the World to Come, for great is the reward of him who performs a service for the community (cf. Avot 5:18) through publishing books which are great in quantity as well as in quality, as the Almighty has taught me to do. Amen.

235 May God's will be done! And may I fulfill that which is written, "He does righteousness at all times" (Ps. 106:3). This refers to him who writes books and lends them to others (Yal. II. 864, 477b).[44]

tiqqun le-kol ha-mizvot (l. 225) may be the only explicit kabbalistic terms in the *Or.* Cf. Scholem, *Major Trends in Jewish Mysticism,* p. 233 and *passim.* Dr. Marcus has called my attention to an unpublished doctoral dissertation of Lawrence Fine, "Techniques of Mystical Meditation for Achieving Prophecy and the Holy Spirit in the Teachings of Isaac Luria and Hayyim Vital" (Brandeis University, 1975), pp. 53, 58–75, on this use of the term *tiqqun.* Cf. my Intro. pp. 39–43 on Sabbatian usage of *tiqqun.* In his *Margaliot Tovot,* where Zahalon attempts to teach the *Hovot ha-Levavot,* in his chapter "The Gate of Repentance," our author advises his reader to pray that our Creator grant him a "*tiqqun* (redemption) to redeem his erring through [the process of] *teshuvah.*" He adds, "and what is *teshuvah*? It is *taqqanat ha-adam* (the redemption of man)," p. 45b.

[43] The author has deleted the section beginning with ll. 215–226, "And also in my *Zohola ve-Rina*" until here, with the note explaining the deletion found in ll. 227–229. See above, n. 41.

[44] Cf. above, ll. 199–201. What follows here in our translation is not the order as found in the Cas. MS., which is obviously the earliest MS., apparently with the author's own instructions and emendations. On the recto of the page bearing "the Precautions the Preacher Should Keep in Mind" (ll. 239–240) are the author's instructions (see above, Intro., n. 243), rearranging the *Or* according to the order later to be found in the JTS MS. and the Oxford MS. The original order, as we see from the Cas. MS., was as follows: the title page (ll. 1–24), the chapter headings (ll. 236–255), the preacher's manual (ll. 256–756), and then, following the end of Chap. 13, the introduction to the index of the *Yalqut* (ll.

The Following Are the Precautions the Preacher Should Keep in Mind so that His Sermons Will Be Acceptable in the Sight of God and Israel, written by the devoted preacher to his people (see Est. 10:3), the physician, our honored master and teacher Jacob, son of our honored master and teacher Isaac 240 Zahalon, "may the memory of the righteous be for a blessing" (Prov. 10:7):

1. What Should Be the Content and the Subject of the Sermon?
2. The Quality of the Sermon.
3. The Length of the Sermon.
4. The Order of the Sermon.
5. The Manner of Composing the Introduction.   245
6. On the Use of One's Voice.
7. Concerning One's Manner of Speaking
8. On the Use of Gestures.
9. What the Preacher Should Do before He Goes Up to Preach.
10. The Purpose of Preaching Sermons.   250
11. On Concluding and Closing the Sermon.
12. Caring for One's Health as a Means to More Effective Preaching.
13. After Concluding the Sermon.

The explanation for these matters is found in the following 255 chapters:

26–235). And, clearly, in the Cas. MS. what followed that introduction (ll. 26–235) was the full text of the index. By combining that introduction with his preacher's manual, Zahalon sought to incorporate it into a smaller work than the large index it had been a part of, a much less ambitious work to publish. Perhaps, too, Zahalon anticipated the potential problem that his work on the *Yalqut* might encounter at the hands of the Holy Office, as in fact it did (see above, Intro., pp. 94–95).

1. The Content and the Subject of the Sermon

1) It is extremely essential in homiletics that the [general] content and the subject [of the sermon] be both attractive and novel. Afterwards one may decorate the sermon, garbing it with pleasing interpretations [of biblical verses]. The subject at 260 times will be completely about a verse or [a rabbinic] interpretation, a lesson or a good attribute which is deserving of praise, or a bad trait [which ought to be] condemned in order to show its offensive and injurious consequences from every point of view.[45]

[45] In this suggestion concerning praising and condemning, and below in ll. 303–305, and ll. 650–653, Zahalon's stress on the sermon motivating good deeds is, according to Reuben Bonfil, indicative of a major change in emphasis within Jewish preaching, which came about during the Renaissance. Prior to that, exegesis and philosophical meditation were the principal subject matters of sermons. Now, he explains, preachers "regarded themselves as the spiritual shepherds of their generation" and, therefore, emphasized deeds and ethics (*musar*). The same shift in homiletic emphasis can be seen in the Christian world, where ethics and political science replaced logic and metaphysics as the main preoccupation of sermons (*Ha-Rabbanut be-Italia bi-Tekufat ha-Renaissance* [Jerusalem, 1979], p. 202).

O'Malley bears this out in his description of epideictic preaching with its goal to aid the individual in "the art of good and blessed living." He notes that the ultimate purpose of such preaching, which evokes sentiments of admiration, gratitude, and praise which will foster a desire to imitate certain positive qualities and shun negative ones, was to practice what Cicero called *ars bene beauteque vivendi* (*De officiis*, I. 6. 19), meaning "the art of good and blessed living." O'Malley explains that "the preacher's learning and all his proficiency in the art of oratory were to be directed to this single goal of aiding his listeners in their efforts to master" this most essential aim in life. The sacred orators of the papal court during the Renaissance gave this Ciceronian expression a Christian interpretation. When Zahalon defined the purpose of preaching as "to teach the *Torah* of the Lord" through drawing the people *closer to* certain religious paths and *further away* from others which were transgressions (ll. 650–653), he followed, perhaps without being aware of it, the same Ciceronian goal. He thereby specifically advised using *derashot* as instruments of guidance for promoting certain patterns of behavior, and discouraging others. Sermons for him, as for the sacred Christian orators earlier, provided a kind of balance so needed in a turbulent world. As O'Malley

[Further, a sermon might deal with] a basic principle of faith, demonstrating how essential it is and what tends to substantiate it. [A sermon, too,] might seek out an entirely new content which appears both astonishing and yet true, while 265 afterwards proofs [for the new thought which might] be brought will not be lacking,[46] as [it is said,] "Study the *Torah* again and again, for everything is in it" (M. Avot 5:22). [A preacher] should not discuss a subject which is [overly] simple [or obvious] to a large congregation of people.[47]

[The necessity of having an attractive and novel] subject is comparable to adorning an [already] attractive woman with 270 beautiful jewelry. How very apparent her beauty becomes! On the other hand, when an unattractive woman is bedecked with beautiful jewels, or the opposite, [when a lovely woman is garbed in an untasteful fashion,] she will never appear completely pleasing to those who see her.

The eminent preacher, the author of the *Aqedah*[48] and other works, [avoided these pitfalls,] as one can see in his sermons.

puts it, sermons gave "a sense of order, stability, and personal identity in a world where these values were, perforce, under some threat. The sermons were meant to cast light on the mystery of man's life and to equip the listeners with the inspiration they needed to face life's problems" (*Praise and Blame in Renaissance Rome* [Durham, 1979], pp. 70–71, 124, and 162).

[46] The thought here is that once you are innovative with a new and *true* interpretation, people will later find proofs, treating your innovation as an established interpretation. That it should not be a forced idea, see above, Intro. n. 110.

[47] R. David Darshan had explained the various rhetorical devices preachers use in order to "enhance the value of the *derashah* in the eyes of the people: because of their [natural] impatience they are not [always] appreciative of [the preacher's citing additional biblical] verses [as support] or [his citing] the *peshat* (the plain meaning of a verse)." Darshan goes on to justify embellishing the verses cited in various ways (*Ketav Hitnazlut le-Darshanim*, 4:2, as quoted in Ben-Sasson, *Hagut ve'Hanhagah* [Jerusalem, 1959], pp. 42–43 and cf. *Or*, ll. 377–379). See my Intro., n. 261, and below, n. 54 on R. Joel Ibn Shu-aib's suggestion.

[48] The *Aqedat Yizhaq* (Venice, 1573), by R. Isaac Arama (b. northern Spain, 1420, d. Naples, 1494). This is the one *darshan* and book of *derashot* cited in the *Or*. He refers to the *Olat Shabbat* (Venice, 1577), in the *Ozar*. See Intro., n. 183.

275 He did as the servant of Abraham had done when he took a
golden nose-ring and gold bands and handed them to Rebec-
ca, an attractive young girl. Likewise, the rabbi [Isaac Arama],
of blessed memory, took [for the subject matter of his sermons]
that which was [at once] novel, attractive, [containing an
element of] surprise, and [yet perfectly] true for the subject
matter of his sermons. He then proceeded to adorn each
sermon with pleasant and new interpretations. From him we
ought to learn!

280   2) [A preacher] must avoid having too many parts in [his]
sermon. One, too, or three parts, [at most, are sufficient,] for
when one makes too many sections within a sermon, [his]
listeners become irritated and confused, as wise men have
remarked, "Where there is excess, there is confusion."[49]

285   3) He should seek to learn what it is that [his] congregation
is most anxious to hear about, for example, whether [they are
concerned] about [the prospect for] *Geullah* (redemption) and
the reasons for the length of the *Galut*. [They might want to
hear about] *Teshuvah* (repentance) and to be admonished,
[thereby inspiring them to repent. Still, they might want to
learn new] explanations for some biblical verses, or [suggested]
answers for some problematic verse. [They might want to hear
an interpretation of some seemingly] strange [rabbinic] say-
290 ings.[50] [Or, they might prefer hearing] an account of some
events [which occurred and what can be learned from them,]
or the explanation of some laws together with the verses [on
which they are based,] or something similar [to these things].

---

[49] I have not been able to find this quotation in any Jewish source. Dr. Tovia
Preschel has suggested that this may have been a local saying of scholars, not
related to Jewish literature. O'Malley records that Pope Calixtus III included "a
special admonition [in his constitution of November 13, 1456] that the Master of
the Palace take care that the sermons be not tiresome by being too long" (*Praise
and Blame in Renaissance Rome*, p. 18 and n. 42). See below, n. 112.

[50] *Ma'amarim zarim.* Could this be a veiled reference to the use of such rabbinic sayings in Sabbatian preaching? Cf. Intro., Chap. 6.

[Attempt to] adjust your will according to the wishes [of your congregation] (cf. M. Avot. 2:4).

4) He should try to make his subject matter one of timely interest. For example, during the days of *Sukkot,* the season for our rejoicing, one ought not to deliver sermons reproving [the people. On the other hand,] if it is a period for repentance, [it would be inappropriate] to spend much time [in his sermon] 295 on joyous matters. [Further,] if there is a bridegroom or a baby boy [born within the community and] about to enter the covenant [of Abraham,] or if [there are those in] mourning— [it should] not [happen] to us—[the preacher] ought to make mention of these events, for "A word in due season, how good it is!" (Prov. 15:23). This is what our Sages, of blessed memory, have taught: Moses cautioned the Israelites that they should expound "the laws of *Pesaḥ* on *Pesaḥ* [the laws of *Aẕeret* on *Aẕeret* (*Shavu'ot*), and the laws of the Festival on the Festival (*Sukkot*)"] (Meg. 4a and 32a). We should not be like those who expatiate at great length in sermons which do not 300 relate to timely [appropriate] issues, and, [only] as an after-thought, append a few words about the matter [which is on people's minds].

5) He should try to make the subject matter [of his sermon] something of value which will bear fruit, as [inspiring] good deeds among the people. [That is to say, his aim must] not [be] to exhibit his profound wisdom or [merely] to relate matters 305 [of no practical importance] without [some] novel interpreta-tion.[51]

6) [The preacher] should pray to the Lord that He bestow upon him wisdom and understanding, that He look down from His holy habitation (see Deut. 26:15) to teach him true interpretations. [He should also pray for the Lord to enable him] to recall what he learned at the revelation at Mount

---

[51] The words *be-li ḥidush,* "without some novel interpretation," have been added in the Cas. MS. See above, nn. 12 and 45 on *derashot* inspiring good deeds, and cf. below, l. 653 on showing off one's wisdom.

310 Sinai.[52] This is what our Sages, of blessed memory, have said, "Everything which a faithful disciple would teach in the future was [already] taught by the Lord to Moses and Israel" (cf. Meg. 19b, T.J. Peah 2:6, 17a, and Lev. R. 22:1). All of the souls of Israel were there [at Sinai]; they all heard the words of the living God.[53]

2. The Quality of the Sermon and the Manner [of Composing It]

    1) [A preacher] should seek to include in [his] sermon
315 something [which is] profound and stimulating in order to please the learned and thoughtful [members of his congregation.[54] He should also include that which] is pleasant and

---

[52] This is reminiscent of Zahalon's words in the physician's prayer, asking God to aid his memory in recalling what he has learned: "Especially I beseech You, God of the spirits of all flesh, concerning one thing, namely, that You will strengthen the power of my memory so that when I go to visit a sick person [You will] remind me immediately of the proper cure for him whether I have studied it or not" (*Margaliot Tovot*, p. 6b). Perhaps what Zahalon meant by asking for divine aid in remembering even what he might *not* have studied is similar to the concept here of requesting God's aid in recalling what he learned at Sinai (see n. 53). Concerning the matter of memory, see also *Or*, ll. 197, 640–642, 702–705, and n. 14 to the text on *zekhira*.

[53] I could not find this exact source. The first half is based on Ex. R. 28:6. The language of the second half may have been influenced by Jer. 23:36, Erub. 13b, or Git. 6b. Cf. below, n. 83. R. Zev Wolf Einhorn, in his comment on Ex. R. 28:6, notes that "all Israel was in a certain place in the wilderness, necessarily implying that all those generations who were later to be created—*all of them* were there [at Sinai]" (*Midrash Rabbah* [Vilna, 1853–1858], 50b). It may be that Zahalon was influenced by this and other Jewish sources, and he might also have been familiar with Plato's statements about learning as recollection or reminiscence (see *Phaedo* 72 E, *Meno* 81 D) from his studies in philosophy.

[54] In his *Olat Shabbat* (Venice, 1577), R. Joel Ibn Shu-aib, in the introduction, urges *darshanim* to be sure that their words have value for all their listeners. If their sermons are very profound, they should explain them, so that the masses will be able to understand. And when the matters that a preacher talks about are

readily understood in order to appeal to the majority of the people. [Let the preacher, too,] relate something which will be appreciated by those who are not learned [in the study of *Torah,*] as well as the women, young people, and elderly folks, in order that everyone [present] may derive some benefit [from his sermon. This is] in accord with our Sages, of blessed memory, [who interpreted the verse,] "'Thus you shall say to the house of Jacob' (Ex. 19:3) this refers to the women, 320 'and tell the children of Israel' (*ibid.*) this refers to the men" (Mekh., Lauterbach ed., II, 201; Yal. I, 276, 84b).

2) If he is delivering a eulogy, he should be very cautious not to praise the deceased beyond what is due him, for to do otherwise would actually bring shame and disgrace [to the dead rather than praise]. This is [the way the talmudic passage is] explained: "Be fervent in my funeral eulogy, for I will be standing there" (Shab. 153a), that is, be fervent in expounding 325 my praises to say what I have actually accomplished, as if I am actually there. If you, however, praise me for what I am not [and have not accomplished], it will seem as if you are eulogizing someone else in my place (cf. Rashi *ad locum*).

well known, he should also include material from which the learned individuals who are present will derive benefit. (See above, Intro., pp. 62 and 84). Steven Langton (d. 1228), a very influential English churchman who served as cardinal and was one of the most distinguished scholars of his day, urged his students to preach to the laity as well as the learned, and to beware of devoting their sermons to those on their own intellectual and religious level. "See!" Langton wrote, "a preacher should not always use polished, subtle preaching, like Ehud's sword (Jud. 3:21), but sometimes a ploughshare, that is, rude, rustic exhortation [like Shamgar, who slew 600 Philistines with his ploughshare, or oxgoad, *ibid.*, v. 31]. Very often a popular story [*exemplum vulgare*] is more effective than a polished, subtle phrase." Quoted in Beryl Smalley, *The Study of the Bible in the Middle Ages* (Oxford, 1952), pp. 254–255. Smalley notes that Langton contrasted "the *exemplum vulgare* of the popular sermon with the 'polished phrase' of the sermon to clerks," p. 256.

[55] For this saying, which was apparently a popular saying in the Middle Ages, see I. Davidson, *Oẓar ha-Meshalim ve-ha-Pitgamim mi-Safrut Yemei ha-Baynaim* (Jerusalem, 1956/1957), p. 188, no. 3084.

3) He should not rely on what he finds in texts for his entire
330 sermon. Rather, he should add some nuance of his own, an
insight or interpretation according to his own opinion and
understanding. [Of course,] he should have access to many
texts, for no one can be a scholar without the aid of many good
books.[55] At times he will find his subject matter [by looking
further] in an additional book, and he will [thereby be able to]
335 incorporate some secular wisdom into his sermon.[56] These
[forms of knowledge] are the "auxiliaries of wisdom" (M.
Avot 3:19), such as zoology and similar kinds of learning. He can then immediately [relate this teaching from other
disciplines] to a verse or rabbinic statement which made the
same point, for nothing is hidden from [the biblical and rabbinic sources].

4) When he wants to introduce a certain novel interpreta-
340 tion, he ought not to plunge into the subject all at once.
Rather, through properly laying out [his sermon], his preface
should serve to elucidate [his subject]. He should not engage in
a lengthy introduction [and presentation], which is one of the
main obstacles to wisdom, as Maimonides, of blessed memory,
has written in his *Guide* (I, 34, 73–76).[57]

5) He should not belabor the obvious in a [rabbinic] saying
or in telling a story, for it is not fitting that he devote half of his
345 sermon to citing [biblical] verses or [rabbinic] statements
according to their plain explanation. It is unwise to include
within a sermon a simple verse or saying into which he has not
infused some new meaning, unless it is to prove a certain point.

6) If you subdivide a subject, [separating it into different
350 parts,] be careful that all of the parts add up together to equal
the whole. You should not [find yourself] saying, "This matter
may be divided into four parts," when in reality there are

[56] See in the *Or,* ll. 458–459 (Chap. 3:3), where Zahalon also refers to extra-
neous, or secular, sources for sermon illustrations.

[57] See above, n. 26.

additional sections as well. However, if you do not care to refer to all of the [different] parts, clearly state that you [have intentionally] made reference to only those sections which pertain to your subject.

7) When [the preacher] begins to sense that his congrega- 355 tion is becoming tired and restless, he should [at this point] relate some suitable story that will awaken [interest in] the people and delight them. Our Sages spoke of this in the saying of a certain rabbi who, when he noticed that the people were becoming drowsy, remarked: "The time will come when a woman will bear a child every day" (Shab. 30b).[58] To remedy this [problem of drowsiness,] he might also say something humorous (*ibid.*). Naturally, he must not carry on at great 360 length [this way. Such diversions should be used] in a rather offhand manner.[59]

8) He should always attempt to incorporate into a sermon the most suitable interpretations, never those [which appear] forced.[60] Never trouble the people with overly complex explanations, posing difficult questions in their presence. Similarly, he should not bring up many subtle textual difficulties concerning a [rabbinic] saying or [biblical] verse. Instead, let him mention [only those teachings which are] most essential 365 to his subject and leave the rest [for people] to study on their own. Notice, too, that the rabbinical author of the *Aqedah,* and

[58] The authority cited is Rabban Gamaliel, and he bases it on a novel interpretation of Jer. 31:7. Other examples in the *Talmud* of *darshanim* employing attention-getting devices to arouse their drowsy congregations include R. Aqiba (Ber. R. 58:3) and R. Judah ha-Nasi (Song R. 1:15:3).

[59] David Darshan had spoken of the use of deliberate exaggeration as permitted to preachers as "needed in order to awaken the drowsy" (*Ketav Hitnaẓlut le-Darshanim,* 3:1, as quoted in Ben-Sasson, *Hagut ve-Hanhagah* [Jerusalem, 1959], p. 43). See my Intro., n. 261.

[60] This appears to be directly aimed at some of the distorted Sabbatian preaching. See Intro., Chap. 6, n. 110. Other references to that which is *be-doḥak* (or "forced") appear in the *Or,* ll. 603–604 (Chap. 7:6) and ll. 636–638 (Chap. 9:1).

others like him,[61] did not elaborate on [all possible] problems
and precise details when he explained a verse or saying.
Rather, when he wants to explain a section by mentioning
370 many [possible] interpretations of a verse or saying, he
will refer beforehand rather quickly to those [comments which
are] not relevant to his subject. Finally, [after these preliminaries,] he will deal with one explanation which is [most]
appropriate to his subject.

9) [You can] elucidate a [biblical] verse or [rabbinic] saying
either by means of another verse or saying, or by [referring to]
375 an insight or a particular law which the Sages have mentioned.
Of course, when [the preacher] cites another verse or saying, he
should include some personal observation, or new interpretation originated by others, which goes beyond the plain meaning of the text.[62] Concerning this it has been said, "There can
380 be no homiletic interpretation without some new insight."[63] He
should always quote a teaching in the name of its author in
order that [people] will reliably assume that, when he does not
make reference to [another] author [for a particular saying], it
is only because that saying is his own new interpretation.
David followed this practice [of referring to original authors]
385 in his *Psalms* of the sons of Koraḥ and others. Our Sages of
blessed memory say, "Whosoever reports a thing in the name
of him that said it brings deliverance into the world" (M. Avot
6:6; Meg. 15a).

10) When he refers to a certain matter or incident, he ought
to add some of the [pertinent] details, such as where the event
390 took place, what time [it happened,] and who the people

---

[61] *U-ke-yoẓei.* This word was a later addition by the author, written above the
line, in the Cas. MS. Maybe in his later life Zahalon became aware of other *darshanim* who measured up to his standards, such as R. Joel Ibn Shu-aib. Cf. above,
n. 48.

[62] See above, ll. 268–271; and n. 47 on R. David Darshan, and also n. 12 on l.
22 on the subject of originality, or new themes.

[63] A variation of Hag. 3a, "There is no *Beit ha-Midrash* without some new
insight."

[involved were. Through doing] this his words will have greater credibility.

11) He ought to be very careful in delivering a sermon before the public not to include in it anything which will raise theological doubts or impart a particle of suspicion in the 395 minds of his congregation that what [he] is saying is [not] according to accepted opinions.[64] It was because of [such doubts and suspicions being raised] that the Sages sought to exclude the book of *Koheleth* [from the canon] (Shab. 30b; Lev. R. 28:1; Koh. R. 1:3).

Even if you ultimately [include in your sermon] appropriate answers [to the disquieting questions you have asked, you will still] have reason to worry that your congregants will [in the future] remember [only] the doubts [which you raised in 400 their minds,] and that they will forget the [proper] answers [which you later gave to dispel those doubts]. Concerning this [very matter] it has been said, "Learned people, be careful with your words, etc." (M. Avot 1:11), and "The subject of the *Ma'aseh Merkavah* (the mystery of the divine chariot) may not be expounded, etc." (M. Ḥag. 2:1, referring to Ezek. 1).[65]

---

[64] This is another caution aimed at preachers who might have used distorted and forced interpretations to support the Sabbatian heresy. Cf. above, n. 60.

[65] It is possible that Zahalon here is trying to guide darshanim away from disquieting interpretations, such as some of the eschatalogical teachings prevalent in the wake of the Sabbatian movement. In urging clarity and the avoidance of raising unnecessary doubts, he is assuming the role which Maimonides did five centuries earlier in his *Epistle to the Jews of Yemen,* which he wrote in 1172 to counter the messianic preaching of a false prophet who had stirred up considerable anxiety among Yemenite Jewry. See Scholem, *Sabbatai Ṣevi,* p. 14, and my Intro., n. 110. R. Leone da Modena, in a responsum on whether a preacher who said in his sermon that the world would never end should be punished, stated: "it is better not to raise such profound subjects before a congregation . . . for our *Torah* is as wide as the ocean and there are not lacking 'less complicated' subjects that are more appropriate for the souls of the listeners than this subject (*She'elot u-Teshuvot Ziqnei Yehudah,* ed. S. Simonsohn [Jerusalem, 1956], no. 16, p. 30). As to Zahalon's hesitation to include *Kabbalah* as a source of enrichment of the sermon, see below, n. 72.

12) To embellish the sermon [the preacher] should try to
405 include in it an incident found in [one of] the holy texts, giving
it a [slightly different] twist in order to enhance [the quality of]
the homily, for all people naturally derive joy from hearing
about actual events which have occurred. All the more [do
they relish learning of] incidents [or happenings] from the holy
410 texts, as they are [considered] extremely reliable. Our Sages, of
blessed memory, have said concerning the verse, "Refresh me
with apples" (Song 2:5): "R. Isaac said, 'Formerly, when
everyone had enough income [for his necessities], people were
eager [to learn something of] *Mishnah, halakhah,* or *Talmud.*
Now, [however,] that [they] do not have enough [for their
415 necessities], and still further, that [they] are sick of the [oppres-
sions of the Roman] government,[66] they are eager to hear
[only] words of Scripture and *haggadah*" (Yal. II,
986, 535a; cf. Sof. 16:4; Song R. 2:5), [i.e., now that the people
are oppressed economically and worn out with persecution,
they want only light and easily understood spiritual food, such
as biblical and other stories].

13) If [the preacher] intends to raise a question regarding a
particular verse or saying, he should raise the question before
420 he begins to explicate the rabbinic or biblical text. It is not
proper while he is [in the midst of] explaining the [difficult]
verse to confuse the explanation by raising a question or fine
point. Rather, [he should raise textual] difficulties at one time,
and answer them, [interpreting the verse or saying] at another
time [not simultaneously, thereby confusing questions with
answers].

425·   14) A young man who is beginning to compose sermons
ought to read all twenty-four books of *Torah, Prophets,* and
Writings together with the commentary of Rashi or some other
commentator. Furthermore, he ought to [study and] reflect
upon all of the rabbinic sayings of *Ein Yisro'el*[67] together with
the commentary, and he should read the *Yalqut.*

---

[66] See above, ll. 196–197, and n. 33.
[67] See above, n. 28.

3. Concerning the Length and Substance of the Sermon   430

1) [The preacher] should not make his sermon too long, in order not to burden the congregation.[68] However, he should not [make his homily] too short either, for it is not right to trouble the people by having brought them [out of their homes] to hear something which is too brief. Rather, he ought to ponder over four [principal] considerations: the time, the subject matter, the place, and the man himself. Now if the 435 weather is very warm, he ought to speak briefly.[69] If it is quite chilly, [he should speak for] a longer period of time. If it is almost time for dinner, he should limit his words. [So much regarding time.]

Regarding subject matter, if his subject matter is very painful, arousing anxiety, he should be brief. On the other hand, if 440 his subject is a cheerful matter, he may speak more at length.

Concerning the place, [if the congregation is very] cramped, and the people are standing there[70] uncomfortably crowded together, his sermon should be kept short.

Regarding the preacher himself, if he is possessed of unusual charm and grace, then even if he speaks at some 445 length, the people will not tire of him. The opposite would hold true of one who does not possess such an attractive personality. [Likewise,] if he is an eminent scholar, renowned for his

---

[68] Renaissance sources on sermons given at the papal court indicate that "brevity at times seems almost the measure of excellence," according to O'Malley (*Praise and Blame in Renaissance Rome,* p. 22). On sermon length, see below, n. 112.

[69] O'Malley notes from a Vatican MS. that "Roman fear of the summer heat seemingly eliminated the possibility for a sermon on the feast of Assumption, and on August 15, 1505, old hands at the court smiled at the thought that somebody might propose a sermon in such a season" (*ibid.,* p. 15 and n. 29).

[70] Here is an indication that most people apparently stood during the sermon, although Zahalon alludes to the scholars and important community leaders who might walk in in the middle of the *derashah* and for whom the *darshan* should wait "until the prominent person has taken his seat." See 1. 562 (Chap. 6:4), and ll. 610–612 (Chap. 8:1). See below, notes 95 and 112.

wisdom, people will not object to his speaking longer, whereas
they would [be impatient] if an [ordinary] student was deliver-
450 ing a [lengthy] sermon.

2) If he would divide his sermon into two parts, let the first
section be the longer of the two. [This makes sense, as] once
the people will have listened to the first part, it might be
455 especially burdensome and tiring for them if the second part
tends to be too long.

3) Within the sermon he ought to include traditional
interpretations,[71] *Notarikon* [acrostics, an interpretive device
whereby the letters of a word are made to stand for whole sen-
tences], actual incidents [which would serve as illustrations],
laws, biblical verses, rabbinic sayings, *Gematriot* [numerolo-
gies, the use of the numerical value of Hebrew words and the
search for possible connections with other words or phrases of
the same value], and some secular wisdom, for all of these
forms of knowledge are "auxiliaries of wisdom" (M. Avot
3:19).[72] If one's explanation [of a subject might tend to

---

[71] The idea here in the use of the word *masorah* seems to be that the *darshan* in
his *derashah* may veer from the *masorah* (traditional interpretation) to give a
ḥidush, but, nevertheless, somewhere ahead of time he should still give the traditional interpretation. Cf. l. 491 and l. 703.

[72] *Gematriot*, or *Gematria*, are an early method of interpretation, "not Kabbalistic in the strict sense of the word" (Scholem, *Major Trends in Jewish Mysticism* [New York, 1954], p. 100). The same applies to *Notarikon*. The term
Gematriot is mentioned in M. Avot 3:18. R. Johanan b. Zakkai is said to have
studied *Gematriot* among other methods of learning (Suk. 28a, B.B. 134a). From
M. Shek. 3:2 there is evidence that the numerical value of letters, both Hebrew
and Greek, was used in the Temple itself. *Gematria* appear in many *Midrashim.*
One of the best known is that cited by Rashi on Gen. 32:4, which was taken by
Moses ha-Darshan from *Gen. Rabbati,* 145. *Notarikon,* traced by some to Gen.
17:5 on the derivation of the name of Abraham, is found, together with *Gematria,*
in the *Baraita of 32 Rules,* or hermeneutical principles for interpreting Scripture
(nos. 29 and 30). Both methods assumed much wider usage and significance within *Kabbalah,* and *Gematria* especially became an essential means of proving Sabbatai Ẓevi's messianism. See Scholem, *Kabbalah,* pp. 337–343.

Nevertheless, the absence of *Kabbalah* per se from Zahalon's list of sources for
preaching would seem to be a conspicuous omission. Perhaps our author was

become] too complex, he may clarify it through the use of 460
an illustration. We find this done in rabbinic sources, and
especially in the incidents related in the *Torah, Prophets,* and
Writings [the three divisions of the Scriptures], as we have
mentioned above [2:12]. It is also a pleasing device to cite biblical verses or rabbinic sayings which [appear to] contradict
each other, to explain them, and then to reconcile [the apparent contradictions.] (Incidentally, please note what I shall
write at the end of this work concerning the length of the 465
sermon, or a hot spell [and how that ought to
affect a preacher's plans].[73]

4. Concerning the Order of the Sermon

1) One of the essentials of an effective sermon is that it have

trying to steer a very clear path away from more openly mystical interpretations.
If so, there were precedents for this. R. Leone da Modena stated, "I testify concerning myself that for 33 years in the holy work of preaching the word of the
Torah in a great Jewish city where I reside and in other principal holy congregations in Italy I have never quoted any of the divine wisdom and mysteries except
in bare outline" (*She'elot u-Teshuvot Ziqnei Yehudah,* ed. S. Simonsohn [Jeru-
salem, 1956], no. 55, pp. 76–78). Reflecting on his concern regarding *Kabbalah,*
da Modena states in the same responsum as to whether a preacher who teaches
Kabbalah in public should be silenced: we must first ask whether most of the *Kabbalah* we now have "deserves to be called 'the secrets of the *Torah*' and whether it
is permitted to study it even privately." An earlier precedent for Zahalon's omission of *Kabbalah* is cited by Werblowsky: "Karo's non-halakhic, homiletic
novellae, exactly like those of Joseph Taytazak, show no trace of kabbalistic
influence. . . . Karo excluded kabbalism from his public teaching and preaching
(*Joseph Karo: Laywer and Mystic* [Philadelphia, 1977], p. 145 and n. 4). That
Zahalon reflected this same approach to teaching *Kabbalah* publicly may also be
deduced from Chap. 2:11 of the *Or,* especially ll. 402–403. Cf. Intro., n. 110. Yet
see l. 225 of the *Or* (and n. 42) where he uses the kabbalistic term *tiqqun.* Cf.
Intro., pp. 39–43.

[73] See below ll. 588–596. Aside from l. 436 above there is no other mention of
hot weather. Zahalon was editing his own copy of the MS. in adding this sentence. It is written in the space between the chapters in a different handwriting.
Perhaps he intended to add further to his MS., but did not manage to do so.

a well-ordered quality [which is evident throughout. The sermon should appear] to proceed in a straight line, and if
occasionally the preacher veers from his subject, he should
470 immediately return to the original line of reasoning. Now if
you should happen to find an [interesting] interpretation of a
verse or saying, cite it quickly, making reference to the author,
even if it is not [immediately] relevant to your subject matter.[74]
Afterwards, explain this interpretation in its relationship to the
475 general order of your sermon. If it is properly arranged
[according to a clear plan, there is more of] a reason
for people to remember all of [your] sermon.

2) It is wise and appropriate to place one's best illustrations
at the beginning and at the end of the sermon.[75] Otherwise, if
you should put rather uninteresting and colorless material at
the beginning [of your sermon, your] listeners will assume that
480 such is indicative of your entire sermon. Then they might
become impatient and leave, or they might fall asleep. Likewise, it is advisable to place a very beautiful interpretation at
the end of the sermon in order that it should seem a pleasurable experience for the people to hear [all of your words]. This is
what those who plan banquets do at the end, namely, they
485 bring out sweet things [which have an especially pleasant
aroma] and "there is always room for a spicy dish"
(Erub. 82b).[76] In the middle [section of the sermon] you should
place the least attractive material, but you must limit [such

---

[74] R. Yedidiah Gottlieb (d. 1645) justified his long sermons by explaining that
he "at times spoke at length when he should have been brief" because he wanted
to provide the reader with additional explanations and innovative interpretations
"which have no direct need or relevance at all to the present matter" (*Ahavat
ha-Shem* [Cracow, 1641], p. 3a, as quoted in Ben-Sasson, p. 44). See my n. 114
below for Gottlieb's other reasons for lengthiness.

[75] See above, in n. 14, Messer Leon on *seder* and this same point.

[76] Rashi's explanation in Erub. 82b of this saying helps us to understand why
Zahalon quoted it as applying to pleasing examples which are used after most of
the sermon has come to an end. Said Rashi: "One's stomach can always make
additional room for something sweet."

content] in order that time will not be lacking afterwards for explanations, other fine points, and [interesting] new interpretations.

3) The order of things should be as follows: subject matter, 490 biblical verse, rabbinic saying, illustrative incident, traditional interpretation of the verse, *Notarikon,*[77] and a citation from secular wisdom. [Such order is essential] as it is not a pleasing style to lump all relevant verses together one after another, nor similarly to cite all rabbinic sayings together at once. At times it is [stylistically] a good practice to repeat the subject one 495 began with in every single section of the sermon. Occasionally, it is helpful to summarize briefly the views of the commentators, and afterwards [to give] one's own interpretation.

4) There are times when he should mention his proposition first, followed by the verse or saying which serves to substantiate it, especially when the proposition seems rather improbable. At other times he ought to quote the verse first and afterwards [indicate how it bears out] his proposition, 500 [especially] when it is not apparent from the plain meaning of the verse.

5) He ought to begin each verse or saying in a pleasant, imaginative manner and a suggestive, original touch in order 505 to awaken the interest of his listeners through his novel interpretation [of the subject], according to [the biblical example of] "they shall prepare that which they bring in" (Ex. 16:5), as that very suggestive device [will serve as] a preparation for the interpretation [which the preacher will use subsequently] and make it that much easier for it to be understood. 510

5. Concerning the Introduction of the Sermon

1. The introductory section of the sermon ought to be brief, for if it tends to be lengthy, then one's sermon [may possibly seem] like a man whose head is larger than his entire body. 515

---

[77] See above, n. 72.

136   GUIDE FOR PREACHERS

2) An introduction should be something novel and inventive which *appears* to be rather remote from the subject matter of the sermon.[78] [Only] after [thus arousing the attention of the listeners, the preacher] will attach it and integrate it properly with the [essential] theme of his sermon.

520   3) He should not explain verses or sayings at length in the introductory section in order that the introduction should not [appear to] be an entire sermon in itself. [Rather] it should be merely a beginning and a suggestion [of what he is going] to preach about.

4) In his introduction he should pray to the Lord for divine aid. He should in all humility and contrition with his heart and soul request permission to speak from the Holy One, praised
525 be He, from His holy *Torah,* and from the scholars and leaders of the day.[79]

[78] Messer Leon in his *Nofet Zufim* describes this hidden or indirect introduction in his seventh chapter. See above, n. 14. R. David Darshan had justified such a remote or distant way of approaching a subject among the various devices by which the preacher is able to reach his listeners (*Ketav Hitnazlut le-Darshanim* 4:2, as quoted in Ben-Sasson, *Hagut ve-Hanhagah,* pp. 42–43; cf. above, n. 47).

[79] R. Bahya b. Asher in his *Kad ha-Qemah* (a popular collection of sixty sermons alphabetically arranged on theological topics and specific commandments, written sometime after 1291 in Saragossa and published numerous times, including Constantinople, 1515, and Venice, 1545) explains in his chapter entitled *Reshut* (*Kitvei Rabbeinu Bahya* [Jerusalem, 1970], pp. 356–369, ed. C. B. Chavel) the background of this custom. Based on M. Avot 5:7, that "the wise man does not speak before one that is greater than he in wisdom," Bahya also proves this in many ways; e.g., (1) the priests, when they are giving their priestly blessing, "face the people and have their backs toward the Sanctuary," meaning that all the more so an Israelite "must today show respect and fear for the public by speaking before them only with their permission" (p. 359); (2) from Deut. 6:13, "Revere the Lord your God," R. Aqiba proved that we must have special reverence for the Sages (Pes. 22b), again requiring their permission, as well as that of the general public (p. 361); (3) preparation of what one is going to say, and brevity in saying it, as well as caution in one's words, are deduced from Eccles. 5:1 (pp. 362–363); (4) from Prov. 16:20 Bahya concludes that "a person [must] first contemplate [very carefully] the theme he wishes to speak about or the goal he wishes to accomplish and consider the ways by which he will succeed . . . [and] not rely

5) He ought to begin his sermon with words which are at
once clear and pleasant and attractive according to [the parti-

upon himself, but only upon God [in a sense, seeking His permission], to bring his
desired goal to complete success" (p. 363); (5) we learn the hesitation to speak
without first receiving permission from our listeners from David in Ps. 119:46 (p.
364); (6) silence is preferable to speaking in the presence of the great (i.e., any
congregation), as we learn from Prov. 25:6, though we must still speak out, for
the experience of doing so will also teach us any errors we may make, and, therefore, be instructive (pp. 364–365); (7) just as the High Priest could only enter the
Holy of Holies to ask atonement for all of Israel on Yom Kippur after many
preparations had been completed and, according to Lev. R. 21:8, with many different kinds of merit, "how much more does this principle apply to the common
people, devoid of wisdom, knowledge, and merit as they are, who desire to speak
before a large assembly . . . thus, with the permission of God, and with the permission of the wise men and those assembled here . . ." (pp. 368–369); (8) as
much as deference for the congregation is required, the preacher should learn
from Prov. 22:17, as explained in Hag. 15b, that one who teaches Scripture and
preaches in public is acting as a vehicle of God, as if he were Moses himself
(*Sifrei,* ed. Horowitz-Finkelstein, *Ekev,* p. 86). In this last comment, Baḥya urges
the *darshan* to be cognizant of his divine role and at the same time to show respect
for his listeners (cf. *Or,* Chap. 6:3, ll. 549–557). With all Baḥya's deference, he did
not hesitate to give strong reproofs, as is evident from his indictment of those who
fail to pay their taxes (in his sermon entitled *Gezeleh,* "Robbery"). We are not,
however, able to find any parallel to Zahalon's suggestion to ask permission of
the *Torah,* l. 524. Cf. the later parallel in R. Ezekial Landau of Prague
(1713–1793), who *did* ask for the consent in a *reshut* with which he was accustomed to begin his *derashot,* as Dr. Tovia Preschel notes in his "'*Reshut' Derashah,"* in *Sinai* LXXXIX (1981), 93–94. (Trans. of Baḥya based on *Encyclopedia
of Torah Thoughts* [New York, 1980], Eng. trans. of the *Kad ha-Qemaḥ,* pp.
562–584, "Deference to the Congregation One Addresses.") I am indebted to
Jack Nelson for his insights on Baḥya's view of *reshut.* Zahalon's advice concerning asking *reshut* is part of what was the *exordium* section of a sermon, or, as Bonfil describes it, "expressions of humility and apology along with aspects [leading
into] the main body of the sermon." He refers to Judah Moscato's *Nefuẓot Yehudah* (Venice, 1588) as an example of this classical form, and he includes among his
documents a sermon by R. Azriel Tarbut which illustrates a *darshan*'s deference
for his listeners (*Ha-Rabbanut be-Italia bi-Tekufat ha-Renaissance,* p. 194 and
290 [no. 64]). Nevertheless. see the *Or,* ll. 549–559, where Zahalon appears to
give the opposite kind of counsel to preachers. Obviously, the *reshut* sought by
the *darshan* was an important part of the introduction of the sermon and the state

cular standards of] the language [in which he is preaching].⁸⁰

6. Making [Effective] Use of One's Voice

530   1) When [the preacher] begins his subject, his first [rab-
binic] citation, or the sermon itself, instead of speaking at once
quite loudly, he should start off softly. He should use his
normal voice without any singsong quality. Likewise, in the
middle of the sermon, when he is reading verses or sayings, he
535 should do so naturally, just as he would speak with friends,
without any chant or melody. Chanting is appropriate with
prayers, not in a sermon.⁸¹

of mind of the preacher. From then on, he was to be as "bold as a leopard" (M.
Avot 5:20). Cf. I. Elbogen, *Ha-Tefillah be-Yisro'el* (trans. from the German by
Joshua Amir [Tel Aviv, 1972] from the Leipzig, 1913, 3d ed. of *Der Judische
Gottesdienst in seiner geschichtlichen Entwicklung*), p. 217, for his suggestion that
the *piyyutim* filled the same function in the synagogue as the *derashot*. The *paytan*
saw himself with the same spiritual responsibilities as the *darshan,* to enlighten the
people and give encouragement, and also to provide that which was innovative
and creative. Considering that the *piyyut* form known as *reshut* was so prevalent,
it may be that the use of that concept within sermons was borrowed from the
realm of the *paytanim*.

⁸⁰ See below, n. 114. It is my impression that Zahalon may have been referring
here to the need for avoiding the awkwardness of literal translations, not to mention their inaccuracy (cf. R. Judah's comment in Kid. 49a: "If one translates a
verse literally, he is a liar; if he adds to the meaning of the verse, he is guilty of
blasphemy"). But above all, the emphasis here is on *style* and proper usage. See
below, l. 592 and n. 92.

⁸¹ The reference here seems to be to the custom originating with the statement
in Meg. 32a, "R. Shefatiah said in the name of R. Joḥanan: 'If one reads the
Scripture without a melody (*ne'imah*) or repeats the *Mishnah* without a tune
(*zimra*), of him the Scripture says, "Wherefore I gave them statutes that were not
good" (Ezek. 20:25).'" *Tosafot* comments there, "they were accustomed to repeat
the *Mishnah* in a tune because they learned it by heart, and through the use of the
singsong method they were able to remember it better." This is an interesting
comment in the *Or* on what must have been one preaching style in Zahalon's day,
clearly *not* the one he recommended.

Israel Abrahams refers to the suggestions for studying made by Profiat Duran

2) He should vary the tone of his voice according to the subject matter, for he should not deliver his entire sermon in a monotone. For example, if he is relating the words of a king, 540 he should speak with an authoritarian manner, "for the rich answers impudently" (Prov. 18:23), as if he himself is the king commanding his people.[82] Yet if he is relating the words of the [common] people, he should speak plaintively, "for the poor uses entreaties" (*ibid.*), like a servant addressing the king. If he 545 is discussing a matter which might provoke worry and pain [on the part of his listeners], he should speak with a [sad and] subdued voice, even weeping as he speaks and with tears in his eyes. Yet if he is discussing a joyful matter, he should speak with [obvious] delight and a happy face.

3) [The preacher] should have absolutely no trepidation, but rather he should preach cheerfully, confident that his words 550 are [certainly] attractive and fitting and pleasant to his listeners. In this matter he should not be at all anxious but rather

to his Hebrew grammar (*Ma'aseh Efod* [Vienna, 1865], written in Spain in the fourteenth century) among which was that one should *sing* as he read the Bible, as had been done in earlier years with the *Mishnah* when it was studied (see Erub. 54a). The practice of singing during one's study, says Abrahams, "was common to Jews everywhere" (*Jewish Life in the Middle Ages* [Philadelphia, 1958], p. 355; cf. Steinschneider, *Jewish Literature,* p. 154). Also see Eccles. R. 7:3, describing the *meturgemanim,* or interpreters, who conveyed the words of *darshanim* in a singsong style to the congregation, which they did, according to R. Zev Wolf, Einhorn, in order to sweeten the otherwise strong reproofs (*Midrash Rabbah* [Vilna, 1853–1858], 19a).

Professor Jose Faur has confirmed in private conversation with this writer the custom still prevailing today among people educated in the traditional schools of the Ottoman Empire, of using a special *niggun,* or melody, in delivering regular *derashot,* as well as a distinctive *niggun* for eulogies. Sefardic congregations expect and enjoy this tradition, which can have a powerful emotional effect on the congregation. Dr. Faur believes that Zahalon here was attempting to discourage a very well entrenched custom, which appears to have survived his criticism. (Clearly, in Zahalon's day it was being practiced, or he would not have had to speak against it.)

[82] Cf. above, n. 14, on speaking authoritatively or plaintively.

"bold as a leopard" (M. Avot 5:20), for it is most essential in preaching to deliver his sermon enthusiastically, as if all of his words are indeed, "the words of the living God" (Jer. 23:36).[83]
555　There should be no fear of people [whatsoever].[84] At times he should speak with great vivacity, and afterwards he should read the verse or saying [a bit gently and] in a relaxed manner. Then once again he should resume the very lively delivery, depending upon the requirements of his subject matter.

　　　4) If a scholar or rabbi or important person [within the
560　community] should come [into the congregation] in the midst of his sermon, he should interrupt his speaking until the [prominent] person has taken his seat.[85] [He should do this both] out of respect for the Torah and [also out of consideration for] that important individual. [He should pause, too,] in order that his own voice not become drowned out by the voices of those acknowledging the [presence of this] person who has
565　just entered.

---

[83] Cf. Erub. 13b and Git. 6b, where the phrase is used in reference to the halakhic controversies of Beit Hillel and Beit Shammai. Cf. above, l. 312 and n. 53.

[84] The use of the term morat anashim here is reminiscent of Ber. 28b, where before his death R. Joḥanan b. Zakkai blesses his disciples with the blessing, "may your fear of the Lord be as great as your fear of human beings." Zahalon's use of the phrase may be influenced by the Shulḥan Arukh, Oraḥ Ḥayyim, 1:1, in the text and the notes of Isserles. The first words of the text are a reference to M. Avot 5:20 (to being strong as the lion rather than bold as the leopard, because R. Joseph Karo is interested in the strength required to get up in the morning rather than in the boldness, or azzut, required to speak publicly). Isserles explains how a person's constant awareness of the presence of God will cause him "not to be ashamed in the presence of people who ridicule him when he is engaged in the service of God."

[85] In the Midrash Moses interrupts in the middle of his teaching when Joshua enters as a special sign of respect, waiting until Joshua has taken his seat before resuming the lesson (Sifrei Num., Horowitz ed., p. 186). Aside from the honor due to entering dignitaries, it is clear from the context that Zahalon's advice here is very practical in enabling the darshan to deal sensibly with an interruption of his derashah.

5) He should take care not to squander his vocal power by straining his voice beyond its natural limits. Rather, he should raise his voice only according to its normal range and in keeping with the needs of his subject, as mentioned above. After [having raised his voice for effect,] he should then resume immediately his normal [speaking] voice.

7. The Preacher's Manner of Speaking   570

1) He should speak with ease, yet a definite dynamism, for if he should deliver his sermon in a sluggish manner, it will [only serve to] irritate his listeners. At times he should speak hurriedly,[86] as if he is uttering many [biblical] verses, novel interpretations, plain explanations and their implications,[87] all with apparent ease.   575

2) Whenever you quote from the *Torah, Prophets,* or rabbinic literature in order to prove a point, you should mention the names [of the illustrious biblical or rabbinic personages together] with words of praise and reverence. For example, one might say, "Did not that [ever-flowing] spring of wise utterances,[88] Solomon, may he rest in peace, say this . . . ?" Or, "the divine poet, King David, of blessed 580 memory," or, "the man of such rare patience, Job." Or, "the brightly shining sun, Maimonides."[89] Or, "the exalted

---

[86] The Hebrew reads, literally, "in one breath."

[87] *Inyanim* is translated "implications" instead of "context" or "matter," in accordance with its use in *Kuzari* 3:35 and *Moreh Nevukhim* I, 65. The other meanings would imply that the *darshan* was using too many subjects at once, thus violating Zahalon's own style.

[88] Cf. M. Avot 2:8, where R. Johanan b. Zakkai describes Eleazar b. Arakh as an "ever-flowing spring." Rashi quotes Sot. 13b in his comment on Deut. 31:2 on Moses as having "well-springs of wisdom closed up for him."

[89] *Encyclopaedia Judaica,* XI, 757, notes that in the *Megillat Zuta* Maimonides is called "the light of East and West and unique master and marvel of the generation."

dialectician, Naḥmanides." Or, "the very spiritually eminent[90] Rashi," etc.

3) When you are saying something which is obvious, well
585 known, and simple to understand, say it quickly. First, give the literal meaning of the verse directly, and then follow it with your own interpretation.

4) Be careful in your speaking that you are not at all repetitious.[91] Rather, you should speak with enthusiasm and without
590 excess verbiage, for "in the multitude of words, transgression is not lacking" (Prov. 10:19). Utter no words which are not straightforward, in good taste, and in proper usage of the language.[92] One should not multiply words without a [specific] purpose [in mind]. Now there are certain subjects [for which it is necessary] to bring a progression of sayings in order to cause the people to pay attention. Let him be sure that the people are
595 following his line of reasoning [closely, as he is in the process of quoting these various sayings,] and [let him also be certain] that they will easily grasp his words.

5) When he explains one verse with another, or one saying with a different saying, he should [take care to] discuss the second quotation very briefly, lest the people forget the first.
600 On the other hand, he should not spend too much time on any one verse or saying, for people are always eager to hear something new at every moment.

6) He ought to be careful if he says something which is a bit forced,[93] or [which brings to mind] a certain difficult question,
605 to preface his remarks by clearly indicating, "I have already

---

[90] Literally, "the spiritual eagle."

[91] Literally, "be careful in your speaking that you do not repeat [even] one word."

[92] Here again Zahalon expresses his concern for the *style* of the preacher's use of a particular language. Conveying important subjects succinctly with telling illustrations, etc., cannot be done effectively without sensitivity for the language and its proper usage. See above, l. 528 and n. 80.

[93] See above n. 60, and Intro., n. 110.

been aware of this difficulty, and it is possible to deal with it in such-and-such a way." In explaining a verse which consists of several parts, he should state in advance the [different] parts of the explanation [so that the people will know what to expect].[94]

8. Concerning the Preacher's Body Movements [or Gestures]

1) He ought to direct his glance in every direction in which 610 the people are standing,[95] and especially to where the scholars and community leaders are sitting.

2) He should be careful not to jump up or down or pound the rostrum,[96] nor to stand constantly in one fixed position like a tombstone. Rather, he should move about, gesturing with his 615 hands and arms, according to what might be appropriate for this subject matter.

3) If his words are [directed] to the Lord, then he should raise his head and eyes upwards towards God in heaven. If he

[94] Here, as in the previous sentence, Zahalon is suggesting that the *darshan* anticipate any difficulty his listeners might have, and share with them the outline of what he is about to explain when it is somewhat complex, or let them know of his own awareness of a difficulty and his personal attempt to grapple with it. Cf. n. 107 to l. 604 of the Heb. text for a possible comparison with the talmudic practice of noting a difficulty in advance of speaking about it.

[95] This would seem to be further clear evidence that the people *stood* while the *derashot* were being given, while the scholars and community leaders were given seats. See above, n. 70. The presence of many listeners standing would, it seems, make the *darshan* all the more anxious to speak as effectively as possible, that is, with brevity and directness. Besides, restlessness or mild annoyance with the speaker would be all the more noticeable in standees. Cf. below, n. 112, on R. Joseph Karo sitting while preaching.

[96] While Zahalon counseled dynamic preaching (see ll. 549–554, 571, 573), here he cautions against the *darshan*'s being overcome with emotion or being dynamic to a fault, as with these practices. Yet he does counsel continual movement and changing of one's position *behind* the rostrum, as he indicates immediately after this.

is reproving the people, he should lower his head, [focusing]
620 his eyes directly at the people themselves.[97]

9. What the Preacher Should Do Before He Goes Up to
Preach

1) After he has composed his sermon, and its written text is
before him, he should look it over carefully to be sure that it
625 has a well-ordered quality, as well as to improve upon any
particular interpretations, [being very certain] that they are as
completely appropriate as possible. Furthermore, if he comes
across something which is forced, he can either correct it or
delete it [altogether].[98]

[97] Zahalon's focus on the eye contact of the darshan with his congregation, the
felt presence of the preacher being a necessity for establishing rapport with his
people, particularly in the sensitive area of seeking to affect the lives and behavior
of those who are hearing words of reproof, recalls a similar statement of an earlier
darshan from Venice. Azariah Picho analyzed the unique impression made by the
preacher, which no written word can compare to, in a comment on Prov. 15:31 on
"the ear that hears the reproof of life": "He who hears from the mouth of the
teachers and reprovers who are living and moving about . . . [i.e.,] when to the
contents of the words themselves is added the power in the felt word both from
the sound of the pronunciation and from the motions and other aspects of the
darshan's presence, his words will be very much engraved on the hearts of his listeners, who will be moved by the words into action. Such words of admonishment
will accomplish great value . . . such a strong impression will not easily leave the
congregants" (Binah le-Ittim [Lemberg, 1797], II, Ser. 48, 16c, fifth sermon for
the second day of Shavu'ot).

[98] While Zahalon is offering some sound advice for his colleagues in the
preparation of their derashot, the fact that this is the third time he uses the term
dohaq, referring to a forced point or explanation (see ll. 362 and 603), might have
wider significance. If, for example, after much review the preacher improves upon
an interpretation, making it more na'eh (fitting, attractive, appropriate), it would
be much less likely that some bizarre, crude, or "unfitting" Sabbatian material
would be used (see Intro., n. 110, and cf. above in text, n. 60). His emphasis on
that which is fitting or attractive—found at least twenty-five times in the Or—
seems aimed at bringing about a responsible, thoughtful, careful method of
homiletics, in which much extravagant preaching would tend to be eliminated

2) He should try delivering his sermon in a small, quiet place with learned and perceptive friends present before he 630 delivers it publicly, as our Rabbis said, ["Every single statement which the Holy One, blessed be He, made to Moses, He said twice to himself and only then to Moses. What is the proof? 'Then did He see it, and declare it' (Job 28:27) denotes once;] 'He established it, yea, and searched it out' (*ibid.*) [denotes a second time, and then] 'and to man He said' (*ibid.,* 28) [which refers to Moses]" (Gen. R. 24:5).

3) If it is his custom to write out an outline of the structure of his sermon, he should write a very brief outline in order that 635 the sermon should not appear to his own eyes[99] to be too

(see Intro., n. 185). The reference in the following section to God Himself reviewing His words carefully before saying them to Moses, counsels responsible preaching in its own not so subtle way. (Zahalon could, in fact, have made an even stronger point by citing the view of R. Aḥa, instead of that of the Rabbis, who, in the same text in Gen. R., argued that God reviewed His words *four* times before saying them to Moses (cf. Yal. II, 916, 508a, and Baḥya b. Asher's emphasis on preparation, above n. 79, 3).

Obviously, many *darshanim* did not have any written text or outline in front of them when they preached. So popular a preacher as R. Moses Alshekh (1520–ca. 1600) preached regularly for years in Safed extemporaneously on the Sabbath after having spent time studying the weekly portion on Fridays, and large numbers of people flocked to hear him. He did record his sermons after the Sabbath. Sh. Shalem in his *Rabbi Moshe Alshekh* (Jerusalem, 1966) describes the mystical preacher's practice, pp. 23, 28, and 39, which, after due preparation on Fridays, seemed to rely heavily on divine inspiration (see p. 28). Zahalon must have been aware of such successful extemporaneous *darshanim,* but his advice is more conservative for the average preacher, who, he thought, required a carefully worked written text.

[99] The actual Hebrew here in ll. 636–637 is in the second person, reading, "that it should not appear to your eyes . . ." Zahalon has changed from having used the third person in ll. 634–635. It is uncharacteristic of his writing style. We might imagine that he is pointing his finger, as it were, at the individual *darshan* and cautioning him to make a preliminary outline of his sermon in order to determine the length in advance by this device. The jarring effect of the second person is to make the *darshan* self-critical. Considering that this is already the sixth reference to the danger of making the sermon or its parts too long, one would assume

lengthy and [that he can, through that outline,] exercise
caution [against the danger] of irritating the people, [by giving
too long a sermon].[100]

4) He should take care before he delivers his sermon publicly to review all of the verses and sayings and not to rely [solely]
640 on his memory. [Otherwise,] perhaps he will err in the interpretation of a verse, [in the event that] his sermon is [partly] based
on [a certain word in that verse], and [it could be that] that
specific word may not be found in the actual verse.[101]

5) It is a very [good practice] to see first of all what the
[classical] commentators have said concerning a verse or say-
645 ing, for they invariably will reveal to you the [essential] truth
contained in the verse or saying, and they will also point the
way for you to give [your own] new interpretation.

10. The Preacher's [Objective] Purpose and His [Private]
Intentions Concerning His Sermons

650   1) The objective and intention of the preacher should be to

that Zahalon's direct approach to the *darshan* is due to excessive wordiness being,
in his mind, the most common pitfall of the preacher (see 1:2; 2:5, 7; and 3:1,
where there are two warnings).

[100] Zahalon leaves the matter of the outline to the particular custom of the
individual *darshan,* but he was very explicit earlier about the need for a prepared
text, ll. 623–628. Such a prepared written version might be good insurance
against too long a sermon, with or without an outline. He also appears to assume
that even with the fullest preparation in advance, the *darshan* will add other
material extemporaneously. Hence his counsel to "write down his entire sermon
plainly [and fully]" after preaching, ll. 738–739.

[101] Zahalon's advice here, to check one's sources carefully in order not to err
by placing too much reliance on one's memory (cf. above, n. 52), as well as his
counsel in ll. 643–646, to review ahead of time all the classical commentators who
will "invariably reveal ... the [essential] truth," would seem to be further
thoughtful restraints with which to enable preachers to curb some of the excesses
they might otherwise be given to.

refine the people and to draw them ever closer to the service of the Lord. [At the same time it is] to draw them away from transgressions and to teach them the *Torah* of the Lord, all for the sake of heaven, and not for [the preacher's] own glorification or to show off his intellect.[102]

2) Whenever he is reproving [the people,] he should indicate to them that he is [at the very same time] chastising himself.[103] He ought to speak with respect for the people, never 655 in a contemptuous or insulting manner if there [happen to be some who are known to] be wrongdoers present. That which our Rabbis, of blessed memory, have said concerning Moses, who was punished for having said, "Hear now, you rebels" (Num. 20:10), and concerning Isaiah, who said, "and in the midst of a people of unclean lips I dwell" (6:5), and Elijah, who 660 said, "for the people of Israel have forsaken your covenant" (1 Kings 19:10), is surely familiar [to you]. So, [too,] if there is one individual present who has committed a grievous sin which is generally known about, [the preacher] should not

[102]The original text of l. 651 was, it seems, as we have translated V. note to Hebrew text. Cf. Deut. R. 7:5, where Moses is praised for having "brought closer those who are distant." R. David Darshan, in his *Ketav Hitnazlut le-Darshanim* (Lublin, 1574), had written that "the ways of sermons, which are principally strong admonitions for the masses of the people are to *draw near* [or encourage] that which is fine and to *make distant* [or discourage] that which is ugly" in Jewish life (par. 4, see my Intro., n. 261, italics added). Even earlier, after 1455, the Spanish philosopher Joseph Ibn Shem Tov had defined the purpose of the sermon from the point of view of the listeners as well as the preacher as "to remove spiritual ills from the souls of the people and guard their [spiritual] health" (*Ein ha-Kore*, p. 92b, and see p. 102b). See Intro., n. 261, and *Or*, ll. 260–263, and n. 45. The phrase *le-harot hakhmato* ("to show off his intellect") in l. 653 also appears earlier in ll. 304–305 concerning the choice of a sermon topic, which Zahalon urges be something with *to'elet* ("value"), l. 303.

[103] Azariah, Picho, in his *Binah le-Ittim*, II (Lemberg ed., 1797), ser. 66, 40d wrote that his sermons were addressed to himself. "How can I open my mouth in words of *tokheha* which I am personally, doubly, and many times more in need of?" See above, intro, n. 261 on Ben Bassa.

chastise him publicly but rather only when the two of them are alone.[104]

665   3) He should be extremely careful to avoid preaching in such a way as to rebuke or shame others—God forbid—for it is not right "to make unworthy use of the crown" of *Torah* (M. Avot 1:13) to take vengeance against one's enemies. Rather, in his reproofs [the preacher] should speak pleasantly and not in a harsh manner, or in a haughty way, but [acting] as a father who is [lovingly] chastising his own children. [Concerning this]

670   our Rabbis, of blessed memory, have said, "I wonder if there is one in this generation who is worthy enough to reprove!" (Ar. 16b).[105] Also, "let a person adorn himself in that matter that he

---

[104] This entire last sentence is found only in the Cas. MS. and was written in the margin by the author, apparently as a later refinement of his thinking. The sentence was obviously not in the MS. at the time that the Oxford and JTS MSS. were copied.

[105] The actual quotation by R. Eleazar b. Azariah is, "I wonder if there is one in this generation who knows how to reprove!" Rabbi Judah Loew of Prague (1512–1609) wrote of the difficulty of admonishing properly in his *Netivot Olam* (Prague, 1596): "Great wisdom is needed to reprove a person so that he will accept the admonition of the person reproving him. The wrongdoer is drawn to wrongdoing, and if one wishes to release him from what he has done, he needs great wisdom to speak to him pleasantly and sensibly until the words will enter his heart. Similarly, to influence him not to do what it is improper to do, one needs words of sense, words of truth which enter the heart, which break through the hardness of the heart. . . . At the present time in these countries those who preach to the public interpret biblical verses as well as statements of the sages in a manner that distorts their meaning. . . . Their only objective is to show the uninformed public that they are innovators in the teaching of the *Torah*. They claim that if they did not act thus, in what way would we add new elements beyond what other people know. . . But will people accept such pronouncements? Falsehood is without cogency. They will say, these words are not wisdom but the contrivances of his own heart. If a preacher delivered such discourse without proof texts it would be preferable, since the people would then regard them as the preacher's own teaching" (Netiv 17a, *Tokheḥa* 3, trans. by B. Z. Bokser in *Rabbinical Assembly Proceedings*, XL [1978], 134–135). Zahalon in the *Or* cautions against allowing explanations of a text to obfuscate the true message of the *darshan* (Chap. 2:8, ll. 361–373). See above, n. 74, R. Yedidiah Gottlieb's point of view in marked contrast to the advice of R. Judah Loew.

would seek to adorn others" (B.M. 107b), as our Rabbis, of blessed memory, have interpreted, "Gather yourselves together, yea, gather" (Zeph. 2:1).[106] [Further, concerning the opposite extreme, the preacher] may praise the rest of the scholars present along with his friends, but he should praise 675 them very briefly in their presence in order that he should not appear to be a flatterer.[107]

4) When he is ready to begin the sermon he should pray to the Holy One, praised be He, with all his heart and soul that He help him in delivering the sermon, that he may bring "from potentiality to actuality" (Maimonides, *Moreh Nevukhim,* II, 18, Ibn Tibbon trans.) that which he wants to say in order that [the sermon might] earn him approval and a sympathetic 680 response before the Lord as well as with his congregants, that his words should be acceptable, heeded, and acted upon. [He should pray, too,] that he will not have exerted himself [in preparing and delivering the sermon] "in vain and to no purpose" (Isa. 30:7). [He should seek divine aid] that he may concentrate on the good purpose [of his sermonizing efforts, namely,] to reconcile the people with the Almighty, that they 685 should perform good deeds and that all who have sinned should repent. [Thereby, he prays] that he should become one who "preaches well and acts well" (Ḥag. 14b).[108] I

---

[106] The wording in B.M. 107b by Resh Laqish is, "First, adorn yourself, and then adorn others." It is also found in B.B. 60b; Sanh. 18a, 19a; and Yal. II, 302, 825b. The root *q-sh-sh* ("gather") is connected with *q-sh-t* ("adorn"). The meaning is: adorn, or *reprove,* yourselves first. Later, reprove others. See "Prayer for One Who Preaches Publicly," *Margaliot Tovot,* 4a and note.

[107] Just as one may go too far in admonishing one's enemies, abusing his position as *darshan* and teacher of *Torah,* so he may go too far in the other direction, by praising his friends and scholars who are present, thus appearing to be false. In Sot. 41b and 42a, there are several warnings against flattery.

[108] This is a part of the compliment paid by R. Joḥanan b. Zakkai to R. Eleazar b. Arakh, *viz.,* "There are some who preach well but do not act well, others act well but do not preach well, but you preach well and act well." Cf. below, "Prayer for Preachers," Appendix C, 4a.

have already written in my book *Margaliot Tovot* a lovely prayer which would be appropriate for one who preaches [regularly] to recite.[109]

690 11. How to Conclude and Complete the Sermon

1) When he completes his sermon, he should not end it off with [an apparent] slackening of ardor. On the contrary, he should place at the end an even more attractive explanation and novel interpretation than any he has included thus far in the sermon. He ought to conclude either with a prayer that the Lord may cause his listeners to take his words to heart, or with 695 a plea to the people that they should fulfill the words of the Lord, and of His Prophets and Sages.

2) He should always place at the end of the sermon a verse of comfort and redemption for Israel, which gives promise of future salvation [for the Jewish people].

700   3) At times [it is good] toward the end to review the sermon briefly and only indirectly in order to remind [one's listeners of its salient points] in a rather cursory way.

4) At the end of his sermon he ought to quote a [biblical] verse or [rabbinic] saying or teaching [from the Jewish tradition], in which are clearly included, or from which may be deduced, all the parts of the sermon in order that it remain 705 [vividly] in the memory [of those assembled].[110]

[109] Although his use of the word *na'eh* in describing the prayer for preachers might sound as if Zahalon is praising his own work, it may be, rather, that he regarded his prayer as a conglomeration of biblical and rabbinic quotations and prayers. Zahalon's attitude about his work, as seen in the introduction to the *Or,* seems rather modest and unassuming; see ll. 190–193. Cf. Intro., p. 26 and n. 58.

[110] Baḥya, in his *Ḥovot ha-Levavot,* includes at the end of his work ten Hebrew couplets, each with the theme of one chapter. "I am ending this book of mine with them, in order that they be for you a reminder, so that once you know them by heart, and keep them in your mind and thought, day and night . . . you will think of the contents of this book and will remember its principles" (Ibn Tibbon trans., A. Ẕifroni ed. [Tel Aviv, 1959], p. 582). Cf. above, notes 14 and 34.

5) If he is going to preach another sermon not long after this one, it would be a good idea, and quite proper for him, to invite the people in a pleasant way to come and hear his second sermon, the subject matter of which he should also indicate.   710

12. Concerning the Personal Health of the Preacher

1) The preacher should be very careful during the time which precedes [the delivery of] the sermon not to overtax either his body, his mind, or his heart. He should not go for a walk in the marketplace [at this time],[111] or ponder [excessive- 715 ly] over a matter which grieves and disturbs him.

2) He should not eat that which would be difficult to digest [and cause him discomfort. For example,] he should not eat olives, nuts, or salty foods, or cheese or legumes, for all of these [foods] are [rather] harsh and harmful to the voice, and 720 even tend to restrict [free] movement of the lips and the tongue.

3) He should drink a little fine, unadulterated wine, which [tends to] induce a pleasant mood and [also] strengthens the voice and the body organs. He should eat sparingly only that which is easy to digest, which strengthens his heart and mind, and [foods which at the same time] are healthful for the throat, the chest, and the stomach.   725

4) After he has finished preaching, he should go immediate-ly to rest on his bed.[112] He should drink a little fine wine or

---

[111] Literally, "go for a walk in the marketplace at night."

[112] The *darshan* that Zahalon was describing delivered his sermons indepen-dently of the synagogue service, which was the common practice. The late Dr. Cecil Roth in a letter to this writer on February 20, 1970, wrote: "Of course, the sermon was then not an exhortatory interlude in the Sabbath morning service, but a two-hour set piece in the late morning or early afternoon." Cf. his book, *The Jews in the Renaissance* (Philadelphia, 1959), pp. 35–36, where he adds addi-tional interesting details about Jewish preaching in Renaissance Italy, which he

chicken soup,[113] and, after an hour or two, he could eat a full meal.

730 13. What He Should Do After He Has Finished Preaching His Sermon

1) After he has preached, he should ask a certain trusted friend to tell him truthfully, if he [happened to] err in any of the matters mentioned [in his sermon]. In this way he will be 735 able to improve [his preaching skill] for the future, for "a man may examine all leprosy signs except his own" (M. Neg. 2:5), [i.e., one cannot be objective about his own imperfections].

calls "the golden age of the Italian sermon." From what we know, sermons in Zahalon's time had generally lost much of this high esteem. In his letter, referred to above, Roth added that in Zahalon's day the ghetto of Rome "was in a period of full decadence." Werblowsky, in his biography of R. Joseph Karo, quotes from a Yemenite traveler, Al-Dahari, who witnessed the academy of Karo on the Sabbath, when about two hundred students would come to his *derashot* during the afternoons (R. J. Zwi Werblowsky, *Joseph Karo: Lawyer and Mystic* [Philadelphia, 1977], p. 140, and see A. Yaari, *Masa'ot Yisro'el* [Tel Aviv, 1945–1946], Chap. 13). Al-Dahari describes how the elderly Karo would sit on a chair and preach to the assembled students, sitting on benches. When Karo had finished his words, he would motion to one of the students sitting opposite him to stand and speak, extemporaneously repeating some of the lessons Karo himself had taught (*Sefer ha-Musar,* ed. Y. Retzahabi [Jerusalem, 1965], pp. 116–117). Two hours was considered a justifiable length for a sermon before Pope Sixtus IV "provided that the preacher had something truly original to say," according to O'Malley, who in this case was describing a particular sermon by an outstanding preacher on Good Friday, 1481. This was obviously the exception, however. Pope Leo X ruled in 1514 that sermons in the papal court should not exceed a half-hour. Yet O'Malley reports that during the following three years Leo came to adopt a stronger position regarding sermon length, "seemingly in consultation with the cardinals," fixing on a limit of fifteen minutes. "The idea may have been to aim for fifteen minutes," he adds, "in the hope of actually containing the sermon within a half-hour" (*Praise and Blame in Renaissance Rome,* p. 23, and cf. p. 27 on the "notoriously prolix" sermons of Giles of Viterbo; see above, n. 68).

[113] Intro., pp. 57–58.

2) He should write down his entire sermon very plainly
[and fully]¹¹⁴ in order that it should be of use to him in his old

¹¹⁴ *Be-biur,* or "very plainly," as in Deut. 27:8, where the use of the root *b-a-r*
is similar, i.e., writing down and recording *after the event* as a clear record. (It is
interesting that the English "to bare" all the facts has the same sense, i.e., to
reveal the *full* story, to leave nothing to interpretation if at all possible.) Bonfil
notes the short, dry, schematic quality of most of the medieval Hebrew sermons
which have come down to us up to the second half of the sixteenth century.
Totally lacking in relevance to the specific events and circumstances of the periods in which they had been delivered, they are, he maintains, positive proof that
what we have in these sermons is not the actual sermons as preached, but notes
written after the fact. If we were to accept these written sermons as the actual
form of the original live *derashot,* we would have to assume, based on their
length, that they lasted no more than five minutes! This we know was certainly
not the case. Besides, since most of the sermons were given on the Sabbath or
Festivals, they had to be written down later on the basis of memory, not beforehand in notes. Further, we know that during the entire Renaissance and afterwards in Italy sermons were given in the vernacular, as they were in the non-
Jewish world, and not in Hebrew or in Latin (see above, my n. 39 on da Modena's
detailed account). Cf. above in the *Or,* 5:5 and 3, 11. 591–592. This, too, provides
additional proof that the records of Renaissance Hebrew sermons in our possession are not at all transcripts of what the *darshanim* actually spoke (*Ha-Rabbanut
be-Italia bi-Tekufat ha-Renaissance,* p. 193 and especially n. 141 for additional
sources and facts about recording sermons). In contrast, according to Ben-
Sasson, in Poland at the end of the Middle Ages those sermons originally
delivered in Yiddish spiced with Hebrew and Aramaic, when later written down
completely in Hebrew, were *expanded* to include additional citations. Ben-Sasson
maintains that there was, nevertheless, basic similarity between the content of the
sermon as delivered and as later written down with very few differences (*Hagut
ve-Hanhagah,* pp. 39–40). Some preachers, such as Yedidiah Gottlieb, who lived
in Poland in the first half of the seventeenth century, included many frankly
irrelevant interpretations in their printed sermons—apparently a common practice—for three reasons: (a) he wanted to provide additional sources for the reader
whose library may have been limited and for whom these interpretations would
have been otherwise inaccessible; (b) he might have no other opportunity to publish his new explanations; and (c) he simply did not want to allow his innovations
on biblical and rabbinic texts to be hidden and, therefore, unknown to the general
public (*Ahavat Ha-Shem* [Cracow, 1641], p. 3a, as quoted in Ben-Sasson, p. 44,
and see above, my n. 74). Werblowsky notes that Joseph Karo would preach on

age or to those who come after him, such as his children or
740   students, as Job said, "Oh that my words were now written!
Oh that they were inscribed in a book! That with an iron pen
and lead they were graven in the rock forever!" (19:23–24).

3) He should give thanks to and praise the Holy One, praised
be He, "that he had come forth from the sanctuary in peace"
745   (M. Yoma 7:4).[115] He should not take pride in his wisdom, but
rather he should think that "the Lord gives wisdom, out of His
mouth comes knowledge and discernment" (Prov. 2:6) and
"the Lord was pleased, for His righteousness' sake, to magnify
the *Torah,* and make it glorious" (Isa. 42:21). And may that
750   day come soon about which it is written, "And all your children shall be taught of the Lord; and great shall be the peace of
your children" (*ibid.,* 54:13). And for the completion of the
holy work written above I shall explain, with the help of the

Sabbath afternoons and then write down the *derashot* Saturday evening after sun-
down (*Joseph Karo: Lawyer and Mystic,* p. 146, n. 4, and cf. above, n. 112). R.
Moses Alshekh followed a similar practice, studying the weekly portion of the
Bible carefully on Fridays, preaching extemporaneously on the Sabbath, and
writing down his sermons after the Sabbath (Sh. Shalem, *Rabbi Moshe Alshekh*
[Jerusalem, 1966], p. 28), and see above, my notes 98 and 100.

[115] Zahalon uses a phrase out of the *Mishnah* which described the moment
when the High Priest took leave of the Holy Temple after the completion of his
special duties on *Yom Kippur.* Although we cannot attach too much significance
to this use of a mere phrase from that context, it is interesting to note that
Zahalon associates the delivery of the *derashah* with the extremely sacred tasks of
the High Priest. The sermon was not given in the midst of a worship service,
though it was surely regarded as a holy occasion; cf. n. 112. Perhaps Zahalon was
also attracted to this source in the *Mishnah* by the drama and adulation surrounding the *Kohen Gadol,* who had just completed a sacred task with which much
preparation and anticipation were associated. The entire congregation em-
pathized with him in his efforts on their behalf. Other priests ministered to him
with deep respect. As the same *Mishnah* tells us, "they would accompany him to
his house. He would arrange for a day of festivity for his friends whenever he had
come forth from the sanctuary in peace." The completion of a moving sermon
might have had a similarly dramatic conclusion.

Lord, the verses, "The Lord God has given me the tongue of them that are taught, etc." (*ibid.,* 50:4), and the verse, "Cry aloud, spare not, lift up your voice like a horn, etc." (*ibid.,* 58:1), which are proof texts for what is written above.[116]

[116] Here the author has deleted a Hebrew abbreviation which stands for "finished and completed, praised be the Lord, creator of the universe!" The fact that this common inscription at the end of a religious book is crossed out would appear to indicate that Zahalon had not completed what he intended to write. Perhaps he had meant to explain Isa. 50:4 and 58:1 in some detail. He did make use of the former verse in his prayer for *darshanim.* Yet there is another more plausible explanation: the last lines here, ll. 751–756, found only in the Cas. MS., and written apparently by the author himself later on, may represent Zahalon's effort to follow his own advice in Chap. 11:4. He may have wanted to leave his readers with two verses in Isa. which would sum up much of what he had written and serve as a mnemonic for them. Isa. 50:4, referring to the *training* of the tongue, sums up much of the educational, religious, and spiritual purpose of the *Or.* The latter verse, alluding to getting one's message across in a dynamic, clear, and effective way, reminds us very succinctly of some of the technical lessons on elocution which the *Or* teaches. On that verse, 58:1, v. Marc Saperstein's article "Your Voice Like a Shofar" in *Conservative Judaism* XXXVIII (1985), 83–90 and his forthcoming book on the history of Jewish preaching in the Yale Judaica Series.

755

751

Appendix A

English Translation of Israel Foa's *Haskamah* to the Casanatense Manuscript of the *Or ha-Darshanim*.

[Page one]

PRAISE AND COMMENDATION OF THE COMPOSITIONS
AND BOOKS [COMPOSED] BY OUR HONORED MASTER
AND TEACHER JACOB ZAHALON, MAY HIS ROCK AND
REDEEMER WATCH OVER HIM, BY THE JERUSALEM
SCHOLAR, OUR HONORED MASTER AND TEACHER,
ISRAEL FOA, MAY THE ALL-MERCIFUL PROTECT AND
REDEEM HIM.[1]

Inasmuch as we are privileged to [be able to hold] this great book
in our hands [and examine it], let us say about it, "a garment is
precious to its wearer" (Shab. 10b), [i.e., a student likes to quote
the works of his teacher]. [I refer to] a precious gem of inestimable
value, [my teacher, who is a] superior source of light "who enlight-
ens the earth and all who dwell thereon."[2] As is its name, so is it, *A
Light for Preachers.* Although "for Moses it may have seemed like
a small thing" (Ber. 33b), he who is our master and teacher, the

---

[1] These words have been written in at the top of the page above the *haskamah*
apparently by the author of the *Or* in the Cas. MS. At the
same time, in the right-hand corner, has been added: "This is not to be printed
here," referring to all of the words of Israel Foa. In keeping with
the instructions, two vertical lines have been drawn through the entire body of the
haskamah on each of the two pages.

[2] Baer, *Avodat Yisro'el,* p. 76. Foa refers to Zahalon here as his teacher.

159

rabbi who wrote this work, has the *Sifrei,* the *Sifra,* and the *Beraita* very clearly in his mind. He constantly occupies himself with the study of *Torah,* understanding the different points of view between one *Mishnah* and another, making refutations in the discussions of the *Talmud,* learning always with [the utmost] clarity.[3] He decides a tradition according to the *halakhah,* as his valuable compositions prove—those great lights which shine and glow and illuminate as the sun or the moon in its newness, not in any general sense, but very specifically [in the genuine aid that they provide for scholars.

For example,] his work *Morashah Qehilat Ya'aqov* on the Rambam, whose words should not be as laws without [proper] explanations, but rather having an "improved taste"[4] [as a result of Zahalon's explanations of them]. It is our duty to praise[5] this "Jacob as a mild man, who dwelled in tents" (Gen. 25:27), "set aside for jubilation" (Lev. 19:24), one who "expounds[6] upon each smallest part of the Hebrew letters of the *Torah* heaps and heaps" (Men. 29b) of specific applications and general rules—such is his work [entitled] *Titen Emet le-Ya'aqov.* [In it] one can recognize words of truth.[7] "The *Torah* of truth was in his mouth" (see Mal. 2:6) concerning all of the weekly *Parshiot* "sought out[8] by all who desire them" (Ps. 111:2). [Zahalon] "would not stir from out of the tent" (Ex.

---

[3] Cf. Git. 70b, Yeb. 113a.

[4] Cf. A.Z. 39b.

[5] Baer, *Avodat Yisro'el,* p. 131.

[6] Foa intends a play on words here, as Dr. Jose Faur has explained to this writer, and this is indicated by the use of two small dots on top of the word or name. Foa calls our attention through this Sefardic custom to his using the word *doresh* as a pun, meaning both "expound" and "preach." We have indicated the marks in our Hebrew text of the *haskamah* in every instance that Foa has used them. Cf. *Or,* l. 16, where Zahalon used the same play on words, but without the markings on any of the MSS.

[7] Cf. Eccles. 12:10.

[8] Here again, as shown in n. 6 above, Foa uses the root *d-r-sh* to refer to the preacher's art.

33:11)—so is [his work entitled] *Ohalei Ya'aqov,*[9] an extremely valuable [work which] contains all the various forms of wisdom. The divine spirit has truly revealed itself in the "tents of Jacob" (Jer. 30:18).[10] [We might say that] a learned scholar is superior to a prophet[11] in explaining the words of Isaiah the prophet. [I refer here to Zahalon's work] entitled *Yeshu'ot Ya'aqov.*

May the Lord save him, and may God bless Jacob[12] with children, with a long life, with [good] sustenance, and with precious pearls,[13] [dealing kindly with him] "in the same measure as he has dealt kindly with us" (M. Sot. 1:7). His work *Margaliot Tovot* is an abbreviated version of

[Page two]

the *Hovot ha-Levavot.* Our author is, [indeed, a man with] a pure heart who, out of a heartfelt [sense of] duty,[14] "undertakes the task" (Ex. 36:2) to publish this great light.[15] It is a [virtual] necessity for preachers, as is well known to anyone who researches and takes pains with his sermons. How very much of his time[16] is needed just to find even one rabbinic saying, and before long an entire day is gone. [Furthermore,] even after all the effort and trouble [one might have taken to find a rabbinic source,] he [still] might not [be able to] locate it. Therefore, "everyone depends on the owners of wheat" (Ber. 64a),[17] [i.e., everyone is dependent

---

[9] The original title of the *Ozar.* Cf. Intro., n. 132.

[10] This is the exact translation of the work just cited, *Ohalei Ya'aqov.*

[11] Cf. Meg. 3a.

[12] Cf. Gen. 35:9.

[13] An allusion here to the work *Margaliot Tovot,* which Foa is about to cite.

[14] Here he uses the words of the title *Hovot ha-Levavot* literally to describe Zahalon's motivation in seeking to publish the *Or.*

[15] An allusion to the *Or.*

[16] Cf. Est. 9:27, 31, where these words are found.

[17] The meaning of the metaphor is this: sound learning is the bread, while dialectics and homiletics are but the spices and less essential ingredients.

upon the true scholars of *Torah* like Zahalon for such a resource as this in composing their sermons]. He is an honored physician,[18] an outstanding one, who includes all branches of wisdom [within the framework of his learning. This work is but one of] the "fruits of the goodly tree" (Lev. 23:40) [of his vast erudition]. "May You be exalted above the heavens" (Ps. 57:12; 108:6), Lord, who has created Your world the way You have, in which "everything has been created as a staff in the service of each [human being]" (Ber. 6b). Further, if I were not afraid of being among those who unwisely attempt to complete all Your praises,[19] I would finish praising [Zahalon].[20]

So said by one who stands in awe of and has compassion for rabbis and their students. "Such knowledge is too wonderful for me,"[21] who have not even reached [the step of becoming] a teacher, but who is the servant of the Almighty, laden with trouble, in need of healing.[22]

Israel Foa
Servant of the All-merciful
From the holy city of Israel
Jerusalem may it be rebuilt and reestablished beautifully
Spoken in his time
Spoken by the dust[23] of the oven[24]
Ready is he *Y-F-H*

[18] Cf. T.J. Tan. 3:66d.

[19] Cf. Ber. 33b. The reference is to those who seek to encompass all of God's praises by endless adjectives.

[20] Foa clearly means that there is much more he could add about Zahalon if it were not in bad taste to do so.

[21] Cf. Ps. 139:6.

[22] Foa may or may not have been ill, but he means here, as he indicates by the dots over *li-refuah,* to refer to Zahalon, who was also a physician.

[23] A reference to the abbreviation below, *A-F-R.*

[24] An expression indicating Foa's humility in the presence of Zahalon and referring to abbreviation below, *K-Y-R-H.*

Jerusalem—may it be rebuilt and reestablished
The little one from the city of Jerusalem
Explanation of abbreviations:
A-F-R (literally meaning "dust")—I am the poor Foa[25]
K-Y-R-H (literally, "oven")—I have written may these words find favor
Y-F-T—Israel Foa a resident
Y-F-H—Israel Foa the speaker of these words

If it were possible to write some cheerful words about this holy man, the author who is so very good humored in this world [and deserves to be cheerful] in the next [world, I would say,] as is his name (Zahalon), so is he for "rejoicing[26] and for joy" (Est. 8:15).

[25] Using *Notarikon* here, Foa explains the word *A-F-R* to stand for the words after it, as he does in the later lines. Cf. n. 72, English translation of *Or*.

[26] The Hebrew root of this word is the same as Zahalon's name, *z-h-l*. See Intro., pp. 90–91.

Appendix B

Prayer for One Who Preaches Publicly or for a Head of a *Yeshiva*
[From the *Margaliot Tovot* (Venice, 1665), pp. 3a–5a.]

[3a]

"Lord, open my lips and my mouth shall declare your praise" (Ps. 51:17).

You are the Lord God who "is great and whose name is great in might" (Jer. 10:6), "the God great, mighty, awesome" (Deut. 10:17), "great in counsel and mighty in deed; whose eyes are open to all the ways of men" (Jer. 32:19). "From [Your] dwelling-place [You] gaze on all the inhabitants of the earth. [You who] fashion the hearts of them all, who discern all their doings" (Ps. 33:14–15), [You] nourish and sustain all, "from the horns of wild oxen" (*ibid.,* 22:22) to the eggs of gnats. "The eyes of all look to You, and You give them their food in due season" (*ibid.,* 145:15), according to the needs of each individual creature. Your providence is revealed and widely known in the eyes of all Your creatures both collectively and individually. Prominent over the work of Your hands is man, whom "You visit every morning and test every moment" (Job. 7:18). You see his ways, and You count each of his footsteps. "I had heard of You by the hearing of the ear, but now my eyes see You" (*ibid.,* 42:5). You have watched over every individual [person, even as You watch over] every insect and worm, every passing shadow and fading blossom, every grain of dust and ashes, even as I myself am, dealing kindly with me in lifting me up from the dust and from the dunghills "to make me sit with princes, with the

167

princes of Your people" (Ps. 113:8). You "have exalted one chosen out of the people" (*ibid.*, 89:20), and "from following the ewes that give suck" You have brought me "to be shepherd over Jacob [Your] people and Israel [Your] inheritance" (*ibid.*, 78:71). Now "what shall I render to the Lord for all Your bounty to me?" (*ibid.*, 116:12). "Were my mouth filled with song like the sea," etc., I would still "be inadequate to thank You, etc." (cf. Baer, *Avodat Yisro'el*, pp. 206–207). "Therefore, I have put my hand on my mouth" (Job 40:4) because "for You silence is praise" (Ps. 65:2, as in Meg. 18a). Because Your acts of grace are truly gracious, and because those with whom You have been merciful have indeed known Your compassion, therefore, with that talent for which I am not deserving, do I beseech You. [I] pray that You will answer my prayer and that You will listen to my petition as You [in the past] accepted the prayers of Solomon, Your servant, when You appeared to him in a dream. You said to him, "Ask what I shall give you" (I Kings 3:5), and You were gracious to him concerning what he asked and what he did not ask.

[3b]

Be gracious also to me, my Father: "Now, Lord my God, You have placed me in a position of authority, and You have appointed Your servant in place of my father, and I am only a small lad, with no experience in leadership. Your servant is in the midst of Your people whom You have chosen, a people too numerous to be numbered or counted. Grant, then, your servant an understanding mind to judge Your people, to distinguish between good and evil; for who can judge this vast people of Yours?" (*ibid.*, 3:7–9). You have given Your servant "a wise and discerning mind" (*ibid.*, 12) to explain to Your people the reasons of Your *Torah*, to guide them to serve You and to bring them near to Your teaching, "for in these things do I delight" (Jer. 9:23). You have given to Your servant "a skilled tongue, to know how to sustain with a word him that is weary. Morning by morning You waken, You waken my ear to hear as those who are taught" (Isa. 50:4). Cause Your divine spirit to emanate to me. "Open my eyes that I may see the wonderful teachings of Your *Torah*" (Ps. 119:18), and that "I may rejoice in Your statutes, and not forget Your words" (*ibid.*, 16), and that I shall preach to Your people "a good word at the appropriate time" (cf. Prov. 15:23), from day to day, "from Sabbath to Sabbath" (Isa. 66:23), on festivals, appointed days, and at all the different times, to preach to them [only] that which is fitting and proper. May they take to heart my words, and "may they wait for me as for the rain; and open their mouth wide as for the latter rain" (Job. 29:23). May my words be sweet to the ears of those who hear them. May Your people come to hear my words "with a whole heart and ready mind" (I Chron. 28:9). May they thirst to hear words of Your *Torah* from my mouth, and may they find satisfaction in my words to slake their thirst and to strengthen hands which are weakened and legs which are feeble from the anguish of *Galut,* as it is said, "Strengthen the weak hands, and make firm the feeble knees" (Isa. 35:3). Let it be clear before the throne of Your glory that I ask not for my honor but for Your honor, after whose name I am called. I pray, Lord, teach me to be of benefit [to others], guide me in the paths I should take to aid Your people and guide them to serve You. May my words fall on attentive ears. May those who hear me not turn aside my words, my reproofs, and my admonitions from their hearts, but may they accept them always and take care to heed them and not veer to the right or to the left. "Let me teach transgressors Your ways" (Ps. 51:15). "Show favor to Your servant" (*ibid.,* 31:17), and enlighten me in Your *Torah.* Help me hold fast to Your commandments, and unite my thoughts with singleness of purpose to love and revere Your name that I may never be ashamed in this world or in the world to come (Baer, *Avodat Yisro'el,* p. 80). Bring not upon me any

[4a]

disgrace or *hillul ha-shem* (profanation of the name of God). Keep
me far from sin, transgression, or iniquity now or at any time.
[Protect me from] any evil report being spread about me or what I
do. Help me not become easily angered or overly strict, or cruel
with any human being. [Rather, I pray that I may be] a tolerant
and compassionate person so that my words and reproofs will be
taken to heart, and that people will not say to me, "Take the beam
from between your eyes" (B.B. 15b, Ar. 16b).* Instead, cause me
to be worthy in their eyes, [and I pray] that I may be among those
righteous individuals to whom it is said, "Preach, Rabbi, preach,
because for you it is appropriate to preach" (Sanh. 100a), for "you
preach well and practice well" (Hag. 14b).—They are paragons in
Israel because of their wisdom and their way of expressing themselves. People will rise up and praise them, queens and concubines
shall call them happy (cf. Song 6:9)—May I find "grace and good
favor in the eyes of God and man" (Prov. 3:4), and guard me from
self-righteousness [or smugness], heaven forbid! "Let not the foot
of the arrogant tread on me, or the hand of the wicked drive me
away" (Ps. 36:12). Rather, I lift up my eyes and my heart to You,
for "from You comes greatness" (see I Chron. 29:11), and You are
the source of all my good (cf. Ps. 16:2). I shall make light of myself,
for I am small, but now You have made me worthy and You have
lifted me up. "Your care has made me great" (*ibid.,* 18:36). May all
of my efforts be for the sake of Your name and Your glory. May
You always be in my thoughts, deeds, and words. Let whatever I
utter show an awareness of You, and may I constantly ponder that
which is for [You and] Your name's sake. Purify my thoughts, and
may I never lift my eyes except to find favor in Your sight. May my
senses only function for the sake of Your glory. May the words

---

* The sources in the Talmud refer to a judge who is unfit to judge. He accuses
the defendant of having a small particle between his eyes, when he himself has a
beam between his. The prayer is that the preacher should not be guilty of such
hypocrisy in his reproving others. See *Or,* ll. 670–674.

which I utter both privately and publicly be for a worthy purpose and not provoke others or put them to shame. May no one humiliate or provoke me, but may all judge me "in the scale of merit" (M. Avot 1:6). Save me from the evil eye, from the evil inclination, and from the hatred of mankind. May no one ridicule me or my words. Let me not fail in [the objective of] my words [lest my enemies] see and rejoice [over me]. Guide my lips in what I say according to the occasion and the subject matter, that I speak without any hesitation. Remove from me "any deceitfulness in speech, and keep me far from any trace of dishonesty" (Prov. 4:24). May all those who would rise against me to do evil quickly find their plans frustrated and their designs come to naught (see Ber. 17a). "And may my head be raised above my foes on every side, and may I offer sacrifices in Your tabernacle with trumpet-sound; I will sing, yea, I will sing praises unto the Lord" (Ps. 27:6). I pray that You in Your compassion will lengthen my days and years. May they not say about me, "Woe to the rabbinate

[4b]

which buries its own members" (Pes. 87b), but may they rather say, "Length of days is in her right hand; in her left hand are riches and honor" (Prov. 3:16), and "Reverence for the Lord prolongs one's days" (*ibid.*, 10:27), "The teaching of his God is in his heart; his feet do not slip" (Ps. 37:31). And may no one be envious of me, and may I not be envious of others except [in a good sense, as] with the envy of scholars and those who do good and act for the sake of heaven in order that serving You and Your *Torah* should be enhanced and exalted (cf. B.B. 21a, 22a). May neither young nor old despise me as a result of my admonishing them on religious matters. Rather, help me to be loved "above" [by You] and respected "below" by [human beings,] Jews and non-Jews alike. Now should I utter a word against the liars and scoundrels, may it be Your will that I not accidentally incriminate either Israel, Your people, or myself. Help me not to be the object of a talebearer, a revealer of secrets, a slanderer, or a would-be informer. Make me strong and determined against such people at any time I may encounter them. Teach me what to answer a self-avowed heretic (M. Avot 2:14) and how to sanctify Your name with my words and answers—though they fight against me, they shall not prevail against me, for You, O Lord, are with me to save me (cf. Jer. 1:19 and 15:20). Cause me to be an instrument for good for Israel [which is] peace (M. Uk. 3:12). Help me bring about compromise and peace between husbands and wives, between one individual and another, and between parents and children. Help me to decide "justly between any man and a fellow Israelite or stranger" (Deut. 1:16). May it be Your will, O Lord, my God and God of my fathers, that You send blessing, relief, and prosperity through all of my endeavors, and may I see the fruits of my efforts. Let me not struggle in vain, and keep me from bringing forth confusion (cf. Isa. 65:23). From the riches and possessions in this world which You graciously give me, may I support Your needy and all of those whom it will be my duty to support, in performing commandments, good deeds, and endeavors wholly for the sake of Your *Torah*. Especially I pray, Lord of all hosts above and below, that I shall be worthy of fathering children and [be privileged] to see grandchildren. May my children achieve all that I have accomplished and many times over. May that scriptural verse be fulfilled in me that "My words which I have put in your mouth, shall not depart out of your mouth" (*ibid.*, 59:21). May I and my descendants, and their descendants to the end of all generations, love and revere Your name, and study and teach Your *Torah* for its own sake, that they be called Your people forever. Help me to be a source of new interpretations and to write books about Your *Torah* which will always be studied by Israel,

[5a]

and which will enhance and glorify Your teaching (cf. *ibid.*, 42:21). Through such endeavors cause me to be responsible for increasing the number of scholars in Israel. May none of my words or sermons be burdensome to Your people, but rather may they be regarded with special affection, even loved from beginning to end. Hear my prayer as You accepted the prayer of Jabez, who prayed before You: "'May You indeed bless me, enlarge my territory, let Your hand be with me and prevent evil from hurting me.' And God granted what he asked" (I Chron. 4:10). May I be worthy of truly helping the general welfare in this world as Your righteous and prophets who brought Your children close to Your service, and who enlightened Israel through their teachings which they taught to such large numbers of people. May my portion be with them in this world and in the world to come. Grant that I may "behold the prosperity of Your chosen ones, and share in the joy of Your nation, and glory in Your very own people" (Ps. 106:5). Help me to "see Jerusalem a peaceful habitation" (Isa. 33:20), and the cities of Judah rebuilt, as well as Mount Zion and the glory and the location of Your tabernacle. In my days "may Judah be saved and Israel dwell safely" (Jer. 23:6), "and a redeemer come to Zion" (Isa. 59:20). "Do not thwart my expectation" (Ps. 119:116), but hear my prayer and be gracious to me. Turn me not away unanswered, for You hear the prayers of all mankind.

May it be Your will, etc.

And one should say Psalm 40, "For the Leader. A Psalm of David. I waited patiently for the Lord, and He inclined toward me and heeded my cry," until the end of the Psalm.

Bibliography

Manuscripts for text of *Or ha-Darshanim*

Or ha-Darshanim, Adler coll., no. 84a (1339), Library of the Jewish Theological Seminary, New York.
Or ha-Darshanim, Bodleian Library, no. 2268.1, Oxford University.
Qol Ya'aqov, Biblioteca Casanatense, no. 217, Rome.

Other Manuscripts by Jacob Zahalon Consulted

Ohalei Ya'aqov Oẓar ha-Ḥokhmot, Vatican Library, no. 466, Rome.
Oẓar ha-Shamayim, Kaufman coll., no. 293, Hungarian Academy of Sciences, Budapest.
Morashah Qehilat Ya'aqov, Gaster coll., Or. 10044, British Museum, London.
Shuvu Elai, Ferrara *Talmud Torah* coll., no. 14; Hebrew University microfilm no. 2391, Jerusalem.
Ẓohola ve-Rina, Ferrara *Talmud Torah* coll., no. 48; Hebrew University microfilm no. 2428.

Published Works by Jacob Zahalon

Margaliot Tovot, Venice, 1665.
Oẓar ha-Ḥayyim, Venice, 1683.

Other Sources

Abrahams, Israel. *Jewish Life in the Middle Ages.* Philadelphia, 1896.
Abramson, Shraga. "Defusei *Musar Haskel* ve-*Toldot Adam* le-R. Yeḥezkel Feivel." *Sinai,* LXXII (1973).

Al-Dahari, Zechariah. *Sefer ha-Musar.* Ed. Y. Retzahaby. Jerusalem, 1965.

Amram, D. W. *The Makers of Hebrew Books in Italy.* Philadelphia, 1909.

Apfelbaum, A. *Toldot R. Yehudah Moscato.* Drohobycz, 1900.

———. *Azariah Figo.* Drohobycz, 1907 (in Hebrew).

Arama, Isaac. *Aqedat Yizhaq.* Pressburg, 1849.

Aristotelis opera cum Averrois commentariis. Venice, 1562–1594; repr. Frankfurt a. M., 1962.

Azikri, Elazar. *Sefer Haredim.* Brno, 1795.

Bahya Ibn Paquda. *Hovot ha-Levavot.* Ibn Tibbon trans., ed. A. Zifroni. Tel Aviv, 1959.

Baer, Zeligman. *Avodat Yisro'el.* Roedelheim, 1868.

Baron, Salo W. *A Social and Religious History of the Jews.* 17 vols. to date. New York, 1952–83.

———. *The Jewish Community.* 3 vols. Philadelphia, 1948.

Bartolocci, Giulio. *Bibliotheca Magna Rabbinica de Scriptoribus et Scriptis Hebraicis.* 4 vols. Rome, 1675–1694.

Barzilay, Isaac. *Between Reason and Faith: Anti-Rationalism in Italian Jewish Thought, 1250–1650.* The Hague, 1967.

Bass, Sabbatai. *Siftei Yeshenim.* Amsterdam, 1680.

Benayahu, M. *Haskamah u-Reshut bi-Defusei Venizia.* Jerusalem, 1971.

———. *Rabbi Hayyim Yosef David Azulai.* Jerusalem, 1959 (in Hebrew).

———. *Sefer Toldot ha-Ari.* Jerusalem, 1967.

———. "Yediot mei-Italia u-mei-Holland al Reshita shel ha-Shabbeta'ut." *Erez Yisro'el,* IV (1956).

Ben Bassa of Blanes, Moses ben Samuel. *Tena'ei ha-Darshan.* Columbia University Library Manuscript Collection, no. X893T 15Q, New York.

Ben-Sasson, H. H. *Hagut ve-Hanhagah.* Jerusalem, 1959.

Berliner, A. *Geschichte der Juden in Rom.* 2 vols. Frankfurt a. M., 1893.

———. *Ketavim Nivharim.* Jerusalem, 1949.

Bettan, Israel. *Studies in Jewish Preaching.* Cincinnati, 1939.

Bonfil, Reuben. *Ha-Rabbanut be-Italia bi-Tekufat ha-Renaissance.* Jerusalem, 1979.

Braude, W., and Kapstein, I. *Pesikta de-Rav Kahana: R. Kahana's Compilation of Discourses for Sabbaths and Festal Days.* Philadelphia, 1975.

The Catalogue of Hebrew Manuscripts in the Collection of Elkan Nathan Adler. Cambridge, England, 1921.

Chavel, Charles B. *Encyclopedia of Torah Thoughts.* New York, 1980.

———. *Kitvei Rabbeinu Baḥya.* Jerusalem, 1970.

Cohen, Boaz. "Mazkeret Meḥabrei ha-Teshuvot be-Sefer *Paḥad Yiẓḥaq.*" *Sefer ha-Yovel li-Khvod Professor Alexander Marx.* New York, 1943.

Corradi, Alfonso. *Annali Delle Epidemie Occorse in Italia dalle Prime Memorie Fino al 1850.* 5 vols. Bologna, 1865–1894.

Davidson, I. *Thesaurus of Medieval Hebrew Poetry.* 4 vols. New York, 1924–1933. (Also cited as *Oẓar ha-Shirah ve-ha-Piyyut.*)

———. *Oẓar ha-Meshalim ve-ha-Pitgamim mi-Safrut Yemei ha-Baynaim.* Jerusalem, 1956/1957.

Elbogen, Ismar. *Ha-Tefillah be-Yisro'el.* Tel Aviv, 1972. Trans. J. Amir, from *Der Judische Gottesdienst in seiner geschichtlichen Entwicklung.* 3d ed., Leipzig, 1913.

Encyclopaedia Judaica. Jerusalem, 1971.

Encyclopaedia Hebraica. Jerusalem, 1950.

Finkelstein, Louis. *Jewish Self-Government in the Middle Ages.* New York, 1964.

Friedberg. Ch. B. *Beit Eqed Sefarim.* 4 vols. Tel Aviv, 1952.

Friedenwald, H. "Jewish Physicians in Italy." *American Jewish Historical Society,* XXVIII (1922).

———. *The Jews and Medicine.* 3 vols. Baltimore, 1944.

Graetz, Heinrich. *Divrei Yemei Yisro'el.* 8 vols. Trans. S. P. Harkavy from *Geschichte der Juden.* Leipzig, 1873–1900.

———. *History of the Jews.* Philadelphia, 1891–1898.

Gregorovius, F. *The Ghetto and the Jews of Rome.* New York,

1966. Trans. Moses Hadas from *Der ghetto and die Juden in Rom.* Berlin, 1935.

Guedemann, Moritz. *Sefer ha-Torah ve-ha-Ḥayyim be-Arẓot ha-Ma'arav bimei ha-Beinayim.* Warsaw, 1896. Trans. A.S. Friedberg from *Geschichte des Erziehungswesens und der Cultur der abendlaendischen Juden.* 3 vols. Vienna, 1880–1888.

Ha-Levi, Yiẓḥaq Barukh. *Sefer Toldot Yiẓḥaq Lampronti.* Lyck, 1871.

Heineman, J. *Derashot be-Ẓibbur bi-Tequfat ha-Talmud.* Jerusalem, 1970.

Heller-Wilensky. R. *Yiẓḥaq Arama u-Mishnato.* Jerusalem, 1956.

Hyamson, Albert M. "Solomon da Costa and the British Museum." In *Occident and Orient (in honor of Moses Gaster).* London, 1936.

Ibn Shu'aib, Joel. *Olat Shabbat.* Venice, 1577.

Jellinek, Aaron. *Qunteres ha-Mafte'aḥ.* Vienna, 1881.

――――. *Qunteres Virmiza u-Qahal Vina.* Vienna, 1880.

Kalonymus, Jacob ben. *Qol Ya'aqov.* Columbia University Library Manuscript Collection, n. X893J 151Q.

Lampronti, Isaac. *Paḥad Yiẓḥaq.* Venice, 1750.

Landshuth, L. *Amudei ha-Avodah.* Berlin, 1857.

Leibowitz, Joshua O. "Jacob Zahalon, a Hebrew Medical Author of the XVIIth Century (1630–1693)." in *Actes du Septième Congrès International d'Histoire des Sciences.* Jerusalem, 1953.

――――. "Magefat ha-Dever be-Ghetto Roma (1656) lefi Zahalon ve-ha-Cardinal Gastaldi." *Qorot,* IV (Jerusalem, 1967).

――――. "R. Ya'aqov Ish Roma u-Fizmono le-Shabbat Ḥanukkah mi-Shnat 1687." In *Sefer Zikhron le-Ḥayyim Enzo Serini, Ketavim al Yahdut Roma,* ed. by A. Milano, Sh. Nakhon, and D. Karpi. Jerusalem, 1971.

Loew, Judah (of Prague). *Netivot Olam.* Prague, 1596.

Luzzatto, Moshe Ḥayyim. *Sefer Lashon Limmudim.* Mantua, 1727.

McKeon, Richard, ed. *The Basic Works of Aristotle.* New York, 1941.

Maimonides. *Sefer ha-Miẓvot*. Trans. with notes by Charles B. Chavel. New York, 1967.

———. *The Book of Knowledge* (first section of *Mishneh Torah*). Trans. and with notes by M. Hyamson. Jerusalem, 1962.

———. *The Guide of the Perplexed*. Trans. by S. Pines. Chicago, 1969.

Marcus, Ivan. *Piety and Society: The Jewish Pietists of Medieval Germany*. Leiden, 1981.

Marcus, Jacob R. *The Jew in the Medieval World*. Philadelphia, 1938.

Margolit, David. *Ḥakhmei Yisro'el ka-Rofaim*. Jerusalem, 1962.

Messer Leon, Judah. *Nofet Ẓufim*. Ed. A. Jellinek. Vienna, 1863.

Milano, Attilio. *Il Ghetto di Roma*. Rome, 1964.

da Modena, Leone. *Beit Leḥem Yehudah*. Venice, 1625.

———. *Ḥayyei Yehudah*. Kiev, 1911.

———. *Riti*. Trans. into English by Edmund Chilmead as *The History of the Rites, Customes, and Manner of Life, of the Present Jews throughout the World*. London, 1650.

———. *She'elot u-Teshuvot Ziqnei Yehudah*. Ed. S. Simonsohn. Jerusalem, 1956.

Mortara, M. *Mazkeret Ḥakhmei Italia*. Padua, 1886.

Moscato, Judah. *Nefuẓot Yehudah*. Warsaw, 1871.

Neppi, N., and Ghirondi, Sh. *Toldot Gedolei Yisro'el ve-Gaonei Italia*. Trieste, 1853.

New Catholic Encyclopedia. Washington, 1967.

Ockley, Simon. *The History of the Present Jews throughout the World*. London, 1707

O'Malley, John W. *Giles of Viterbo on Church and Reform: A Study in Renaissance Thought*. Leiden, 1968.

———. *Praise and Blame in Renaissance Rome: Rhetoric, Doctrine, and Reform in the Sacred Orators of the Papal Court, c. 1450–1521*. Durham, 1979.

Perelmutter, Hayim Goren. *Shir haMa'alot l'David (Song of the Steps) and Ktav Hitnaẓẓelut l'Darshanim (In Defense of Preachers) by David Darshan*. Cincinnati, 1984.

———. Once a Pun a Preacher—a Study in Paranomasia from

Biblical Times to Sixteenth Century Poland, Suggested by the Works of David Darshan." *Journal of Reform Judaism,* XXVII (1980).

Picho, Azariah. *Binah le-Ittim.* Lemberg, 1797.

Popper, William. *The Censorship of Hebrew Books.* New York, 1899.

Preschel, Tovia. " 'Reshut' li-Derashah," *Sinai,* LXXXIX (1981).

———. "Od al Reshut li-Derashah," *Sinai,* XCII (1982).

Rabinowitz, Hayyim Reuben. *Dyuqanut shel Darshanim.* Jerusalem, 1967.

Reusch, Heinrich. *Der Index der verbotenen Bücher.* 2 vols. Bonn, 1883–1885.

Rivkin, Ellis. "Leon da Modena and the *Kol Sakhal,*" *JQR,* n.s., XXXVI–XLI, 1947–1951.

Rosenthal, Gilbert S. *Banking and Finance among Jews in Renaissance Italy.* New York, 1962.

Rodocanachi, Emmanuel. *Le Saint-Siège et les Juifs le Ghetto à Rome.* Paris, 1891.

Roth, Cecil. *History of the Jews of Italy.* Philadelphia, 1946.

———. *The Jews in the Renaissance.* Philadelphia, 1959.

Sacerdote, Gustavo. *Cataloghi dei Codici Orientali di alcune Biblioteche D'Italia,* VI, *Catalogo dei Codici Ebraici della Biblioteca Casanatense.* Florence, 1897.

Savitz, Harry A. "Jacob Zahalon, and His Book 'The Treasure of Life.' " *New England Journal of Medicine,* Vol. 213 (July 25, 1935).

Scholem, G. *Kabbalah.* Jerusalem, 1974.

———. "Le-She'elat Yahasam shel Rabbanei Yisro'el el ha-Shabbeta'ut." *Zion,* XIII–XIV (1948–1949).

———. *Major Trends in Jewish Mysticism.* New York, 1954.

———. "Redemption through Sin." In *The Messianic Idea in Judaism.* New York, 1972.

———. *Sabbatai Ṣevi: The Mystical Messiah, 1626–1676.* Princeton, 1973.

———. *Shabbatai Zevi ve-ha-Tenu'ah ha-Shabbeta'it bimei Hayyav.* 2 vols. Tel Aviv, 1957.

Shalem, Shimon. *Rabbi Moshe Alshekh.* Jerusalem, 1966.

Shulvass, Moses A. *Roma ve-Rushalayyim.* Jerusalem, 1944.

―――. *The Jews in the World of the Renaissance.* Leiden, 1973. Trans. Elvin Kose from *Hayyei ha-Yehudim be-Italia bi-Tekufat ha-Renaissance.* New York, 1955.

Simonsohn, Shelomo. *Toldot ha-Yehudim be-Dukhsot Mantova.* 2 vols. Jerusalem, 1962–1964.

Smalley, Beryl. *The Study of the Bible in the Middle Ages.* Oxford, 1952.

Sosland, Henry A. "A Rabbi-Physician's Prescription for Effective Sermons: the Earliest Hebrew Preaching Manual." *Judaism,* XXVIII (1979).

Steinschneider, M. *Die Hebraeischen Uebersetzungen des Mittelalters.* Berlin, 1893.

―――. *Jewish Literature.* London, 1857.

―――. *Ozrot Chajim; Katalog der Michael'schen Bibliothek.* Hamburg, 1848.

Stow, Kenneth R. *Catholic Thought and Papal Jewry Policy, 1555–1593.* New York, 1977.

―――. "The Burning of the Talmud in 1553 in the Light of the Sixteenth Century Catholic Attitudes toward the Talmud." *Bibliothèque d'Humanisme et Renaissance,* XXXIV (1972).

Strack, H. L. *Introduction to the Talmud and Midrash.* Trans. of 5th ed. of Berlin, 1920. New York, 1959.

Tishby, I. "Te'udot al Natan ha-Azzati be-Kitvei R. Yosef Hamiẓ." *Sefunot,* I (1956).

Vogelstein, H. *Rome* Trans. Moses Hadas. Philadelphia, 1941.

―――. and Rieger, P. *Geschichte der Juden in Rom.* 2 vols. Berlin, 1895–1896.

Werblowsky, R. J. Zwi. *Joseph Karo: Lawyer and Mystic.* Philadelphia, 1977.

Wirszubski, H. "Ha-Idioligia ha-Shabbeta'it shel Hamarat ha-Mashiah lefi Natan ha-Azzati ve-Igeret *Magen Avraham,*" *Ẓion,* III (1938).

―――. "Ha-Teologia ha-Shabbata'it shel Natan ha-Azzati," *Knesset,* VIII (1944).

Wolfson, Harry A. *Philo: Foundations of Religious Philosophy in Judaism, Christianity, and Islam.* 2 vols. Cambridge, 1948.

——. *The Philosophy of Spinoza.* Cambridge, 1948.

Yaari, Avraham. *Masa'ot Erez Yisro'el.* Tel Aviv, 1946.

——. *Sheluhei Erez Yisro'el.* Jerusalem, 1951.

——. *Ta'alumot Sefer.* Jerusalem, 1954.

Ibn Yaḥya, Gedaliah. *Sefer Shalshelet ha-Kabbalah.* Jerusalem, 1962.

Yalqut Shimoni. Frankfurt a. M., 1687.

III. A Critical Edition of the *Or ha-Darshanim* Based on Three Manuscripts

INDEX OF SOURCES

Scripture

185

Mishnah

Jerusalem Talmud

Babylonian Talmud

Midrashim and Other Texts

Moses Maimonides

SUBJECT INDEX

190

חלק א' על התורה

מורה כאצבע הסימנים

מכל דברים וענינים

שֶׁבְּיֵלְקֻ֑וטַ בפנים שונים

מועיל לבחורים וזקנים

להקל טורה הנבונים

ישֶׁר מדליק לפניהם נרות

מלאכת הדרשה מורות

יינ֟ע כפיו של מעלת הרופא מובהק

יעקב בכמהרר יצחק צהלון ז''ל

לשם בורא

Title page of Cas. Ms. of *Or ha-Darshanim*

אור הדרשנים

מאת

יעקב צהלון

יוצא לאור מתוך שלשה כתבי יד
עם מקורות והערות
מאת

יצחק אבי סוסלנד

בית המדרש לרבנים באמריקא
תשמ"ו

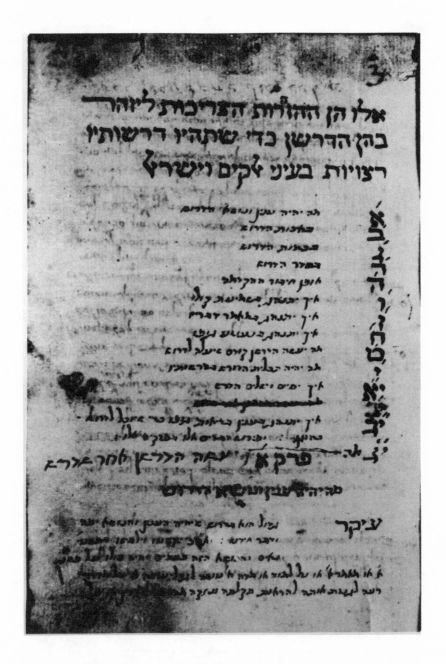

Table of Contents from Cas. Ms. *Or ha-Darshanim*

ב"ה

ספר קול יעקב

חלק א' על התורה

וספר שמו אור הדרשנים

מורה באצבע הסימנים   5

מכל דברים ועניניים

של מאמרי נאמנים

שבילקוט בפנים שונים

מועיל לבחורים וזקנים

להקל טורח הנבונים   10

ועוד מדליק לפניהם נרות

מלאכת הדרשה מורות

בחיבור יפה ובאמירות

לעשות דרשות יקרות

יגיע כפיו של מעלת הרופא   15

המובהק ודורש טוב לעמו[1])

בכתב יד **נ'**, אשר כנראה נעתק מכתב־יד **ק'** לפני שצהלון תיקן את זה, או נעתק מכתב יד מאד דומה לזה בהתחלה, יש הרבה שינויים: 2. ליתא ספר קול יעקב. 3. **נ'** חלק ראשון. 4. **נ'** ספר. 10. **נ'** המבינים. 12. **נ'** מאירות במקום מורות. 16. **נ'** מובהק דורש.

1.   האותיות „ב"ה" בתוך מסגרת בכתב יד **ק'**, וכל השורות 25־1 **בק'**.
2.   המחבר העביר קו על המילים „ספר קול יעקב."
3.   העביר קו על המילים „וספר שמו אור הדרשנים", ומעל למילים „אור הדרשנים" הוסיף נקדות — סימן להשאיר אותן.
7.   העביר קו על המילים „של מאמרי נאמנים."
13־14.   העביר כמה קווים על המילים „בחיבור יפה ובאמירות לעשות דרשות יקרות."
16.   העביר קו על המילים „דורש טוב לעמו".

1)   **דרש טוב לעמו** אסתר י:ג.

ברומא בכנסת

קק״י[2]) קאטאלני וארגוניסי י״ץ[3])

כ״ז שנה ואח״כ בקק״י פיראא

כמה״רר יעקב בכמה״רר יצחק · 20

צהלון ז׳צ׳ו׳קל[4]) לשם בורא

חדשים גם ישנים

יוציאנו לרוחה

[צריך להדפיס בע״ה קודם ההקדמה

ואח״כ ההזהרות של דרשנים] · 25

הקדמת המחבר כמה״רר יעקב

בכמ״הרר יצחק צהלון זצ״ל

מדרך החכמים בכל החכמות להשתדל בכל

עוז לבקש דרך קצרה וקלה בביאור

---

17. נ׳ קאטאלאני.   19. נ׳ ליתא כ״ז שנה ואח״כ בקק״י פיראא.   21. נ׳ ז״צ״ל הבורא.

22. ליתא חדשים גם ישנים בשער של נ׳ נמצאות עוד שתי שורות: „הועתק על יד הבחור שלמה בלא״א יצחק דא קושטה עטיאש נר״ו בלונדרש בשנת התע״ז. גם בנ׳ ההקדמה באה לפני ההזהרות של דרשנים, כפי שצהלון בקש בכתב יד ק׳.

17-18.   על המילים „ברומא בכנסת קק״י קאטאלני וארגוניסי י״ץ העביר קו, ואחר כך הוסיף נקדות מעל למילים לקיים אותן. כנראה אחרי זה העביר קו על הנקדות.

19.   המחבר כתב את המילים „כ״ז שנה ואח״כ בקק״י פיראא״ בכתב ידו על הצד והראה להכניס את אלה בתוך השער, אחר כך העביר כמה קוים על המילים האלה.

22.   המילים „חדשים גם ישנים״ נמחקו.

23.   המילים „יוציאנו לרוחה״ נכתבות בכתיבה אחרת בין השורות עם חמש נקדות.

26-27.   נ׳ א׳ ליתא כמה״רר יעקב בכמ״הרר יצחק צהלון זצ״ל.

27.   ק׳ מדרך נ׳ א׳ דרך.

---

2) קהלת קודש ישראל.

3) ישמרם צורם.

4) זכר צדיק וקדוש לברכה.

החכמות להקל המשא ולהסיר הקושי   30
מעל המעיינים כפי האפשר והוא
לימוד מוסכם ושגור בפי רז"ל
לעולם ילמד אדם לתלמידיו דרך קצרה[5]
וכן אמרו דבר הכתוב בהוה[6]) ודברה
תורה כלשון בני אדם[7]) וכ"כ למה   35
להקל כובד משא החכמה מעל המעיין
והלומד הן בלשון קצר או בצחות הלשון
או בהמשיל משלים וגם הנביאים ע"ה
הוצרכו להשתדלות הזה וכמו שאמר
הרמב"ם ז"ל בהלכות יסודי התורה   40
שלכל א' כפי מעלתו היה מראה
לו הנבואה וסגנון של זה אינו
כסגנון של זה. זה בברור וזה
במשל וזה בצורות וזה במראות[8])

---

31. ק' כפי נ' א' בכל. ק' נ' האפשרי א' האפשר.
33. ק' א' לתלמידיו דרך נ' את תלמידיו בדרך.
35. א' כלשון ק' נ' בלשון.
36. ק' נ' משא א' המשא.
38. ק' א' ע"ה נ' עליהם השלום.
40. נ' התורה ק' א' תורה.
41. ק' שלכל א' נ' שלכל אחד. נ' א' ליתא היה. ק' א' מראה נ' מראין.
42. ק' א' וסגנון נ' וסגנון.
43. ק' א' כסגנון נ' כסגנון ק' נ' בברור א' בבירור.
44. ק' וזה בצורות א' נ' זה הצורות.

5) ראה פסחים ג:, חולין סג:
6) משנה בבא קמא ה:ז.
7) ברכות לא: ומקבילות.
8) עין רמב"ם שם, פרק ז:ב: „כמו שיש בחכמה חכם גדול מחברו כך בנבואה נביא גדול
מנביא". ושם,ג: „הדברים שמודיעים לנביא במראה הנבואה — דרך משל מודיעים לו, ומיד
יחקק בלבו פתרון המשל במראה הנבואה וידע מה שהוא . . . . וכלם . . . במשל ודרך חידה הם
מתנבאים.

כל א׳ כפי כחו וכמו שאחז״ל
קול ה׳ בכח[9]) בכחו לא נאמר אלא
בכח של כל א׳ וא׳[10]) ומי לנו גדול
ממשה רבע״ה רבן של נביאים דכתיב
ביה לא כן עבדי משה בכל ביתי
נאמן הוא פה אל פה אדבר בו ומראה
ולא בחידות ותמונת ה׳ יביט[11]) ואחר כל
הכבוד הזה כתיב ויקרא אל משה
וידבר וגו׳[12]) ותנן בספרא[13]) והביאו
רש״י ז״ל בריש פר׳ ויקרא ז״ל ויקרא
אל משה וידבר וגו׳ הקול הולך ומגיע
לאזניו וכל ישראל לא היו שומעים
יכול אף להפסקות היתה קריאה ת״ל
וידבר לדבור היתה קריאה ולא להפסקות
ומה היו ההפסקות משמשות ליתן רוח למשה
להתבונן בין פרשה לפרשה ובין ענין לענין
ק״ו להדיוט הלמד מן ההדיוט עכ״ל:

45

50

55

60

45. ק׳ א׳ כל א׳ נ׳ כל אחד. ק׳ נ׳ כחו א׳ כוחו.
47. ק׳ א׳ א׳ וא׳ נ׳ אחד ואחד. ק׳ א׳ לנו נ׳ הוא.
48. ק׳ א׳ רבע״ה נ׳ רבינו ע״ה.
49. ק׳ א׳ עבדי משה נ׳ משה עבדי.
53. א׳ וידבר ק׳ נ׳ ליתא.
54. ק׳ פר׳ נ׳ א׳ פ׳. ק׳ א׳ ויקרא ז״ל נ׳ וז״ל.
56. נ׳ ישראל ק׳ ישר׳.
57. ק׳ נ׳ קריאה א׳ קראה.
59. ק׳ א׳ ומה נ׳ ואם. נ׳ א׳ רוח ק׳ ריוח.

9) תהלים כט:ד.
10) ראה שמות רבה כט:א, וראה גם ילקוט שמעוני תהילים תש״ט.
11) במדבר יב:ז-ח.
12) ויקרא א:א.
13) פרק א:ו-ט.

ואפשר שלזה רמז הכתוב באמרו קול
קורא במדבר פנו דרך ה׳ ישרו
בערבה מסילה לאלקינו[14]) מלבד מה
שפרשתי בפרושי בס׳ ישעיה אפשר לומר 65
קול קורא על עסקי התורה שנתנה במדבר
וכמש״רזל על וממדבר מתנה[15]) — אי נמי התורה
נקראת מדבר לשון דבור לפי שבה יהיה
רוב דבורנו שנ׳ ודברת בם[16]) ולא בדברים
בטלים ואמר פנו דרך ה׳[17]) ירצה אתם 70
המלמדים והמדברים תורת ה׳ ודרכיו
ית׳ לרבים צריכים אתם בכל עוז
לפנות כל הבלבולים ולתקן כל
המקולקלים ולהרים כל אבני נגף ומכשול
ממנה ולנקות דרכיה כדי שבנקל יהיו 75
דורכים דרך אמתן והשגתם והיה
העקוב למישור והרכסים לבקעה[18]) וזהו

.64 ק׳ מסילה נ׳ א׳ מסלה. ק׳ א׳ לאלקינו נ׳ לאלדינו.
.65 ק׳ נ׳ שפרשתי א׳ שפירשתי. ק׳ א׳ בפרושי נ׳ בפירושי.
.67 ק׳ וכמש״רזל נ׳ וכמ״ש רז״ל א׳ וכמ״שרזל.
.68 ק׳ א׳ דבור נ׳ דיבור.
.69 ק׳ דברנו נ׳ דְבָרֵינוּ א׳ דבורינו. ק׳ א׳ שנ׳ נ׳ שנאמר.
.70 ק׳ א׳ ואמר נ׳ ואחר. נ׳ ירצה ק׳ יר׳ א׳ ליתא, אבל מקומו נשאר פנוי.
.73 ק׳ א׳ לפנות נ׳ למעט.
.76 ק׳ אמתן נ׳ א׳ אמתם.
.77 ק׳ וזהו נ׳ א׳ וזה.
.78 ק׳ א׳ וכו׳ נ׳ וגו׳. ק׳ א׳ אשרו נ׳ והסירו.

14) ישעיה מ:ג.
15) במדבר כא:יח, וראה עירובין נד. ונדרים נה. וראה גם ילקוט במדבר תשס״ד.
16) דברים ו:ז.
17) ישעיה מ:ג.
18) שם,ד.

ישרו וכו׳[19] יר׳[20]) אשרו איזה קושי ממנה
ומהליכתה ותתקננה באיזה ערבות וקלות
ויהיו הכל דורכים מסילה ומהלך   80
שבילי הדעת לאלקינו ית׳ ועבודתו
ולכן אנכי תולעת ולא איש[21]) — חברתי זה
הספר וקראתיו קול יעקב[22]) אור הדרשנים
המאיר עיני בחורים וחברתיו בבחרותי
כאשר התחלתי להרים קולי לדרוש   85
ברבים מדי שבת בשבתו[23]) ומדי יום
ביומו וכדי להקל מעלי כובד משא
בקשתי העניינים הדרושים השייכים
לאותה פ׳ דברתי אני עם לבי
קום לך וצאי בעקבי הצאן ורעי את   90
גדיותיך על משכנות הרועים[24]) ה״ה

ק׳ ותתקננה נ׳ ותקנה א׳ ותקנינה.   .79

ק׳ א׳ מסילה נ׳ מסלה.   .80

ק׳ ועבודתו נ׳ א׳ לעבדתו.   .81

ק׳ קול יעקב נ׳ א׳ ליתא. בק׳ המחבר הוסיף את המילים „קול יעקב" בין השורות. ק׳ נ׳ א׳   .83
המילים „אור הדרשנים" נכתבות באותיות גדולות.

ק׳ נ׳ בחורים א׳ חכמים. ק׳ בבחרותי נ׳ א׳ בנערותי. בק׳ על המילה „בנערותי" העביר קווים   .84
וכתב בין השורות „בבחרותי".

ק׳ א׳ מדי נ׳ מידי. ק׳ א׳ ומדי נ׳ ומידי.   .86

ק׳ נ׳ העניינים א׳ העניינים. ק׳ הדרושים נ׳ א׳ הדורשים.   .88

ק׳ א׳ פ׳ נ׳ פרשה.   .89

ק׳ א׳ הרועים נ׳ הלעים.   .91

---

19) שם,ג.

20) ירצה.

21) תהלים כב:ז.

22) בראשית כז:כב.

23) ישעיה סו:כג.

24) שיר השירים א:ח.

קדמונינו אשר למדונו לסקל בערבה

מסילה לאלקינו והקלו מעלינו טורח

הדרך בלתי סלולה והנה שמעתי לקול

מורי ומדי עברי במים אדירים[25])

בים ס' ילקוט עיינתי בכל מאמר עם

העניינים שיכולים לדרוש בו בב'

או ג' מקומות או יותר כפי העניינים

הרמוזים בו כדי שכאשר ארצה לחבר

דרוש א' מאיזה ענין אמצא בנקל

כל המאמרים שנכתבו בילקוט השייכים

ונכנסים תחת הענין ההוא אשר

קראתיו בשם: ומלבד זה אשתמש מחיבור

זה ג"כ ללמוד בו כל הילקוט בקצרה

כי כתבתי רוב המאמר בקיצור

נמרץ כי הנחתי מלכתוב ראיית

הפסוקים ושאר מלות לקצר הדרך: ועוד

כיוונתי לתת סדר לעניני מאמרי

חז"ל כי מחבר הילקוט כתבם על סדר

הפסוקים וחבורי זה הוא על סדר

95

100

105

110

92. נ' למדונו ק' א' למדנו.

93. ק' א' מסילה נ' מסלה. נ' מעלינו ק' א' מעליך.

96. ק' עייתני נ' א' עינתי. נ' א' עם ק' היה כתוב ומחקו.

97. נ' א' לדרוש ק' לידרש.

98. ק' א' ג' נ' בג'.

99. ק' ארצה נ' ארצא א' ארצ'.

100. ק' א' דרוש א' נ' דרוש אחד. ק' נ' בנקל כל א' בנקלה על.

102. נ' א' הענין ק' עניו.

105. נ' א' בקיצור ק' בקצור.

108. ק' כיוונתי נ' כונתי א' כוונתי.

110. ק' וחבורי נ' א' וחיבורי.

25) שמות טו:י.

העניינים כדי שיהיה ס׳ הילקוט שלם

בכל סדריו ודבר גדול הוא הסדר

שכן מצינו גדול שבנביאים קבל באהבה

עצת חותנו יתרו שנתן לו סדר ואופן

115 נאות לשפוט העם באופן נקל לרוב

התלמידים: ולולי הסדר ההוא נבלל גם

הוא גם הם וכד״א וישמע משה לקול

חותנו ויעש כל אשר אמר[26]). גם הפלוסופים

שבחו הסדר בכל הדברים כי ארסט״ו

120 בס׳ השמים שלו וכן בחכמת הטבע

שלו חלק ח׳ פ׳ ט״ו ובספר ההגיון

שלו חלק ששי שבח סדר הדברים עד

שמסדר הנמצאים הביאו החכמים ראיה

על מציאות ה׳ ואחדותו: וכן תמצא

125 שהרב המורה בפ׳ ל״ד ח״א בחמשה

מונעים שהביא שם אמר שאין להתחיל העיונים

מעניינים ודברים קשים או אלקיים: ועמוד

והתבונן הסדר הנפלא שסדר הרמב״ם

בס׳ הי״ד שלו שמלבד עומק חכמתו שפסק

130 כל פסקי דיני הגמרא והתוספתות

---

111. ק׳ העניינים נ׳ א׳ העניינים. ק׳ א׳ ס׳ נ׳ ספר.

113. נ׳ א׳ שבנביאים ק׳ שבנביאי׳.

116. ק׳ נ׳ התלמידים א׳ התלמידי׳. ק׳ א׳ נבלל נ׳ נבל.

118. ק׳ א׳ ויעש נ׳ וגו׳. ק׳ א׳ כל אשר אמר נ׳ ליתא. ק׳ נ׳ הפלוסופים א׳ הפילוסופים.

121. נ׳ פ׳ ט״ו ק׳ פט״ו א׳ ליתא. ק׳ א׳ ובספר נ׳ ובס׳.

122. ק׳ חלק נ׳ א׳ ס׳.

123. ק׳ נ׳ הנמצאים א׳ הנמצאי׳. ק׳ החכמים נ׳ א׳ חכמים.

127. ק׳ א׳ מעניינים נ׳ מעניינים.

128. ק׳ שסדר נ׳ שסידר א׳ שבסדר.

129. ק׳ הי״ד נ׳ יד החזקה א׳ ה׳ יד.

130. ק׳ נ׳ והתוספתות א׳ והתוספות.

26) שמות יח:כד.

ספרא ספרי ומכילתא גם השתדל ברוב
חכמתו לסדרם בסדר יפה ומתוקן עד ששם
כל הדינים של ענין א׳ בפני עצמו ושל
ענין אחר בפני עצמו וגם כי הם

135 מפוזרים בגמרא לפי שהסדר דבר ראוי
והגון הוא ומתחייב בכל הדברים וכמו
שכתבתי בהקדמת ס׳ מורשה קהלת
יעקב[27]) שלי פ׳ על הרמב״ם ז״ל ע״ש[28]) וכן
שהע״ה[29]) חבר ג׳ ספרים בסדר מופלא

140 הלא תראה שכל העניינים הצריכים להנהגת
עצמו ואהבת ה׳ שם בשיר
השירים והצריכים להנהגת ביתו כתב
בס׳ משלי והמחוייבים להנהגת מדינתו
כתבם בס׳ קהלת וכן אמרו חז״ל

145 בערובין פ״ב[30]) אמר עולא אמר ר׳ אלעזר
בתחילה היתה התורה דומה לכפיפה
שאין לה אזנים עד שבא שלמה ועשה
לה אזנים ז״ש אזן וחקר תיקן משלים

---

132. ק׳ בסדר יפה נ׳ א׳ בסדרי פה.
133. ק׳ א׳ הדינים נ׳ הדינין. ק׳ א׳ ענין א׳ נ׳ אחד.
134. נ׳ ענין אחר ק׳ אחר א׳ א׳.
136. נ׳ הוא ק׳ א׳ ליתא.
138. ק׳ פ׳ נ׳ א׳ ליתא.
139. ק׳ א׳ חבר נ׳ חיבר. ק׳ נ׳ בסדר א׳ בספר.
140. ק׳ א׳ העניינים נ׳ העניינים.
144. ק׳ א׳ וכן אמרו חז״ל נ׳ וכאחז״ל.
145. ק׳ א׳ פ״ב נ׳ פ׳ ב׳.
146. ק׳ א׳ בתחילה נ׳ בתחלה.
148. ק׳ נ׳ לה א׳ לו. ק׳ תיקן נ׳ א׳ תקן.

27) ראה דברים לג:ד.
28) עיין שם.
29) שלמה המלך עליו השלום.
30) כא:, וראה יבמות כא.

הרבה[31]): ובמראה מקום זה תמצא
כל המאמרים שבשאר ספרים של
חז"ל עין ישראל[32]) רבות ילמדנו
פ' ר' אליעזר ספרא וספרי ואחרים
כי בעל הילקוט בהביאו המאמר מורה
מקומו שממנו לקטו: ומה שלא קצרתי
יותר לרמוז בלבד המאמר כדרך
שאר מראה מקום של ספרים אחרים
אלא הארכתי קצת דע שזה עשיתי
לב' טעמים א' מפני מה שכתבתי
לעיל כדי שיהיה זה כקיצור כל
ספר הילקוט ועוד כדי שהדרשן יכול
להבין מעצם המאמר הנכתב כאן אם
שייך לעניינו קודם שיטרח לבקשו:
ועשיתי ב' חלקים א' על התורה וב'
על נביאים וכתובים ולא קבצתיו בחלק
א' כדי שלא יקשה בעיני הקורא בו בראותו
יחד לפניו הרבה מאד מאמרים תחת
אות א' וישוב אחור אלא ישתמש ממה

150. ק' נ' המאמרים א' המאמרי'. ק' א' ספרים נ' ספרי. ק' של נ' א' ליתא.
151. נ' ישראל ק' ישר' א' יש'.
152. נ' פ' ר' אליעזר ק' א' פר"א.
153. ק' נ' המאמר א' במאמר.
156. נ' מראה ק' א' מורה.
159. ק' כקיצור נ' א' בקיצור.
160. נ' ספר ק' א' ס'. ק' א' שהדרשן יכול נ' שיוכל הדרשן.
162. נ' לעניינו ק' א' בעניינו.
167. ק' א' נ' אחת.

31) קהלת יב:ט.
32) זה היה שמו של ספר עין יעקב בראשונה.

שימצא בחלק א׳ ואם ירצה לעיין יותר או שלא
מצא בבקשו בחלק א׳ ימצאנו בחלק ב׳:

ואל תתמה אם נכפל איזה מאמר בח״ב   170
הכתוב בחלק א׳ כיון שכפלו בעל הילקוט עצמו:

ומאמר המדבר מהרבה ענינים שמתיו
תחת הרבה אותיות כדי למצוא המאמר
ההוא כפי צורך ענין הדורש: וכן

כתבתי מאמרים שהם מענין א׳ תחת   175
אותיות חלוקות ד״מ)[33] אדמה ארץ
עפר ולא קבצתים תחת אות א׳ הטעם
שלפעמים יש מאמר השייך תחת אות אדמה
ולא תחת אות עפר וכן בהפך

וכיוצא בזה ועוד מפני שיקל יותר   180
למבקש מאמר תחת אות א׳ ימצאנו מיד
ולא יצטרך לחשוב מלה אחרת: ולפי שספר
ילקוט נדפס בדפוסים חלוקים ושונים אני
חברתי ספר זה על דפוס ישן — ודפוסים

חדשים אינם מתאמים בסימנים עם הישנים   185

---

168. א׳ בחלק ק׳ נ׳ בח׳. ק׳ לעיין נ׳ א׳ לענין. ק׳ יותר או נ׳ אחר אחר א׳ יותר אחר.

169. ק׳ נ׳ בחלק א׳ בח׳. ק׳ א׳ ימצאנו נ׳ ימצאהו. ק׳ א׳ בח״ב נ׳ בחלק ב׳.

171. ק׳ א׳ הכתוב נ׳ ליתא. ק׳ בחלק א׳ נ׳ בח׳ א׳ א׳ בח׳ א׳. נ׳ א׳ שכפלו ק׳ וכפלו.

172. ק׳ נ׳ ענינים א׳ עניינים.

173. נ׳ המאמר ק׳ א׳ מאמר.

175. ק׳ נ׳ מענין א׳ א׳ מענין אחד.

177. ק׳ א׳ הטעם נ׳ לפי.

179. ק׳ א׳ בהפך נ׳ בהיפך.

181. ק׳ נ׳ מיד א׳ ליתא.

182. ק׳ נ׳ שספר א׳ שס׳.

183. ק׳ א׳ ושונים נ׳ ליתא.

184. ק׳ א׳ חברתי נ׳ כתבתי. נ׳ ספר ק׳ א׳ ס׳.

185. ק׳ מתאמים נ׳ מותאמים א׳ ליתא. נ׳ א׳ בסימנים ק׳ בסמנים. ק׳ נ׳ הישנים א׳ הישני׳.

(33) דרך משל.

לכן רשמתי ורמזתי ג"כ הקאפיטו"לי שבהם
כל הספרים שוים ולפיכך אם יש לפניך
ילקוט מדפוס ישן רשום בו ותכתוב
הקאפיטו"לי אז תמצא מה שתבקש בלתי
טעות: והאלקים הוא יודע שלא עשיתי זה 190
לכבודי ולא לכבוד בית אבא[34] ולא
להתגדל בו[35] שס' זה הוא של טורח יותר
משל עיון וגם לא לאותם שסוקרים כל
הילקוט בסקרא א'[36]) ואינם צריכים לחבורי
זה כי גלויים להם כל ענייני הילקוט אמנם 195
לאיש כמוני כי מרוב תלאות הזמן נתמעטו
הלבבות והשכחה גוברת — בעונותינו הרבים[37])
ולכן עשיתי אזנים לקופתי[38]) לאחזה בהן
להשתמש ממנה לעבודת ה' ית' שמו: ואקיים
מה שנ' עושה צדקה בכל עת[39]) זה 200

ק' א' הקאפיטו"לי ל נ' הקפיטו"לי. ק' נ' שבהם א' שבהן. .186
נ' שוים ק' א' שוין. .187
ק' ישן נ' א' חדש. ק' ותכתוב נ' א' ליתא. .188
ק' א' הקאפיטו"לי ל נ' הקפי"טלי. .189
ק' בסקרא נ' א' בסיקרא אבל בראש השנה יח. כתוב ככה: „וכולן נסקרין בסקירה אחת". **ק'** .194
נ' לחבורי א' לחיבור.
ק' א' ענייני נ' עניני. .195
ק' נ' מרוב א' לרוב. .196
ק' א' אזנים נ' אדנים. ק' א' לאחזה נ' לאחוז. .198
בכתב יד ק' המחבר הוסיף בכתב ידו המילים „ואקיים מה שנ' עושה צדקה בכל עת זה הכותב .199-200
ספרים ומשאילן לאחרים"ובנ' וא' ליתא.

תענית כ.; מגילה.; בבא מציעא נט: (34
ראה אבות ד:ה. (35
ראש השנה יח. (36
ראה עזרא ט:ו. (37
ראה עירובין כא: ויבמות כא. ראה למעלה הערה 30. (38
תהלים קו:ג. (39

הכותב ספרים ומשאילן לאחרים[40]) וכיון
שספרי זה תכליתו להקל דרך הדרשנים
להאיר לפניהם מסילה בחיבור דרושיהם
חשבתי להוסיף עמו תוספת רב האיכות
ומעט הכמות להורות לבחורים כללים יפים   205
איך יתנהגו בחיבורם ובאמירתם ברבים
הדרושים בהיות שלא מצאו ספר יורה להם
הדרך הם טורחים מאד בתיקונם וצריכים
הרגל ארוך וזמן הרבה ללמוד אופנים
ממלאכת הדרשה והנני כפי קוצר דעתי ממה   210
שהשגתי ונתתי לבי בשנים שדרשתי ברבים
למדתי דרכים ואופנים הצריכים בענין
זה וכתבתים בס׳ הזה בתחילה ועל פיהם
דרכתי בס׳ תתן אמת ליעקב[41]) שלי שהוא דרשות
על כל פרשיות וכן ספר צהלה ורנה[42]) על שיר   215
השירים ועל ס׳ קהלת ודניאל וס׳ דרושי

---

202.   ק׳ שספרי נ׳ א׳ שס׳.
203.   א׳ בחיבור ק׳ נ׳ בחבור. ק׳ נ׳ דרושיהם א׳ דרושים.
206.   א׳ בחיבורם ק׳ נ׳ בחבורם. ק׳ א׳ ובאמירתם נ׳ ובאמירותם.
207.   ק׳ בהיות נ׳ א׳ להיות. א׳ ספר ק׳ נ׳ ס׳.
208.   ק׳ א׳ בתיקונם נ׳ בתקונם.
209.   ק׳ א׳ הרבה נ׳ מרובה.
211.   נ׳ שהשגתי ק׳ א׳ שהשגחתי ונתתי לבי.
213.   ק׳ וכתבתים נ׳ א׳ הכתבתים. ק׳ א׳ בתחילה נ׳ בתחלה.
213-215.   בק׳ העביר קו על המילים „ועל פיהם דרכתי בס׳ תתן אמת ליעקב שלי שהוא דרשות על כל הפרשיות".
215.   ק׳ וכן ספר צהלה ורנה על שיר נ׳ א׳ ליתא בק׳ העביר קו על המילים האלה.
215-226.   כל השורות האלה נמצאות רק בק׳ בנ׳ וא׳ ליתא. ובכתב יד ק׳ העביר קוים על השורות.

---

40) כתובות נ.
41) מיכה ז:כ.
42) ראה ההקדמה שלי למעלה, עמודים 62-63.

הלועזיים ושבתות כי באמת ס׳ זה היה
לי ליד ימין בחיבורם קרוב לחמש מאות
דרושים מלבד — מהדרושים שחברתי על
ס׳ מורשה קהלת יעקב בפי׳ ס׳ מדע   220
אהבה וזמנים של הרמב״ם ז״ל וספר
אוצר החכמות וס׳ שני מאורות התשובה
תיקון כל עון בפרט ודרשות ב׳
על מזמור בבוא אליו נתן הנביא[43]) על
תשובה ותיקון לכל טעות הב״ה[44]) יטיב   225
עמי שיבואו לאור אמן ת״ושלב״ע[45])
[אין צורך לזכור אלו כי כבר זכרתים
בהקדמת ס׳ שני מאורות הגדולים על
התשובה,]
יהי רצון מלפני אלקי השמים בע״ה[46])   230
שיזכני בחסדו שישתמשו בני ישראל בספרי
זה להחיות נשמתי בעה״ב דגדול שכר
המזכה את הרבים[47]) ויביא לאור שאר

227-229. השורות האלה נמצאות רק בק׳. בנ׳ וא׳ ליתא. וכנראה המחבר כתב את המילים 229 — 227
על השורות שנכתבות על הצד הימיני ובתחתית העמוד של כתב-יד ק׳ — — זאת אומרת
השורות המתחילות עם 215 ,,וכן ספר צהלה ורנה על שיר . . .״ עד 226 ,,. . . שיבואו לאור
אמן ת״ושלב״ע״. השורות 229-227 הן נתינת טעם למה העביר קוים על מה שכתב בצד
ולמטה מן ,,וכן ספר צהלה . . .״.

230. ק׳ א׳ יהי רצון מלפני נ׳ ירמ״א שבשמים. ק׳ אלקי השמים נ׳ א׳ אלקינו שבשמים. ק׳ בע״ה
נ׳ א׳ ליתא.

231. נ׳ א׳ ישראל ק׳ ישר׳. ק׳ נ׳ בספרי א׳ מספרי.

---

43) תהלים נא:ב.
44) הקדוש ברוך הוא.
45) תם ונשלם שבח לאל בורא עולם.
46) בעזרת השם.
47) ראה אבות ה:יח.

ספרים רבי הכמות והאיכות שלמדני הוא

יתׄ אכיׄׄר[48])   235

אלו הן ההזהרות הצריכות ליזהר

בהן הדרשן כדי שתהיו דרשותיו רצויות

בעיני אלקים וישראל אשר חבר הדורש טוב

לעמו[51]) הרופא כמהורׄׄר יעקב בכמוהרׄׄר

יצחק צהלון זצׄׄל   240

אׄ   מה יהיה ענין ונושא הדרוש

בׄ   באיכות הדרוש

גׄ   בכמות הדרוש

דׄ   בסדר הדרוש

הׄ   אופן חיבור ההקדמה   245

וׄ   איך יתנהג בשמיעת קולו

זׄ   איך יתנהג במאמר דבריו

חׄ   איך יתנהג בנענוע גופו

טׄ   מה יעשה הדרשן קודם שיעלה לדרוש

יׄ   מה יהיה תכלית הדורש בדרשותיו   250

235. בק׳ אחרי המילים יתׄ אכיׄׄר נמצאות המילים „ואקיים מׄׄש עושה צדקה בכל עת[49]) זה
הכותב ספרים ומשאילן לאחרים"[50]) ומחק אותן. המילים אלה נמצאות למעלה ב1999 —
201.

237. קׄ אׄ שתהיו נׄ שיהיו. קׄ נׄ דרשותיו אׄ דרשיותיו.

238-240. נׄ אשר חבר הדורש טוב לעמו הרופא כמהורׄׄרר יעקב בכמוהׄׄרר יצחק צהלון זצׄׄל קׄ אׄ
ליתא.

245. קׄ נׄ חיבור ההקדמה אׄ חבור הקדמה.

246. קׄ נׄ קולו אׄ קול.

250. קׄ נׄ בדרשותיו אׄ בדרשיותיו.

48) אמן כן יהי רצון.
49) תהילים קו:ג.
50) ראה למעלה, הערה 40.
51) אסתר י:ג.

י"א איך יסיים וישלים הדרש
י"ב איך יתנהג בענין בריאות גופו כדי
שיוכל לדרוש כהוגן
י"ג מה יעשה הדרשן אחר שדרש
ופרוש דברים אלו בפרקים אלו: 255

פרק א' מה יהיה ענין ונושא הדרוש

א) עיקר גדול הוא בדרוש שיהיה הענין והנושא
יפה ודבר חידוש: ואח"כ יקשטו וילבישו
בפשטים נאים והנושא הזה פעמים יהיה כולו על
פסוק א' או מאמר א' או על למוד או מדה א' טובה 260
לגדל ערכה או על מדה רעה
לגנות אותה להראות תקלתה ונזקה
מהרבה צדדים או על עיקר מעיקרי
האמונה להראות הכרחיותיו וראיותיו ויבקש
ענין חדש ומחודד שנראה דבר תמוה 265
ואמיתי כי לא ימנעו אח"כ ראיות להביא
עליו כי הפוך בה והפוך בה דכולה

252. **ק'** י"ב, והמחבר מחק את המספר. המילים „מה יעשה הדרשן אחר שדרש" היו שם והעביר
קווים עליהן. המחבר שינה את המספר י"ג לי"ב לעשות מה שהיה הנושא לפרק י"ג במקום
י"ב. בכתב יד נ' כתוב „י"ב מה יעשה אחר הדרש" בכתב יד א' כתוב „י"ב מה יעשה הדרשן
אחר שדרש".

252. **ק'** י"ב נ' א' י"ג.

255. **ק'** ופרוש נ' וביאור א' ופי'.

258. **ק'** חידוש נ' א' חדוש. **ק'** א' יקשטו נ' יקשיטו.

259. **נ'** בפשטים **ק'** בפשטי'.

260. **ק'** על מדה **נ' א'** על ליתא.

262. **ק' א'** לגנות **נ'** לגרוע.

263. **ק' א'** מהרבה **נ'** מכמה. **א'** צדדים **ק' נ'** צדדין.

264. **ק' נ'** וראיותיו **א'** וראותיו.

265. **ק' א'** ומחודד **נ'** ליתא. **ק' נ'** שנראה **א'** דנר'. **ק' נ'** דבר **א'** ליתא. **ק' נ'** תמוה **נ' א'** תמיה.

266. **ק' נ'** ימנעו **א'** ימוטו.

בה[52]) ולא יקח ענין פשוט אצל המון העם

משל למה הדבר דומה לאדם הלובש[53])

270 אשה נאה בתכשיטין נאין כמה יתראה

יפיה[54]) אבל לקשט אשה כעורה בתכשיטין

נאים או בהפך לא תיישר בעיני כל

רואיה בשלימות ובדרך זו דרך הדרשן

הגדול בעל העקידה וכיוצא כמו שתוכל

275 לראות בדרשותיו עשה כמו עבד אברהם

שלקח נזם זהב וצמידים ונתנם בידי

רבקה נערה טובת מראה[55]) כן הרב ז״ל

עשה ענין חדש נאה תמוה ואמיתי וקשטו

בחידושים נאים וממנו נלמד לעשות:

280 ב׳ עוד יזהר שלא ירבה חלקי הדרוש אלא

אומר א׳ או ב׳ או ג׳ חלקים כי בהרבות

חלקי הדרוש יקוצו השומעים ויבלבל דעתם

כמו שאמרו החכמים[56]) במקום הרבוי שם

הבלבול:

---

269. ק׳ א׳ למה הדבר דומה נ׳ למה״ד.

271. ק׳ א׳ לקשט נ׳ להכשיט. ק׳ נ׳ כעורה א׳ כעור.

272. ק׳ נאים נ׳ א׳ נאין.

274. ק׳ וכיוצא נ׳ א׳ ליתא. בכתב יד ק׳ המחבר כתב את המילה הזאת בין השורות בתור תיקון.

275. נ׳ בדרשותיו ק׳ א׳ בדרשיותיו. ק׳ א׳ עשה נ׳ שעשה. ק׳ א׳ עבד נ׳ בעבד.

278. ק׳ חדש נ׳ הדרש א׳ הדרוש. ק׳ תמוה נ׳ א׳ תמיה.

279. נ׳ א׳ בחידושים ק׳ בחדושים.

281. נ׳ א׳ אומר ק׳ או׳.

285. ק׳ א׳ יבקש נ׳ צריך.

---

52) אבות ה:כב.

53) כך צריך להיות, אבל „הלובש" במובן הפעיל כאילו כתב „המלביש".

54) ע׳ ספרי דברים מהדורת פינקלשטיין עמ׳ 68: משל למלך וכו׳.

55) בראשית כד:כב.

56) כנראה חכמים נכרים, ומאמר ידוע באיטליה.

ג׳ עוד יבקש לידע במה יחפוץ הקהל 285
לידע יותר ד״מ[33]) אם בענין הגאולה וטעם
אורך הגלות, או מתשובה ותוכחות או
בפירו׳ פסוקים ותשובות קושיות
בפסוקים או בפי׳ מאמרים זרים או
בסיפור מעשים או בפי׳ דינים עם 290
פסוקים וכיוצא עשה רצונך כרצונו[57]:

ד׳ עוד יבקש שיהיה הענין כפי הזמן
ד״מ אם ידרוש בימי סוכות זמן שמחתנו
לא תדרוש אז דברי תוכחות ואם
הוא זמן תשובה לא תאריך בדברים 295
של שמחה ואם יש חתן או בן זכר
למול או דבר אבלות ב״מ[58]) יזכיר קצת מהם כי
דבר בעתו מה טוב[59]) וכמו שאחז״ל משה הזהיר

ק׳ א׳ ותוכחות נ׳ ותוכחת. 287.
ק׳ בפירו׳ נ׳ א׳ בפי׳. 288.
נ׳ א׳ מאמרים ק׳ מאמרי׳. 289.
ק׳ או בסיפור מעשים נ׳ א׳ ליתא. בכתב יד ק׳ המחבר כתב את המילים האלה בין השורות 289-290.
בתור תיקון.
ק׳ וכיוצא נ׳ א׳ ליתא. בכתב יד ק׳ המחבר כתב את המילה הזאת בין השורות בתור תיקון. 291.
ק׳ נ׳ א׳ הענין ובכתב יד ק׳ המחבר הוסיף את המילה „הענין" בין השורות בתור תיקון. 292.
ק׳ שמחתנו נ׳ א׳ שמחינו. 293.
ק׳ א׳ תדרוש נ׳ ידרוש. ק׳ אז נ׳ א׳ ליתא. בכתב יד ק׳ הוסיף את המילה הזאת בין השורות 294.
בתור תיקון. ק׳ נ׳ דברי א׳ דבר.
ק׳ א׳ תאריך נ׳ יאריך. ק׳ נ׳ בדברים א׳ בדבר. 295.
ק׳ נ׳ של א׳ ליתא. 296.
ק׳ א׳ ב״מ נ׳ וכו׳. 297.
ק׳ א׳ וכמו שאחז״ל נ׳ וכמשאחז״ל. 298.

57) אבות ב:ד.
58) בר מנן, ז.א. חוץ ממנו.
59) משלי טו:כג.

לישראל שיהיו דורשין הלכות פסח בפסח וכו'[60]
לא כאותם — שמאריכים בדרשות שלא
כענין הזמן ואח"כ מדבקים קצת הדבר
בענין:

ה' עוד ישתדל שיהיה הענין דבר תועלת
ועושה פירות במ"ט[61]) בעם לא להראות
בעומק חכמתו או סיפור דברים בלבד
בלי חידוש.

ו' יתפלל לה' שישפיע עליו חכמה ובינה וישקיף
ממעון קדשו[62]) להורות לו פירושים אמיתיים
ויזכור מה שלמד לפני הר סיני כמו
שאחז"ל כי כל דבר שעתיד תלמיד ותיק
לחדש הורה ה' למשה ולישראל עמו[63]) ששם
היו כל הנפשות[64]) ששמעו דברי אלקים חיים[65])

---

299. נ' א' לישראל ק' לישר'.
300. ק' א' שמאריכים נ' שמאריכין. נ' א' בדרשות ק' בדרשו'.
306. ק' בלי חידוש נ' א' ליתא. בכתב יד ק' הוסיף את המילים האלה בכתב ידו של המחבר.
308. נ' א' פירושים ק' פירושי'.
309. ק' נ' לפני א' ליתא. ק' נ' הר א' בהר. נ' כמו ק' כ' א' כי מה.
310. נ' שאחז"ל ק' אמרו חז"ל א' שאחז"ל.
311. ק' א' ה' נ' הקב"ה. נ' א' ולישראל ק' ולישר'. נ' א' ששם ק' ושם.
312. ק' ששמעו דברי אלקים חיים נ' א' ליתא. בכתב יד ק' המחבר הוסיף את המילים האלה.

---

60) מגילה ד. ולב.
61) במעשים טובים.
62) ראה דברים כו:טו.
63) ראה מגילה יט: וראה גם ירושלמי פאה ב:ו, יז, ומדרש ויקרא רבה כב:א.
64) ע' שמות רבה כח:ו: ולא אתכם לבדכם אנכי כרת את הברית הזאת . . . כי את אשר
ישנו פה עמנו עמד היום . . . ואת „אשר איננו פה עמנו היום" (דברים כט:יג-יד), איננו פה
עמנו עמד היום לא כתוב כאן אלא, איננו פה עמנו היום — אלו הנשמות העתידות להבראות,
שאין בהן ממש, שלא נאמרה בהן עמידה.
65) עירובין יג: גיטין ו: „אלו ואלו דברי אלהים חיים".

פרק ב' באיכות הדרוש ואופן הדרשה

א' יבקש שהדרוש יכנס בו דבר עמוק
ומחודד שייישר לת"ח ומעיינים ודבר מתוק   315
וקל להבין כדי שייישר להמון העם וסיפור
איזה דבר הנשמע גם לע"ה ונשים בחורים
וזקנים כדי שכולם יהנו ממנו כמו שדרשו
חז"ל על כה תאמר לבית יעקב[66] אלו
הנשים ותגד לבני ישראל אלו האנשים וכו'[67]:   320

ב' אם ידרוש דרש של הספד יזהר מאד
שלא לשבח הנפטר יותר מדאי ממה
שעשה שזה לו לגנות ובזיון וכמו
שיש מפרשים אחים לי בהספדאי דהתם
קאימנא[68] כלומר התחמם לפרש שבחי   325
באופן שאני שם באמת לומר מה שעשיתי
שאם תשבחני במה שאין בי הרי כאלו
אתה מהלל לאחר ואיני שם[69]:

ג' לא יאמר כל הדרוש ממה שכתוב
בספרים אלא יחדש מדעתו איזה חידוש   330

א' שייטב ק' נ' שייישר.   316.
ק' א' שכולם נ' שכלם.   318.
נ' א' ישראל ק' ישר'. נ' א' האנשים ק' אנשים. ק' וכו' נ' א' ליתא.   320.
ק' א' של הספד נ' מאיזה ספר.   321.
ק' א' ובזיון נ' ולבזיון.   323.
נ' א' מפרשים ק' מפרשי'.   324.
ק' א' קאימנא נ' קאמנא. נ' כלומר ק' א' כלו'. ק' נ' לפרש א' לפרוש.   325.

66) שמות יט:ג.
67) מכילתא מהדורת האראוויטץ רבין 207. ראה גם ילקוט שמות רעו.
68) שבת קנג.
69) ראה רש"י שם.

ופירו' כפי דעתו וחכמתו ויזמין ספרים
הרבה כי אין חכם בלי ספרים רבים
וְטוֹבים[70]) כי פעמים ימצא ענינו בא'
ולא באחר ויערב בדרושו איזה דבר
מחכמה של חיצוניות שהם פרפראות   335
לחכמה[71]) כמו סיפור טבעי הב"ח[72]) וכיוצא
ומיד ימצא פסוק או מאמר חז"ל שאמרו
דבר ההוא כי לא נכחד מהם דבר:

ד' כאשר ירצה לומר איזה פירוש
וחידוש לא יכנס פתאום לענין אלא ע"י   340
ההקדמה והצעה ופתח דבריו יאירו ולא
יאריך בהצעה כי היא אחד ממונעי
החכמה כמו שכתב הרמב"ם ז"ל במורה:[73])

ה' לא יאריך בספור פשט המאמר או המעשה
כי אין ראוי שתוציא חצי הדרוש בספור   345

331. ק' ופירו' נ' ופי' א' או פ'.
333. ק' נ' וטובים א' וטובי'.
336. ק' הב"ח נ' הכ"ח א' ליתא.
337. ק' א' חז"ל נ' רז"ל.
339. ק' נ' פירוש א' פי'.
340. ק' וחידוש נ' או חידוש א' ליתא.
342. ק' בהצעת נ' א' בהצעה. נ' אחד ק' א' א'.
343. ק' א' שכתב נ' שכתב אבל שם נקדות על מלת דבריו לסימן שיש למחקה. ק' ז"ל נ' א'
ליתא.
344. ק' נ' או המעשה א' ליתא.

70) ראה דאווידסון י. אוצר המשלים והפתגמים מספרות ימי הבינים, 188, 3084.
71) אבות ג:יט.
72) הבעלי חיים.
73) מורה נבוכים א:לד.

פסוקים או מאמר כפשטן כי אין הגון להביא
מעולם פסוק או מאמר בדרש שלא תחדש בו איזה
דבר אם יהיה לראיה איזה דבר.

ו' אם תעשה איזה חילוק באיזה דבר הזהר שיהיו
החלקים כולם שלמים כפי הכל ולא תאמר דבר
זה נחלק לד' חלקים ובאמת יש לו חלקים אחרים
אלא אם לא תרצה לזכור כל החלקים
פרש דבריך ואמור כי אתה הבאת קצת
חלקיו כפי עניניך:

350

ז' כשירגיש ויראה שהעם ייעף וייגע משמוע
אז תספר איזה מעשה נאה להעיר אותם ולענג
השומעים כמו שסיפרו חז"ל במאמר ר' פלוני
שראה העם ישנים אמר עתידה אשה שתלד
בכל יום[74]) וע"ד זה עשה אתה לומר איזה דבר
דבדיחותא[75]) אמנם לא תאריך בו אלא בקלות.

355

360

ח' לעולם יאמר הפירושים יותר נאים ולא יביא
הפירושים הדוחקים ולא יטריח העם להביא

---

348. ק' אם יהיה לראיה איזה דבר נ' א' ליתא. ובכתב יד ק' כנראה המחבר הוסיף את המילים האלה.

350. ק' א' כפי נ' בפי.

352. ק' אלא נ' א' אבל.

355. ק' א' כשירגיש ויראה נ' כשתרגיש ותראה. ק' א' ייעף נ' עייף. ק' נ' וייגע א' ויגע.

357. ק' חז"ל נ' א' רז"ל.

360. ק' דבדיחותא נ' א' שבדחותא.

362. ק' הפירושים נ' א' פירושים. ק' נ' ולא א' שלא.

---

74) שבת ל:

75) שם ופסחים קיז.

פירושים בלתי ישרים ולהקשות נגדם וכן אין
להביא על מאמר או פסוק הרבה קושיות
365 מדקדוקים אלא יאמר היותר צריכים לעניינו
ויניח האחרים שהם יבינו מעצמם וראה
שהרב בעל העקדה וכיוצא לא הרבה
בקושיות ודיוקים בפרשו איזה מאמר או
פסוק אלא כשרצה לפרש הפרשה ואם
370 ירצה לזכור הרבה פירושים על פסוק א׳
או מאמר א׳ יזכור קודם אותם
שאינם מעניינו במהרה ובסוף יביא פי׳
שהוא כפי עניינו:

ט׳ פירוש הפסוק או המאמר יהיה או עם
375 פסוק ומאמר אחר או עם איזה דבר חכמה
ממה שזכרו[76] החכמים או עם איזה
דין ובהביאו פסוק או מאמר אחר יאמר
בו ג״כ איזה חדוש מלבד פשוטן של
דברים מדעתך או מדעת אחרים

---

366. ק׳ נ׳ שהם א׳ ליתא.
367. ק׳ א׳ שהרב נ׳ ליתא. ק׳ וכיוצא נ׳ א׳ ליתא. ובכתב יד ק׳ הוסיף את המילה בין השורות. ק׳ א׳ לא נ׳ שלא.
368. ק׳ בפרושו נ׳ כשמפרש א׳ בפי׳.
370. ק׳ נ׳ ירצה א׳ יר׳. ק׳ נ׳ פירושים א׳ פירושי׳.
371. ק׳ נ׳ או א׳ ליתא. ק׳ נ׳ מאמר א׳ ומאמר. נ׳ א׳ ק׳ א׳ ליתא.
372. נ׳ מעניינו ק׳ א׳ בעניינו. ק׳ א׳ פי׳ נ׳ הפירוש.
373. ק׳ א׳ כפי נ׳ ליתא. ק׳ א׳ עניינו נ׳ כעניינו.
375. ק׳ נ׳ ומאמר א׳ או מאמר.
377. ק׳ פסוק נ׳ א׳ הפסוק. ק׳ א׳ מאמר נ׳ המאמר.
379. נ׳ א׳ דברים ק׳ דברי׳. ק׳ א׳ מדעתך נ׳ מדעתו.

---

76) כך צריך להיות. אבל צריכים להבין את „שזכרו החכמים" במובן הפעיל כאילו כתב
שהזכירו החכמים. ראה למעלה, הערה 53.

עַל זֶה אָמְרוּ אֵין מִדְרָשׁ בְּלֹא חִידּוּשׁ[77]) 380
וּלְעוֹלָם אָמוֹר דָּבָר בְּשֵׁם אוֹמְרוֹ[78]) כְּדֵי
שֶׁיֵּדְעוּ וְיַאֲמִינוּ כַּאֲשֶׁר לֹא תִזְכֹּר שֵׁם
אוֹמְרוֹ יוֹדוּ שֶׁהוּא חִידּוּשׁ שֶׁלְּךָ בִּלְבַד
וּכְמוֹ שֶׁעָשָׂה דָּוִד הִזְכִּיר בַּמִּזְמוֹרִים
בְּנֵי קֹרַח וַאֲחֵרִים[79]) וְאָמְרוּ חַז"ל כָּל 385
הָאוֹמֵר דָּבָר בְּשֵׁם אוֹמְרוֹ מֵבִיא גְאֻלָּה
לָעוֹלָם[80]).

יו"ד בְּהַזְכִּירְךָ אֵיזֶה דָּבָר אוֹ מַעֲשֶׂה
אֱמוֹר פְּרָטֵי הַדְּבָרִים ד"מ[81]) הַמָּקוֹם
שֶׁאֵירַע דָּבָר הַהוּא וְהַזְּמַן וְשֵׁמוֹת 390
הָאֲנָשִׁים כִּי זֶה הוּא נוֹתֵן יוֹתֵר אֲמִיתּוּת
לַדְּבָרִים

י"א יִזָּהֵר מְאֹד שֶׁלֹּא יֹאמַר בִּדְרוּשׁ
בָּרַבִּים דָּבָר הַמְפַקְפֵּק בָּאֱמוּנָה וְנוֹתֵן

ק' עַל זֶה אָמְרוּ אֵין מִדְרָשׁ בְּלֹא חִידּוּשׁ נ' א' לֵיתָא. בִּכְתַב יַד ק' הוֹסִיף אֶת הַמִּילִים הָאֵלֶה 380.
בְּגִלְיוֹן עִם סִימָן לְהַכְנִיס אוֹתָן בְּאֶמְצַע הַשּׁוּרוֹת.
ק' א' אָמוֹר נ' יֹאמַר. 381.
ק' א' תִזְכּוֹר נ' יִזְכּוֹר. 382.
ק' חִידּוּשׁ נ' א' חָדוּשׁ. ק' א' שֶׁלְךָ נ' שֶׁלּוֹ. ק' נ' בִּלְבַד א' לֵיתָא. 383.
נ' א' וְאָמְרוּ חַז"ל כָּל הָאוֹמֵר ק' וְאז"ל אוֹמֵר וּבִכְתַב יַד ק' הוֹסִיף אֶת הַמִּילִים „וְאז"ל אוֹמֵר 385.
דָּבָר בְּשֵׁם אוֹמְרוֹ מֵבִיא גְאֻלָּה לָעוֹלָם" בְּצַד (387-385).
ק' א' שֶׁאֵירַע דָּבָר הַהוּא נ' שֶׁאֵירַע בּוֹ. 390.
נ' א' יֹאמַר ק' לוֹמַר. ק' א' בִּדְרוּשׁ נ' בִּדְרַשׁ. 393.
נ' וְנוֹתֵן ק' א' וְנוֹתְנִין. 394.

77) ר' חֲגִיגָה ג. „אִי אֶפְשָׁר לְבֵית הַמִּדְרָשׁ בְּלֹא חִידּוּשׁ".
78) אָבוֹת ו:ו.
79) תְּהִלִּים מב, מד-מח, צד, צז.
80) מְגִילָּה טו. חוּלִין קד: וְנִדָּה יט:
81) ע' לְמַעֲלָה הֶעָרָה 33.

איזה שמץ פיסול[82]) באוזן השומעים גם
שאתה תספר הדבר כפי דעות
האומרים כן שמפני זה בקשו חכמים
לגנוז ספר קהלת[83]) ועם שאח״כ תאמר
התשובות הגונות יש לחוש שמא
יזכרו העם הספקות וישכחו התשובות
ועל זה אמרו חכמים הזהרו בדבריכם
וכו'[84]) ואמרו אין דורשין במעשה
מרכבה וכו':[85])

395

400

י״ב להידור הדרש ישתדל להביא
בדרושו איזה מעשה הכתוב בכתבי
הקדש באיזה חידוש כדי ליפות
הדרוש כי טבעו של כל אדם להתענג
בשמעו איזה מעשה שאירע כ״ש
מעשים שנכתבו בספרי הקדש שהם
נאמנו מאד אמרו חז״ל בפסוק

405

410

395. נ' א' באוזן ק' באזן. ק' נ' השומעים א' השומעי'.
398. ק' א' שאח״כ נ' שאחר כך.
399. ק' א' הגונות נ' הצריכות.
401. נ' ועל זה אמרו ק' א' ועז״א. ק' א' חכמים נ' חז״ל.
402. נ' א' דורשין ק' דורשי'.
404. ק' להידור נ' לנד א' להדור.
405. ק' נ' בדרושו א' בדרוש.
406. ק' א' חידוש נ' חדוש.
409. ק' נ' בספרי א' בכתבי.
410. ק' אמרו חז״ל נ' א' אחז״ל.

82) ראה פסחים ג:, ומגילה כה: וקידושין עא:
83) שבת ל:, ויקרא רבא כח:א, קהלת רבה א:ג, יא:ט, ומקבילות.
84) אבות א:יא.
85) משנה חגיגה ב:א על יחזקאל א.

רפדוני בתפוחים[86]) אמר ר׳ יצחק
בראשונה כשהיתה הפרוטה מצוייה
אדם מתאוה דבר משנה דבר הלכה
דבר תלמוד ועכשיו שאין הפרוטה מצוייה
וביותר שאנו חולים מן המלכיות אדם   415
מתאוה לשמוע דבר מקרא דבר
אגדה:[87]) ע״כ

י״ג אם ירצה לומר איזה קושיא בפסוק
או מאמר יזכרנו קודם שיתחיל פירו׳
המאמר והפסוק כי אינו נאה   420
בעוד שהוא מפרש הפסוק — לערבב
בתוכו איזה קושיא ודיוק בפסוק כי
עת שאלה לחוד ועת פירו׳
לחוד:

י״ד בחור המתחיל לחבר דרשים יקרא   425
כל כ״ד ספרי׳ תורה נביאים

411. נ׳ אמר ר׳ יצחק ק׳ א׳ א״ר יצחק.
412. ק׳ נ׳ כשהיתה א׳ כשהייתה. ק׳ הפרוטה נ׳ א׳ פרוטה.
414. ק׳ א׳ ועכשיו נ׳ עכשיו.
415. ק׳ א׳ וביותר נ׳ וכיותר. ק׳ נ׳ חולים א׳ ליתא.
416-417. ק׳ נ׳ דבר אגדה א׳ או דבר.
419. ק׳ פירו׳ נ׳ א׳ פי׳.
420. ק׳ א והפסוק נ׳ או הפסוק.
421. ק׳ נ׳ בעוד א׳ כעוד.
422. נ׳ א׳ בתוכו ק׳ תוכו.
423. ק׳ פירו׳ נ׳ א׳ פי׳.
425-429. השורות האלה רק בק׳, ובנ׳ וא׳ ליתא, וברור מן הכתיבה שבכתב יד ק׳ הוסיף את השורות האלה אחר כך.

86) שיר השירים ב:ה.
87) ילקוט שיר השירים תקכה תתקפו. וראה מסכת סופרים טז:ד ומדרש שיר השירים רבה ב:ה.

וכתובים עם פי' רש"י או מפרש
אחר ועוד יעיין כל מאמרי עין ישר'[88])
עם הפירוש ויקרא ס' ילקוט:

פרק ג' בכמות וחומר הדרוש 430

א' לא יאריך דרושו כדי שלא לטרוח
הציבור וגם לא כ"כ קצר שאין ראוי
להטריח העם להביאם לשמוע דבר
קצר אלא יחשוב וישקול בדעתו ד'
דברים הזמן והענין והמקום והדורש 435
וזה אם הוא עת חם יקצר ובעת קר
יאריך יותר ואם הוא סמוך לזמן
הסעודה יקצר: אם בעניין אם
ענינו ודרושו דבר מכאוב
ודאגה יקצר ואם ענין של שמחה 440
יאריך קצת: אם המקום צר
והעם עומדים שם בדוחק ועומדים
צפופים[89]) אז יקצר וכך כל
כיוצא בזה: אם בדורש אם
יש לו חן וחסד גם שמאריך קצת לא 445

432. **ק'** הציבור **נ' א'** הצבור.
433. **ק' נ'** להביאם **א'** להביא.
434-5. **ק' ד'** דברים **נ' א'** ליתא. ובכתב יד **ק'** הוסיף את המילים „ד' דברים" בין השורות בכתיבה אחרת.
436. **ק' א'** וזה **נ'** ליתא. **ק' א'** אם **נ'** ואם.
437. **ק'** לזמן **נ' א'** ליתא.
438. **ק'** הסעודה **נ' א'** לסעודה.
444. **ק'** אם בדורש אם **נ' א'** אם בדורש ז.א. „אם" השני ליתא.

88) ראה למעלה, הערה 32.
89) אבות ה:ה.

יקוץ בו העם וזה שאין כן במי שאין
לו חן כל כך: או אם הוא חכם מופלג
בדורו בחכמתו אם יאריך לא יקוצו
בו בני אדם מה שאין כן בתלמיד
דורש.   450

ב' אם יעשה ב' חלקים בדרש יהיה
חלק ראשון ארוך וחלק ב' קצר כיון
שכבר שמעו העם חלק א' היה
עליהם לטורח וילאו נשוא אם
חלק ב' ארוך יותר מדאי: 455

ג' בתוך הדרוש יביא מסורות
נוטריקון מעשים דינים פסוקים
מאמרים גמטריאות וקצת מחכמות
חיצוניות שהם פרפראות לחכמה[90]) ואם
הפירוש עמוק יבארנו במשל כמו שמצינו   460
במאמרי חז"ל ובפרט מעשים של תורה

ק' נ' שמאריך א' שיאריך. 446.
ק' א' בחכמתו אם נ' בחכמה שאם. 448.
ק' א' מה שאין כן נ' משא"כ. 449.
ק' ראשון נ' א' א'. 452.
ק' נ' היה א' יהיה. 453.
ק' א' חלק ב' נ' ח"ב. 455.
ק' בתוך א' נ' ובתוך. ק' נ' מסורות א' אסורות. 456.
נ' נוטריקון ק' נטריקון א' נוטריוקן. ק' נ' פסוקים א' פסוקי'. 457.
נ' א' מאמרים ק' מאמרי'. ק' גמטריאות נ' גימטראיות א' גמטראיות. 458.
נ' א' חיצוניות ק' חצוניות. ק' נ' שהם א' שהן. 459.
ק' נ' חז"ל א' רז"ל. 461.
ק' א תורה נביאים וכתובים נ' תנ"ך. 461-2.

90) אבות ג:יט.

נביאים וכתובים כנ"ל וגם יפה
להביא קראי או מאמרי דקשיו
אהדדי[91]) ולפרשם ולהשלימם יחד: ראה מה
שאכתוב בסוף בענין אורך הדרש או
עת חום.

פרק ד' בסדר הדרוש

א' מעקרי דרוש הטוב הוא הסדר נאה
שיהיה לו קו ישר ואם לפעמים
יצא חוץ מעניינו יחזור מיד לסדרו
הישר ואם תמצא איזה פירוש נאה
בפסוק ומאמר תאמרהו במהרה בשם
אומרו[92]) גם שאינו כפי ענינך והוא
חוץ ממנו אמור אותו בשמו ואח"כ
באר פירושך שהוא כסדר וטוב הסדר
סיבה שיזכרו העם מכל הדרש:

.463 ק' א' דקשיו נ' דקשה.
.464 נ' א' אהדדי ק' אתדדי.
.464-6 א' ת' ליתא. בק' (על הגליון בכתיבה אחרת): „ראה מה שאכתוב בסוף בענין אורך הדרש או עת חום." ראה למעלה שורה 436 בענין אורך הדרש הוא כותב למטה בשורות 588-596. אחרי המילה „שאכתוב" בהוספה הנ"ל נכתבו המילים: „מטעמים וכו'" והוסיף עליהן קו.
.467 ק' א' מעקרי נ' מעיקרי.
.470 ק' נ' מעניינו א' מענינו.
.471 ק' פירוש נ' א' פי'.
.472 ק' א' תאמרהו נ' תאמר אותו. בק' המילה „במהרה" נכתבה בין השורות כתיקון של „במחילה" שנמחקה.
.473 נ' א' אומרו ק' אומרם. ק' נ' ענינך והוא א' עניינך והר'.
.474 נ' בשמו ק' א' בשמם.
.476 ק' א' מכל נ' כל.

91) ראה ראש השנה ג:, מגילה יב., יבמות מט:, ומקבילות.
92) ראה למעלה הערה 80.

ב׳ וטוב והגון לשים ולסדר הפשטים היותר
טובים בתחילת הדרוש ובסופו לפי
שאם בתחילה תאמר חדושים שאינם כ״כ
יפים וישרים השומעים יחשבו שכן יהיה ‏480
כל פירוש של כל הדרוש: ויקוצו
וילכו להם או יישנו וכן בסוף טוב
לומר פי׳ נאה מאד כדי שישמעו
בנעימות כדרך מסדרי בית משתה
שבסוף מביאים דברים מתוקים ‏485
ורווחא לבסומי שכיחא‏(93) ובאמצע יאמר
היותר גרועים וגם בהם יקצר כדי
שלא יחסר זמן אח״כ לפשטים
ודיוקים וחידושים טובים:

ג׳ סדר הדברים יהיה באופן הזה ‏490
ענין פסוק מאמר מעשה מסרה
נוטריקון או דבר חכמה חיצונית
כי אינו יפה להביא כל הפסוקים
יחד זה אחר זה או כל המאמרים זה
אחר זה ולפעמים יפה לחזור בכל ‏495
חלק מן הדרוש את הנושא שהתחיל

478. **ק׳ א׳** בתחילת נ׳ בתחלת. **ק׳ נ׳** ובסופו א׳ ולסופו.
479. **ק׳** בתחילה נ׳ בתחלתו א׳ בתחלה.
481. **ק׳** פירוש נ׳ ליתא א׳ פי׳. **ק׳ א׳** של כל נ׳ ליתא.
484. **ק׳ א׳** בית נ׳ ליתא.
486. **ק׳ נ׳** ורווחא א׳ ורחווא. **ק׳ נ׳** לבסומי א׳ לכסומי. **ק׳ נ׳** ובאמצע א׳ ובאמצעי.
489. **ק׳ נ׳** וחדושים א׳ וחידושים.
492. **נ׳** נוטריקון ק׳ נטריוקון א׳ נוטריוקון. **ק׳** חיצונית נ׳ מחצוניות א׳ חיצוניות.
494. **ק׳ א׳** יחד זה אחר זה נ׳ ליתא. **ק׳ א׳** כל נ׳ ליתא. **ק׳ א׳** המאמרים זה נ׳ המאמרים יחד זה.

93) ראה עירובין פב: ומגילה:, ועיין פירוש רש״י שם.

בו ולפעמים יביא בקיצור פירוש
המפרשים ואח״כ פירושו:

500 ד׳ פעמים יזכור קודם הענין
ואח״כ הפסוק או המאמר לראיה
כאשר הענין תמוה ופעמים יביא
הפסוק קודם ואח״כ יאמר עליו הענין
אם אינו גלוי בפסוק כאשר יאמר
אותו:

505 ה׳ יתחיל כל התחלת פסוק או מאמר
באיזה המצאה יפה והצעה טובה
ומחודש כדי להעיר לב השומעים אותו
בחידוש ע״ד והכינו את אשר יביאו[94] כי
ההצעה ההיא הכנה לפירוש ההוא
510 ויקל להבינו אח״כ.

פרק ה׳ בענין הקדמת הדרוש

א׳ הקדמת הדרוש תהיה קצרה כי
אם תהיה ארוכה אפשר שדרושו

497. נ׳ פירוש ק׳ א׳ פי׳.
500. ק׳ א׳ לראיה נ׳ ליתא. נ׳ הפסוק או המאמר לראיה. כאשר ק׳ א׳ הפסוק לראיה או מאמר כאשר.
506. ק׳ באיזה נ׳ בתחלת א׳ בתחילת.
509. ק׳ הכנה נ׳ נהכנה א׳ בהכנה.
510. ק׳ נ׳ להבינו א׳ להכינו. ק׳ א׳ אח״כ נ׳ אחר כך.
511. ק׳ א׳ הדרש נ׳ הדרוש.

94) שמות טז:ה.

יהיה כאיש שראשו יהיה גדול מכל
גופו: 515

ב׳ ההקדמה צריך שתהיה דבר חידוש
והמצאה שלכאורה היא רחוקה
מעניין הדרוש ואח״כ ידבק ויצרף
היטב לעניין הדרוש:

ג׳ לא יאריך בה לפרש פסוקים ומאמרים 520
כי לא תהיה ההקדמה דרוש בפני
עצמו אלא התחלה והצעה לדרוש:

ד׳ בהקדמה יתפלל לה׳ שיעזרהו ויקח
רשות מהב״ה ומתורתו הקדושה ומכל
החכמים וגדולי דורו בענוה והכנעה 525
בכל לב ונפש:

ה׳ יתחיל אותה בדברים צחים ונאים
ויפים כפי הלשון ההוא:

פרק ו׳ איך יתנהג בקולו

א׳ כאשר יתחיל נושא ומאמר ראשון 530
ודרוש לא ישא קולו הרבה אלא

516. ק׳ נ׳ דבר א׳ דיברי.
524. ק׳ א׳ מהב״ה נ׳ מהקב״ה.
525. נ׳ א׳ החכמים ק׳ החכמי׳.
527. נ׳ א׳ בדברים ק׳ בדברי׳.
529. ק׳ נ׳ איך יתנהג בקולו א׳ ליתא.
530. נ׳ א׳ א׳ ק׳ ליתא. ק׳ ומאמר ראשון נ׳ א׳ ומאמר א׳.
531. ק׳ ודרוש נ׳ א׳ ודרש.

יתחיל בקול נמוך ולא בקול זמר אלא
בקול שוה כטבעו וכן תוך הדרוש
כאשר קורא הפסוקים ומאמרים
יקרא כדרכו לקרות עם חביריו
בלי קול זמר ושירה: כי בתפלות
מזמרים לא בדרש:[95])

ב' וישנה הברת קולו כפי הענין כי
לא יאמר לעולם דרושו בטעם א' דרך
משל אם יספר דברי מלך ידבר
בממשלה ועשיר יענה עזות[96]) כאלו
הוא המלך המצוה לעם ואם יספר
דברי העם ידבר בתחנונים כי
תחנונים ידבר רש[97]) כעבד המדבר
לפני המלך ואם יספר דבר של
דאגה וצער ידבר בקול דכא
בבכי ודמעות בעיניו ואם יספר דבר
של שמחה ידבר בששון בפנים צוחקות:

533. נ' א' בקול ק' קול. ק' נ' כטבעו א' בטבעו. ק' נ' הדרוש א' הדרושה.

534. ק' נ' ומאמרים א' ומאמרי.

535. ק' נ' חביריו א' חבירו.

537. ק' מזמרים נ' א' מזמורים.

539. ק' נ' בטעם א' בנועם.

539-40. נ' דרך משל ק' א' ד"מ.

546. נ' א' דכא ק' דכה.

547. ק' א' בבכי נ' ליתא. ק' א' יספר דבר נ' ידבר בדבר.

548. ק' א' בפנים צוחקות נ' ובפנים שוחקות.

95) ראה מגילה לב.

96) משלי יח:כג.

97) שם.

535

540

545

ג׳ לא יפחד ולא יירא[98]) כלל אלא
ידרוש בשמחה ויחשוב שדבריו יפים
ונאים ויערבו ודאי לשומעיהם כי
בזה לא ידאג ויהיה עז כנמר[99]) כי
עיקר גדול בדרש לומר ענינו
בשמחה כאלו כל דבריו דברי
אלקים חיים[100]) בלי מורת אנשים[101])
פעמים ידבר בזריזות גדול ואח״כ
ינוח קצת בקוראו הפסוק או
המאמר ואח״כ ירים קולו בזריזות
כפי צורך הענין:

550

555

ד׳ אם בתוך הדרש יבוא חכם או רב
או ממונה וגברא רבה יפסוק קצת
מאמרו עד שישב במקומו[102]) זה לכבוד
התורה ואותו גברא רבה וגם שלא
יתבלבל קולו בשמעו קול הברה מאותם
המכבדים אותו הבא:

560

565

ה׳ יזהר שלא יפזר ויכריח קולו נגד
טבעו אלא ירים קולו כפי טבעו —

ק׳ נ׳ לשומעיהם א׳ לשומעים.   551.

ק׳ נ׳ גדול א׳ ליתא.   553.

ק׳ נ׳ דבריו א׳ דברים. ק׳ נ׳ דברי א׳ ליתא.   554.

נ׳ א׳ המאמר ק׳ מאמר.   558.

ק׳ נ׳ חכם א׳ ליתא.   560.

נ׳ א׳ וגברא ק׳ וגברה.   561.

98) ראה ישעיהו מד:ח.

99) אבות ה:כ.

100) ירמיה כג:לו. וראה עירובין יג: וגיטין ו:

101) ראה ברכות כח:

102) עיין מדרש ספרי במדבר מהדורת האראוויטץ 186.

וכפי הצורך והענין כנ"ל אמנם
מיד יחזור לקולו הראשון כטבעו:

פרק ז' איך יתנהג הדרשן בדבורו 570

א' ידבר בקלות ובזריזות נמרץ
שאם יאמר דרושו בעצלות יקוץ
לשומעים ולפעמים ידבר במרוצה כאלו
מדבר בנשימה א' הרבה פסוקים
חדושים פשטים וענינים בקלות. 575

ב' כאשר תביא ראיה מתורה
נביאים וחכמים תזכיר שמם בהלול
ושבח ד"מ[103]) הלא אמר זה מעין[104])
החכמות שלמה ע"ה או המשורר
האלקי דוד המלך ע"ה או הסבלן 580
הגדול איוב או שמש המאיר הגדול
הרמב"ם או המפולפל הנעלה הרמב"ן או
הנשר הרוחני רש"י וכיוצא:

ג' כאשר תאמר איזה דבר גלוי וידוע
ופשוט לכל יאמר אותו במהירות 585

ק' א' הדרשן נ' ליתא. .570

ק' זה נ' **א'** ליתא. **ק' א'** מעיין נ' מעין. .578

ק' נ' שמש א' השמש. **ק' א'** הגדול נ' ליתא. .581

ק' א' הרמב"ם נ' הרמב"ם ז"ל. **ק' א'** המפולפל נ' המפלפל. **ק' א'** הרמב"ן נ' הרמב"ן ז"ל. .582

ק' א' הנשר הרוחני נ' הנשר הגדול והרוחני. **ק' א'** רש"י וכיוצא נ' רש"י נ"ע[105]) וכיוצא. .583

ק' א' יאמר נ' תאמר. .585

103) דרך משל.
104) אבות ב:ח.
105) נוחו עדן.

ואמור קודם פשט הפסוק בקלות ואח"כ
אמור פירושך:

ד' הזהר בדבורך שלא לכפול מלה
א' אלא ידבר בזריזות בלי מותר
דברים כי ברב דברים לא יחדל
פשע[106]) ולא יוציא מפיו דברים בלתי
ישרים ונאים והגונים כפי לשון ההוא
ולא ירבה דברים בלי תועלת אם
לא באיזה ענין יביא הדרגת אמירות
להעיר העם לשמוע ויחשוב שהעם עומד
בכונת הלב ובקלות יבינו דבריך:

ה' כאשר ידרש פסוק עם פסוק או
מאמר עם מאמר לא יאריך בשני כדי
שלא ישכח העם מן הראשון וכן לא
ישהה מאד בפסוק או מאמר א' כי
העם חושקים לשמוע בכל רגע דבר
חדש:

ו' יזהר שאם יאמר איזה דבר שיש
בו קצת דוחק[107]) או קושיא יקדים הוא

590

595

600

588. ק' א' מלה נ' מילה.
589. ק' א' ידבר נ' תדבר.
590. ק' ברב נ' א' ברוב.
593. נ' א' תועלת ק' מועלת. ק' אם נ' אי.
595. ק' נ' להעיר א' להעיר להעיר. ק' א' ויחשוב נ' דחשוב.
596. ק' א' בכונת נ' בכוונת.
601. ק' נ' חושקים א' חושקי'.
603. ק' איזה נ' א' ליתא.

106) משלי י:יט.
107) עיין בבא קמא מג., קו., וכתובות מב., ושם כתוב: „יכילנא לשנוי לך . . . מיהו
שנויא דחיקא לא משנינא לך".

605 לומר ולפרש גם שיש קושיא פלוני
כבר אני ידעתי ואפשר לתרץ כן
וכן: ויקדים לומר חלקי פי׳ הפסוק
אם יש בו יותר מדבר אחד:

פרק ח׳ איך יתנהג הדורש בנענוע גופו

610 א׳ יפנה פניו לכל הצדדין שעומדים
שם העם ובפרט במקום היושבים
שם החכמים וראשי העם.

ב׳ יזהר שלא ידלג ולא יכה את כפיו
על התיבה ולא יעמוד לעולם על
615 מצב אחד כמצבה אלא ינענע
עצמו ידיו וזרועיו כפי צורך העניין.

ג׳ אם דבריו אל ה׳ ירים ראשו
ועיניו למעלה אל אל בשמים ואם
יוכיח העם ישפיל ראשו ועיניו
620 אל העם:

**פרק ט׳ מה יעשה הדרשן קודם
שיעלה לדרוש**

א׳ אחר שחיבר הדרש והוא לפניו
כתוב יעיין בו הרבה לתת לו

---

608. נ׳ א׳ אחד ק׳ א׳.

609. ק׳ הדורש נ׳ ליתא א׳ הדרשן. ק׳ נ׳ בנענוע גופו א׳ בדבורו.

611. ק׳ במקום היושבים נ׳ לפני המקום שיושבים א׳ לפני המקום היושבים.

613. נ׳ את ק׳ ליתא.

615. נ׳ מצב אחד ק׳ א׳ מצב א׳.

621. ק׳ א׳ הדרשן נ׳ ליתא.

625 סדר טוב או לתקן איזה פירוש
באופן יותר נאה שאפשר ואם
יש בו איזה דוחק יתקנו או
ימחק אותו.

ב׳ ינסה עצמו לומר דרושו במקום
630 צנוע עם אוהביו משכילים ומבינים
קודם שידרוש בפרהסיא כמו
שאחז״ל על הכינה וגם חקרה[108])
ויאמר לאדם:[109])

ג׳ אם דרכו לכתוב ראשי
635 פרקים יכתבם בקיצור שלא
תראה בעיניך דבר ארוך ותפחד
שלא לקוץ העם:

ד׳ יזהר קודם שיגיד דרושו ברבים
לילך לראות כל הפסוקים והמאמרים
640 ואל ישען על זכירתו כי שמא
יטעה ויפרש פסוק ואין בפסוק מלה
ההיא שדרש בה:

---

625. **ק׳** פירוש **נ׳ א׳** פי׳.
627. **נ׳ א׳** יתקנו **ק׳** יבקנו.
631. **ק׳ נ׳** בפרהסיא **א׳** בפהרהסיא.
631-2. **ק׳ א׳** כמו שאחז״ל **נ׳** כמשאחז״ל.
632. **ק׳ נ׳** הכינה **א׳** הכנה.
639. **נ׳ א׳** לילך **ק׳** ללך. **ק׳ נ׳** כל **א׳** על. **ק׳ נ׳** ומאמרים **א׳** והמאמרים.
640. **ק׳ נ׳** על זכירתו **א׳** בזכירתו.
641. **ק׳** ויפרש פסוק **נ׳ א׳** ויפרש בפסוק.

108) איוב כח:כז.
109) שם, כח:כח. וראה בראשית רבה כד:ה.

ה׳ טוב מאד לראות קודם מה
שפירשו המפרשים פסוק או מאמר
כי לעולם יגלו לך האמת ויפתחו
פתח לחדש איזה דבר:

645

פרק יו״ד מה יהיה תכלית הדורש
וכוונתו בדרשותיו

א׳ תכלית וכוונת הדורש יהיה
להשלים העם ולהקריבם לעבודת ה׳
ולהרחיקם מעבירה זרה וללמדם תורת
ה׳ ית׳ הכל לש״ש לא לכבוד עצמו
להראות חכמתו:

650

ב׳ באומרו איזה תוכחה יראה לעם
שהוא מוכיח עצמו וידבר בכבוד העם
לא בביזיון וחירופין עם שיש שם
חוטאים וכבר נודע מה שאחז״ל על
משה שנענש על מה שאמר שמעו
נא המורים[110]) וישעיה שאמר ובתוך
עם טמא שפתים אנכי יושב[111]) ואליהו

655

660

643.　ק׳ קודם נ׳ א׳ ליתא.

644.　ק׳ נ׳ המפרשים פסוק א׳ המפרשים על פסוק. ק׳ א׳ או מאמר נ׳ ומאמר.

648.　ק׳ א׳ וכוונתו נ׳ ליתא. ק׳ נ׳ בדרשותיו א׳ בדרשיותיו.

649.　ק׳ א׳ וכוונת נ׳ וכונת.

651.　הנוסח המקורי כנראה היה „להרחיקם מעבירה.״ מישהוא הוסיף את המילה „זרה״ בין
השורות כאילו היה כתוב „מעבודה׃״

654.　נ׳ א׳ באומרו ק׳ באמרו.

656.　נ׳ א׳ וחירופין ק׳ וחרופין.

657.　ק׳ א׳ חוטאים נ׳ חטאים. ק׳ נ׳ שאחז״ל א׳ שארז״ל.

659.　ק׳ שאמר נ׳ א׳ אמר.

660.　ק׳ נ׳ שפתים א׳ ליתא. ק׳ אנכי יושב נ׳ א׳ וכו׳.

---

110) במדבר כ׃י.

111) ישעיה ו׃ה.

על מה שאמר כי עזבו בריתך
בני ישראל[112]) ואם יש יחיד חוטא
בעון א' ונודע לכל לא יוכיחנו ברבים
אלא בינו לבינו:

ג' יזהר מאד שלא לדרוש ח"ו לקנטר 665
ולהכלים אחרים כי אין ראוי להשתמש
בתגא[113]) של תורה לנקמת שונאיו אלא
בתוכחותיו ידבר בנעימות לא בקושי
שלא יראה גאוה אלא כאב המוכיח
את בניו כי כבר אמרו חז"ל תמה 670
אני אם יש בזמננו מי שראוי להוכיח[114])
וגם יקשט עצמו במה שירצה לקשט
אחרים[115]) כמו שדרשו חז"ל על
התקוששו וקושו:[116]) וישבח שאר תלמידי
חכמים וחביריו אך יקצר בשבחם בפניהם 675
שלא יראה כמחניף[117]):

661. ק' א' מה שאמר נ' מ"ש. ק' א' בריתך נ' בריתך את.
662. נ' א' ישראל ק' ישר'.
662‾664. ק' ואם יש יחיד חוטא בעון א' ונודע לכל לא יוכיחנו ברבים אלא בינו לבינו נ' א' ליתא. ובכתב יד ק' המילים האלה נכתבות על הצד עם סימן להכניס אותן בתוך השורה.
667. ק' א' לנקמת נ' לקנאת.
670. ק' נ' חז"ל א' רז"ל.
673. ק' נ' חז"ל א' רז"ל.
674‾675. נ' תלמידי חכמים ק' א' ת"ח.

112) מלכים א, יט:י.
113) אבות א:יג.
114) ערכין טז:
115) ראה בבא מציעא קז:, בבא בתרא ס:, וסנהדרין יח., יט.
116) צפניה ב:א.
117) עיין סוטה מא:מב. וסנהדרין קג.

ד' כשתרצה להתחיל הדרש התפלל
להב"ה בכל לב ובכל נפש שיעזור
אותו בדרוש ההוא להוציא מן הכח אל
הפועל[118]) מה שירצה לומר ויתן לו חן   680
וחסד ורחמים[119]) בעיני ה' ובעיני לב
השומעים ושיהיו דבריו מקובלים ונשמעים
ונעשים שלא יטרח להבל וריק[120]) ויתן
בלבו תכלית זה הטוב להשלים לב
העם לשמים שיעשו מעשים טובים   685
ויחזרו בתשובה החוטאים ותהיה נאה
דורש ונאה מקיים[121]) וכבר כתבתי בספר
מרגליות טובות שלי תפלה נאה והגונה
לאומרה מי שהוא דורש ברבים.

פרק י"א איך יסיים וישלים הדרש   690

א' כאשר ישלים הדרש לא יחתום
אותו בקרירות דברים אלא בפי' וחידוש

---

677.   ק' **א'** כשתרצה נ' כשירצה. ק' התפלל נ' **א'** יתפלל.
678.   ק' **א'** להב"ה נ' להקב"ה.
679.   ק' נ' ההוא **א'** ההיא.
681-680.   ק' **א'** חן וחסד נ' חסד וחן.
681.   ק' **א'** בעיני ה' נ' בעיניו.
682.   ק' נ' ושיהיו **א'** שיהיו.
686.   ק' **א'** ותהיה נ' ויהיה.
687.   נ' **א'** בספר ק' בס'.
689.   נ' לאומרה ק' **א'** לאומרו. ק' **א'** שהוא דורש נ' שדורש.

---

118) ראה מורה נבוכים ב:יח.
119) ראה סדר עבודת ישראל, ברכת המזון, 559.
120) ראה ישעיה ל:ז.
121) חגיגה יד:, יבמות סג:

יותר יפה ממה שהביא בכל הדרש
ויחתום או בתפלה שיתן ה׳ בלב
השומעים מאמריו או בבקשה מן העם   695
שיקיימו דברי ה׳ ונביאיו וחכמיו.

ב׳ לעולם בסוף הדרוש יביא פסוק
של נחמה וגאולה לישראל המבטיח
אותם לישועה עתידה:

ג׳ לפעמים יחזור בסוף כל הדרש   700
בקיצור ורמז ולהזכיר הכל במהרה.

ד׳ יאמר בסוף דרושו איזה פסוק
או מאמר או מסרה שבו יוכללו
וימצאו כל חלקי הדרוש כדי שישאר
לזכרון: 705

ה׳ אם יקרה שהוא ידרוש דרוש
אחר סמוך לזה טוב והגון שיזמין
את העם בדברים טובים שיבואו
לשמוע דרושו השני וירמוז להם
ענין דרוש שני: 710

פרק י״ב איך יתנהג הדרשן בענין
בריאות גופו

א׳ יזהר הדורש שסמוך לזמן הדרש
לא יטרח לא בגופו ולא בדעתו ולבו

693.‎   ק׳ נ׳ ממה א׳ מכל מה.
697.‎   ק׳ הדרוש נ׳ א׳ הדרש.
698.‎   נ׳ לישראל ק׳ לישר׳ א׳ ליש׳.
703.‎   ק׳ נ׳ יוכללו א׳ יכללו.
706.‎   ק׳ נ׳ שהוא א׳ שהוא שהוא. ק׳ נ׳ דרוש א׳ דרש.
708.‎   ק׳ א׳ שיבואו נ׳ שיבאו.
711.‎   ק׳ א׳ הדרשן נ׳ ליתא.

ולא ילך לטייל בשוק בלילה ולא יחשוב
בדבר המצערו ומבלבל לבו:

715

ב׳ לא יאכל דבר המכביד גופו
ולא יאכל זיתים אגוזים ודברים
מלוחים או גבינה וקטניות שכלם
קשים ורעים לקול ומעכבים מוצא
שפתים והלשון:

720

ג׳ ישתה מעט יין חי וטוב המשמח לבו
ומחזיק קולו ומאמץ אבריו ויאכל מעט
וטוב וקל לעכל ודבר המחזיק הלב
והמוח ויפה לגרון ולחזה ולאצטומכא.

725

ד׳ אחר שדרש ילך מיד לנוח על
מטתו וישתה מעט יין טוב או מרק
עופות ואחר שעה או שתי שעות
יכול לסעוד סעודתו:

**פרק י״ג מה יעשה אחר שדרש
וסיים דרושו**

730

א׳ אחר שדרש ישאל לאיזה אהוב
נאמן שיאמר לו באמת אם טעה

716. נ׳ א׳ בדבר ק׳ לדבר. ק׳ נ׳ המצערו א׳ המצטערו.
718. א׳ זיתים ק׳ נ׳ זתים. ק׳ נ׳ אגוזים נ׳ א׳ ואגוזים.
719. ק׳ א׳ גבינה נ׳ גביע. ק׳ נ׳ וקטניות א׳ וקטניות. ק׳ שכלם נ׳ א׳ שכולם.
723. ק׳ אבריו נ׳ א׳ איבריו.
725. נ׳ א׳ ולאצטומכא ק׳ ואצטומכא.
729. ק׳ נ׳ יכול לסעוד א׳ יסעוד.
730. ק׳ א׳ שדרש נ׳ ליתא.
731. ק׳ א׳ וסיים נ׳ שסיים.

באיזה דבר מדברים הנזכרים
כדי שיוכל לתקן להבא כי כל
735 הנגעים אדם רואה חוץ מנגעי
עצמו:[122])

ב' יכתוב כל דרושו בביאור כדי
שיועיל לו לזקנתו או לבאים אחריו
לבניו ולתלמידיו כמו שאמר איוב
740 מי יתן אפו ויכתבון מלי מי יתן
בספר ויחקו בעט ברזל ועפרת
לעד בצור יחצבון.[123])

ג' יודה וישבח להב״ה שיצא בשלום
מן הקודש[124]) ולא יתגאה לבו על
745 חכמתו אלא יחשוב כי ה' יתן
חכמה מפיו דעת ותבונה[125]) וה' חפץ
למען צדקו יגדיל תורה ויאדיר[126])
ויבוא יום שכתוב בו וכל בניך

734. ק' נ' באיזה א' מאיזה.
735. ק' נ' כדי א' ליתא.
741. ק' אפו נ' א' איפה. ק' נ' מלי א' מילי. ק' א' מי יתן נ' ויתן.
742. ק' נ' ויחקו א' ויוחקו.
745. ק' הקודש נ' א' הקדש.
746. ק' נ' אלא יחשוב א' ליתא.
749. ק' א' ויבוא נ' ויבא.

122) נגעים ב:ה.
123) איוב יט:כג־כד.
124) משנה יומא ז:ד.
125) משלי ב:ו.
126) ישעיה מב:כא.

למודי ה׳ — ורב שלום בניך:[127]   750
ולשלמות המלאכה הקדושה הנ״ל
[אפרש בע״ה פסוקים ה׳ אלקים נתן
לי לשון לימודים וכו׳[128]) ופסוק
קרא בגרון אל תחשוך בשופר
הרם קולך וכו׳[129]) לראיה על   755
הנ״ל]

עמוד א׳
הלל ושבח על חיבורים וספרים שחיבר כמוהר״ר
יעקב צהלון י׳ צ׳ ו׳ מפי חכם ירושלמי כמוהר״ר ישראל פואה נר״ו[1]

הואיל וזכינא דאתא לידן האי סיפרא רבא
נימא ביה מילתא אלבישייהו יקירא[2]
מרגניתא דלית בה טימי אור עליון
המאיר לארץ ולדרים[3] כשמו כן הוא אור[4]

750. ק׳ א׳ למודי נ׳ לימודי.
751-756. השורות האלו נמצאות רק בק׳ ונכתבו בסוף בכתיבה אחרת ובשורה אחרונה היו האותיות
„תושלבע״[130]) והוסיף עליהן קו.
751. בסוף כתב יד נ׳ כתוב: „תושלבע נעתק על יד הבחור שלמה בן לא״א יצחק דה קושטה
עטיאש נר״ו יאיר בלונדרש ביום שלישי י״ב לחדש אדר בשנת התע״ז לפ״ק״ ובכתב יד **א**
נכתב בסוף רק „תושלב״ע״.

127) שם, נד:יג.
128) שם, נ:ד.
129) שם, נח:א.
130) ראה למעלה, הערה 45.

1) נטריה רחמנא ופרקיה. עד עכשיו כתב צהלון למעלה מכל ההסכמה עם ההוראות: „זה
אין להדפיס כאן״ והוא העביר קוים .י׳ גוף ההסכמה.
2) שבת י:
3) תפלת שחרית לחול ושבת.
4) שמואל א: כה:כה.

קול יעקב

הדרשנים אע״ג דלגביה משה מילתא

זוטרתי היא[5] הוא מרנא ורבנא הרב

המחבר דנהירין ליה סיפרי וסיפרא ובריית

עסיק תדירא באורייתא רמי מתניתא

מותיב תיובתא משכי בדעתא צילותא[6]

אסיק שמעתתא אליבא דהלכתא כאשר

יורו חיבוריו היקרים המאורות הגדולים

דנהירי וצהירי ובהירי כשימשא וסיהרא

בחידושא לאו מכללא אלא בפירושא

היא ס׳ מורשה קהלת יעק״ב[7]) על

הרמב״ם שלא יהיו דבריו כהלכתא בלא

טעמא אלא כנותן טעם לשבח[8]) עלינו

לשבח[9]) ליעק״ב איש תם יושב אהלים[10]

קודש הילולים[11]) דור״ש על קוץ וקוץ תילי

תילים[12]) פרטים וכללים הוא חיבור תתן

אמת ליעקב[13] ניכרים דיברי אמת

תורת אמת היית׳ בפיהו[14] על כל

הפרשיות דרושים לכל חפציהם[15] לא ימיש

מתוך האהל[16] הוא אהלי יעק״ב[17] רב האיכות

5) ברכות לג:

6) ראה יבמות קי״ג, קי״ג:, וגיטין ע:

7) על פירוש ״ (המרכאות) האלו עיין בתרגום אנגלי בהערות. שם ספרו של צהלון בא מדברים לג:ד.

8) עבודה זרה לט., סז:

9) תפלה בסדר תפלות.

10) בראשית כח:

11) ויקרא יט:כד.

12) מנחות כט:

13) מיכה ז:כ וגם שם של ספר מאת צהלון.

14) ראה מלאכי ב:ו.

15) תהילים קיא:ב.

16) שמות לג:יא.

17) ירמיהו ל:יח וגם שם של ספר מאת צהלון.

כולל כל החכמות רוח הקודש הופיע
באהלי יעק״ב חכם עדיף מנביא[18] לפרש
דיברי ישעיה הנביא ישועות יעקב[19] שמו
יה יושיעהו ויברך אלהים את יעק״ב[20]
בבני חיי ומזוני ומרגליות טובות[21]
במידה שאדם מודד שימדד לנו[22] חיבור
מרגליות טובות קיצור חובת
עמוד ב׳
הלבבות לב טהור מחברו חובת
הלבבות לקרב למלאכה[23]) ולהדפיס המאור
הגדול הזה כי הוא צורך גדול לדרשנים כאשר
ידוע למי שעיין וטרח בדרושים כמה זמן
זמנים זמנהם[24] צריך לטרוח לבקש מאמר
אחד וילך היום ההוא ואחר עמל וטורח לא
ימצאהו לכן הכל צריכין למארי חטייה[25]
ואוקיר לאסייא[26] הוא הרופא המובהק הכולל
בכל מיני חכמות פרי עץ הדר[27] באילנו היא
רומה על השמיים ה׳[28] שככה ברא עולמו כל
העולם כולו לא ניברא אלא לצוות לזה[29]
ואי לא דמסתפינא דלא יהוי מהנך דסמייתינא

18) בבא בתרא יב.
19) תהילים מד:ה וגם שם ספר מאת צהלון.
20) ע׳ בראשית לה:ט.
21) ספר מאת צהלון.
22) ראה משנה סוטה א:ז.
23) ראה שמות לו:ב.
24) ע׳ מגילה ב.
25) ברכות סד., בבא בתרא קמה:, והוריות יד.
26) ע׳ ירושלמי תענית ג:סו:ד.
27) ויקרא כג:מ.
28) ראה תהלים נז:יב; קח:ו.
29) ברכות ו:, שבת ל:

לשבחיה דמרך[30] הייתי גומר עליו את ההלל
נאום דדחיל ורחים ומוקיר רבנן ותלמידהון דעת
ממני ניפלאה[31] ולא הגעתי להוראה עבדא
דעילאה עמוס התלאה צריך לרפוא"ה
ישראל פואה
שלוחא דרחמנא מקרתא
קדישא דישר"אל
ירושלים ת"ו יפ"ה
דיברת בזמנו
דיברת אפ"ר כירה
מוכן הוא יפ"ה
ירושלים ת"ו
זעיר מתא דירושלים

פירוש ראשי־תיבות

אפ"ר	אני פואה רש
כיר"ה	כתבתי יהיו רצון הדברים
יפ"ת	ישראל פואה תושב
יפ"ה	ישראל פואה המדבר

מי יתן ויכתבון מילי מילי
דבדיחותא על האיש קדוש המחבר דבדיח
טובא בהאי עלמא ודאתי
כשמו כן הוא צהלה ושמחה[32])

30) ראה שם לג:
31) ראה תהלים קלט:ו.
32) אסתר ח:טו.

[3a] תפלה ראויה לאומרה מי שהוא דורש ברבים או ראש ישיבה

אדני. שפתי תפתח ופי יגיד תהלתך[1]
אתה הוא ה' האלהים אשר גדול אתה וגדול שמה בגבורה[2]
האל הגדול הגבור והנורא[3] גדול העצה ורב העליליה
אשר עיניך פקוחות על כל דרכי בני אדם[4] ממכון שבתו
השגיח אל כל יושבי הארץ.[5] היוצר יחד לבם המבין את
כל מעשיהם[6]) הזן ומפרנס מקרני ראמים[7] עד ביצי כינים.
עיני כל אליך ישברו ואתה נותן להם את אכלם בעתו[8])
של כל אחד ואח'. והשגחתך גלויה ומפורסמ' לעיני כל
יצורך בכללם ובפרטם. ובפרט על יציר כפיך הוא האדם אשר
תפקדנו לבקרי' לרגעים תבחננו.[9] ודרכיו אתה רואה וכל
צעדיו תספור. לשמע אזן שמעתיך ועתה עיני ראתך[10]
שבפרט ובפרטות השגחת על רימה ותולע' צל עובר ציץ נובל
עפר ואפר כמוני לעשות עמדי חסד להקימני מעפר ומאשפות
הרימותני להושיבי עם נדיבים עם נדיבי עמו.[11]
הרימות בחור מעם[12]) ומאחר עלות[13] הביאתני לרעו'
ביעקב עמו ובישראל נחלתו,[13])
ועתה מה אשיב לה' כל תגמולוהי עליי[14]) ואלו פי מלא

1) תהלים נא:יז.
2) ירמיה י:ו.
3) דברים י:יז.
4) ירמיה לב:יט.
5) תהלים לג:יד.
6) ראה תהלים לג:טו ,,אל כל מעשיהם".
7) ע' תהלים כב:כב.
8) תהלים קמה:טו.
9) איוב ז:יח.
10) שם מב:ה.
11) תהלים קיג:ח.
12) ר' שם פט:כ.
13) תהלים עח:עא.
14) שם קטז:יב.

שירה כים וכו' אין אני מספיק להודות לך וכו'.[15]
ולכן ידי שמתי למו פי[15a]) ולך דומיה תהלה[16])
ולפי שחנוניך הם חנונים ומרוחמיך הם מרוחמים לכן במתנת
חנם אני מתחנן ומתפלל לפניך שתענה עתירתי ותשמע את
תפלתי כמו שקבלת שאלת שלמה עבדך כשנראת אליו בחלום
ואמרת לו שאל מה אתן לך[17]) וחננתו ממה ששאל וממה
שלא שאל. [3b] תחנני גם אני אבי: ועתה ה' אלהי
אתה המלכת ומנית את עבדך תחת אבי ואנכי נער קטן נער
לא אדע צאת ובא. ועבדך בתוך עמך אשר בחרת עם רב אשר
לא יספר מרוב, ונתת לעבדך לב שומע לשפוט את עמך
להבין בין טוב לרע כי מי יוכל לשפוט את עמך הכבד הזה[18])
ונתחי לעבדך לב נבון וחכם[19]) להבין לעמך טעמי תורתך
ולהדריכם לעבודתך ולקרבם לתורתך כי באלה חפצתי.[20])
ונתת לעבדך לשון לימודים לדעת לעות את יעף דבר
יעיר בבוקר בבוקר יעיר לי אזן לשמוע כלימודים.[21])
והאצל מרוח קדשך עלי. גל עיני ואביטה נפלאות מתורתך[22])
ובחקתך אשתעשע לא אשכח דברך[23]) ואדרוש להם דבר טוב
בעתו[24]) מידי יום ביומו ומידי שבת בשבתו[25])
ובחגים ובמועדים ובכל הזמנים המשונים למדע לדרוש להם
דבר הגון וראוי. ויכנסו דברי בלבבם ויחלו כמטר לי ופיהם
יפערו למלקוש.[26]) ויהיו דברי ערבים באזני שומעיהם.

15) ר' באר, **עבודת ישראל**, עמ' 207-206.

15a) איוב מ:ד.

16) תהלים סה:ב לפי מס' מגילה יח.

17) מלכים א:ג:ה.

18) שם ז-ט.

19) שם יב.

20) ירמיה ט:כג.

21) ישעיה נ:ד.

22) תהלים קיט:יח.

23) שם שם,טז.

24) ר' משלי טו:כג.

25) ישעיה סו:כג.

26) איוב כט:כג.

ויבואו עמך לשמוע דברי בלב שלם ובנפש חפצה.[27]
ויהיו צמאים לשמוע דברי תורתך מפי וימצאו בדברי נחת רוח
לרוות צמאם ולחזק רפיון ידיהם וברכיהם הכושלות מצרת הגלות,
כדבר שנאמר חזקו ידים רפות וברכים כושלות אמצו.[28]
וגלוי לפני כסא כבודך שלא לכבודי אני שואל אלא לכבודך
אשר נקרא שמך עלי. אנא ה' למדני להועיל הדריכני בדרך
אלך להועיל לבניך ולהדריכם לעבודתך. ואהיה מדבר על אזנים
שומעות. ולא ימושו דברי ותוכחותי ואזהרותי מתוך לבבם
ויקבלום וישמרום לעשותם כל הימים ולא יטו ימין ושמאל.
אלמדה פושעים דרכיך[29] וגו'.
והאירה פניך על עבדך[30] והאירה עיני בתורתך ודבק לבי
במצותיך ויחד לבבי לאהבה וליראה את שמך לא אבוש בעולם
הזה ולא אכלם לעולם הבא.[31] ואל תביאני לידי [4a]
בזיון ולא לידי חילול ה'. ולא תמציא לידי שום חטא
ועבירה ועון מעתה ועד עולם. ולא יצא עלי שם רע ולא
על מעשי לעולם. ולא אהיה כעסן וקפדן ואכזרי עם שום אדם
אלא סבלן ורחמן כדי שישמעו דברי ותוכחתי ולא יאמרו לי
טול קורה מבין עיניך.[32] אלא אהיה יראוי[33]
בעיניהם ואזכה שיהיה חלקי עם אותם הצדיקים שיאמר על כל
אחד מהם דרוש רבי דרוש כי לך נאה לדרוש[34] כי אתה
נאה דורש ונאה מקיים.[35] והם מופת בישראל מחכמתם ומלשונם.
יקומו בני ויהללום מלכות ופלגשים ויאשרום.[36] ואמצא חן
ושכל טוב בעיני אלהים ואדם[37] ועל כל זאת לא אתגאה חס

27) דברי הימים א:כח:ט.

28) ישעיה לה:ג.

29) תהלים נא:טו.

30) שם לא:יז.

31) עין באר, **עבודת ישראל**, עמ' 80, וע' נוסח ספרד.

32) בבא בתרא טו:, ערכין טז:

33) הכוונה שיראו מפניו.

34) ר' סנהדרין ק.

35) חגיגה יד:

36) ר' שיר השירים ו:ט.

37) משלי ג:ד.

ושלום. אל תבואני רגל גאוה ויד רשעים אל תנידני[38]
אלא אשא עיני ולבי אליך כי לך הגדולה[39] וממך כל
טובתי.[40] ואהיה מקטין עצמי כי קטן ואתה תגדלני ותרוממני.
ומענוותך תרבני.[41] וכל מעשי ידי לשמך ולכבודך יהיו.
ולא אפנה מחשבותי במעשי ודיבורי כי אם לכבודך.
ולא יהיה בפי אלא זכרך ולא יחשוב לבי אלא לשמך.
ויהיו מחשבותי טהורים ולא אשא עיני אלא לרצונך. וכל חושי
לא יפעלו אלא לכבודך. וכל דברי בין ביחיד ובין ברבים
יהיו לתכלית טוב ולא לקנטר או להכלים אחרים. ולא אחרים
יכלימוני ויקנטרוני אלא ידינוני לכף זכות.[42] והצילני
מעין הרע מיצר הרע ומשנאת הבריות. ולא ילעיגו הבריות עלי
ולא על דברי. ולא אכשל בדברי ויראו וישמחו אלא תהיה עם
פי ותורני מה שאומר לפי הזמן ולפי העניין[43] בלי שום
פקפוק. הסר ממני עקשות פה ולזות שפתי הרחק ממני.[44]
וכל הקמים עלי לרעה מהרה הפר עצתם וקלקל מחשבותם.[45] ועתה
ירום ראשי על אויבי סביבותי ואזבחה באהלו זבחי תרועה
אשירה ואזמרה לה׳.[46] והארך נא ברחמיך ימי ושנותי ולא
יאמרו עלי אוי לה לרבנות [4b] שמקברת את בעליה[47]
אלא יאמרו אורך ימים בימינה בשמאלה עושר וכבוד[48]
יראת ה׳ תוסיף ימים[49] תורת אלהיו בלבו לא תמעד
אשוריו.[50] ולא תהיה קנאתי על אחרים ולא קנאת אחרים

38) תהלים לו:יב.
39) ר׳ דברי הימים א:כט:יא.
40) ע׳ תהלים טז:ב.
41) שם יח:לו.
42) ר׳ אבות א:ו.
43) ר׳ **אור הדרשנים** שורות 41-435.
44) ר׳ משלי ד:כד.
45) ר׳ ברכות יז.
46) תהלים כז:ו.
47) פסחים פז:
48) משלי ג:טז.
49) שם י:כז.
50) תהלים לז:לא.

עלי לרעה אלא קנאת סופרים ועושי טובי ולש״ש כדי שתתרבה
ותתגדל תורתך ועבודתך.[51]) ולא ישנאוני לא קטנים ולא
גדולים על הוכחתי אותם במילי דשמיא. אלא אהיה אהוב
למעלה ונחמד למטה בישראל בין באומות העולם. ואם אומר
דבר נגד השקרנים והרשעים, יר״מ שלא ימשך ממנו דבר רע
לא על ישראל עמך ולא עלי. ולא ימצא רגיל,[52]) ומגלה סוד,
ובעל לשון הרע, המלשין. ונתת פני חזקים נגד פניהם ומצחי
חזקה נגד מצחם בעת ויכוחי עמהם. ולמדני להשי׳ לאפיקורוס[53])
ולקדש שמך בדברי ותשובותי. ונלחמו אלי ולא יוכלו לי כי
אתי אתה ה׳ להצילני,[54]) וזכני להיות כלי מחזיק טובה
לישראל הוא השלום.[55])

ואהיה אמצעי לשים פשרה ושלום בין איש לאשתו ובין אדם
לחברו ובין איש לבנו. ואשפוט צדק בין איש ובין אחיו
ובין גרו.[56]) ויהי רצון מלפניך ה׳ אלהי ואלהי אבותי
שתשלח ברכה רווחה והצלחה בכל מעשי ידי ואראה סימן ברכה
מיגיעי. ולא איגע לריק ולא אלד לבהלה.[57]) וממה שתחנני
בעולם הזה מעושר ונכסים זכני להוציאו בפרנסת עניניך
והמוטלים עלי לפרנס ובמצו׳ ומ״ט[58]) ובעסקי תורתך לשמה.
ואנא ה׳ צבאות מעלה ומטה זכני להוליד בנים ולראות בבני
בנים. ויהיו בני ממלאים את מקומי וגדולתי כפלי כפלים
וקיים בי מקרא שכתוב ודברי אשר שמתי בפיך לא ימושו
מפיך וגו׳.[59]) ואהיה אני וזרעי וזרע זרעי עד סוף כל
הדורות אוהבי שמך ויראי שמך ולומדי ומלמדי תורתך לשמה
אשר יקרא שמך עלינו לעול׳. וזכני לחדש חידושי׳ ולחבר
ספרים בתורתך ויהיו לפני ישראל תמיד[5a] להגות בהם

---

(51) ע׳ בבא בתרא כא. כב.

(52) ע׳ רש״י ויקרא יט:טז, ד״ה „לא תלך רכיל״.

(53) אבות ב:יד.

(54) ר׳ ירמיה א:יט וטו:כ.

(55) ר׳ משנה עוקצים ג:יב.

(56) דברים א:טז.

(57) ר׳ ישעיה סה:כג.

(58) ובמצות ומעשים טובים.

(59) ישעיה נט:כא.

ולהגדיל תורתך ולהאדיר,[60]) ועל ידי ירבו ת"ח[61]) בישראל.
ולא יהיו דברי ודרושי לטורח על עמך אלא יעמדו בחבה יתירה
מתחלה ועד סוף באהבה רבה. ושמע תפלתי כמו שקבלת תפלת
יעב"ץ שהתפלל לפניך אם ברך תברכני והרבית את גבולי והיתה
ידך עמי ועשית מרעה לבלתי עצבי מיד ויבא אלהים את
אשר שאל.[62])

וזכני לזכות הרבים בעולם הזה כמו שעשו חסידיך ונביאיך
אשר קרבו בניך לעבודתך אשר האירו ישראל בתורתם שהרביצו
לרוב. ותן חלקי עמהם בעולם הזה ובעולם הבא. וזכני לראות
בטובת בחירך לשמוח בשמחת גוייך להתהלל עם נחלתך.[63])
ועיני תראינה ירושלים נוה שאנן[64]) וערי יהודה בבנינן
והר ציון והנצח ונוה אפריון. ובימי תושע יהודה וישראל
ישכון לבטח,[65]) ובא לציון גואל.[66]) אל תבישני משברי[67]
ואל תפח נא מלבי את תקותי, ושמע תפלתי ותחנני ברצון.
ואל תשיבני ריקם מלפניך כי אתה שומע תפלת כל פה.
יהיו לרצון וכו'.

ואומר מזמור סימן מ למנצח לדוד מזמור קוה קויתי ה'
ויט אלי וישמע שועתי וגו'[68]) עד סוף.

60) ר' שם מב:כא.
61) תלמידי חכמים.
62) דברי הימים א:ד:י.
63) תהלים קו:ה.
64) ישעיה לג:כ.
65) ירמיה כג:ו.
66) ישעיה נט:כ.
67) תהלים קיט:קטז.
68) שם מ:א-ב.

III. A Critical Edition of the *Or ha-Darshanim*
Based on Three Manuscripts